WITHDRAWN

ALBERT INNAURATO was born in 1948 of first generation Italian-American parents. He received an MFA degree from the Yale School of Drama in 1974. GEMINI, one of the longest running comedies to ever appear on Broadway, has also been produced in Washington, D.C., Chicago, and Montreal. His other plays, which have been performed Off Broadway and in major cities across the United States and Europe, also include LYTTON STRACHEY LUCUBRATES DE RERUM SEXUALIS and PASSIONE. Winner of two Obies for BENNO BLIMPIE and GEMINI, and a Drama Desk Citation, Innaurato has also been a Guggenheim Fellow, a Rockefeller Fellow, and resident playwright at the New York Shakespeare Festival and the Circle Repertory Company. In addition to his plays, Innaurato has written numerous short stories, a novel, WISDOM AMOK, and pieces for American television. His plays have been translated into German, Japanese, and the Scandinavian languages.

BIZARRE BEHAVIOR

Six Plays by
ALBERT INNAURATO

 A BARD BOOK/PUBLISHED BY AVON BOOKS

AVON BOOKS
A division of
The Hearst Corporation
959 Eighth Avenue
New York, New York 10019

INTRODUCTION

The plays here gathered are those I wrote in my twenties. *Urlicht* was conceived in my late teens, but the version printed here was finalized by the time I was twenty-one; similarly, *Ulysses in Traction* was produced four months after my thirtieth birthday, but the play was written in my twenty-ninth year.

There has been little continuity to date in my career. It is still commonplace for me to encounter people who know only one of my plays and who therefore proceed to give me advice as though the play in question were my only one. I well remember the lady director who massacred *Gemini* in its first reading—a total disaster—telling me that *Gemini* was the usual sort of first play that the writer deserved to hear (presumably in a ghastly travesty such as the one she perpetrated) and then ought to put in a drawer. First play indeed—I had already written *Urlicht, Wisdom Amok, The Transfiguration of Benno Blimpie* and *Earth Worms,* plus about ten other plays lost or destroyed. But then again, I still meet people who know me only as the writer of *Benno Blimpie,* although it ran less than two months Off Broadway (and at different times a total of twenty-four performances Off Off), and not as the writer of *Gemini,* although as of this writing *Gemini* has reached its thousandth performance on Broadway.

The reader, too, may feel that there is no continuity in this collection of plays. He may well be dazzled to go from the undeniably bizarre *Wisdom Amok* to the comparatively ordinary *Gemini,* from the outrageous and "absurd" *Urlicht* to the fairly realistic *Earth Worms* to *Benno Blimpie,* which combines elements of narrative dramaturgy with "kitchen sink" realism. Perhaps a unity can be found in this work, but I never experience it that way. I have approached all the plays here as though they were my first and my last each time I have sat down to write; and even where there are very obvious similarities in subject matter, such as in my preoccupation with overeating, I am likely to perceive the plays in question as so different that I am outraged when people point out the similarities.

The most popular of these plays to date in a number of senses has been *Gemini*. For example, it proved possible to sell *Gemini* by dint of a television commercial which probably overstressed the burlesque elements in the play (to this day the play is attacked by certain "intellectuals" who have seen only the commercial and neither the play in production nor a text) but which certainly succeeded in attracting an enthusiastic public. Unfortunately this kind of success, which occurred despite reviewers or the conventional forms of theatrical publicity (such as awards and visibility in columns and on television), tends to backfire. Most people in the theater tend to treat *Gemini* as something to be ashamed of, an aberration of an otherwise serious writer, or proof positive, if proof were needed, that the author in question had neither seriousness nor talent.

One of the common dismissals of *Gemini* is that it was written self-consciously to be a commercial play. Well, it was, I can't deny that, but the cruel irony is that it was turned down everywhere because no one thought it was commercial. The play was sent to nearly every regional theater in this country. It was returned as quite out of the question because of the language and sexual concerns of the play. Those commercial managements who read the play had even more negative things to say about its probable future if produced commercially. Not even the Off Off Broadway theaters would do the play. The terrible reading already alluded to killed *Gemini*'s chances at that particular theater, but other theaters thought the play had no chance of moving to a commercial run, so turned it down. And of course, many of the readers simply hated the play. Ironically, two theaters that would later be instrumental in the play's emergence, Playwrights Horizons and Circle Repertory, turned it down: for that abortive reading was done at Playwrights Horizons, while the kind people at Circle lost the script and thus never responded to it.

How the miracle happened, and this "uncommercial," sick, and brutal play became a long-run success on Broadway (albeit after a rough first six months, and in a small theater) is beyond the scope of this piece. But the attacks on a play that attempted to be a communication of something, and within reason succeeded, is saddening. It is one of the many symptoms that a professional, serious theater in this country is dying, if not dead already, for this contempt is based on a series of misassumptions that clear the way for fads and frauds, driving away the most important audience for a serious theater and resulting in a specious choice between cowardly chosen plays and pointless revivals on the one hand, and an amateurish avant-garde on the other. But all that, too, is beyond the scope of this introduction. Suffice it to say that if anyone knows both sides of this issue it is I, as any reader who leaps from the frankly crazy *Wisdom Amok* to the more straightforward *Gemini* will know. I am not ashamed of these radical shifts in my work: I am rather fond of *Wisdom Amok*, and almost certainly provide its best audience; but I am also proud of *Gemini*, and pleased when audiences are both amused and moved by it.

One thing I do know is that it is easy to mystify an audience, and very difficult to communicate to one—particularly now that theater has become more or less a minority art form, less familiar in its conventions than television or the movies. I hope against hope that authoritative, persuasive productions of *Earth Worms* and *Wisdom Amok* will reach larger audiences, but it strikes me as unlikely. The cowardice and barrenness of vision that dominate the larger American theaters militate against both plays, and neither is likely to be produced on Broadway, if only because of the expense involved. But even when *Earth Worms* has been mounted (with the exception of a truly remarkable production directed by Robert Goldsby at the Berkeley Stage in San Francisco), it has proved almost impossible to cast. And both these plays suffer from the erosion of acting and directorial talent that the far more lucrative worlds of television and the movies have created over the past twenty-

five years. Of course, as the playwright in question, I
assume automatically that the plays are worth doing;
whether they are or not, and whether they ever will be,
must be left to what a producer friend of mine calls
"history's kisses."

Critical comment about *Gemini* has often taken dis-
appointing forms. One of the greatest bones of contention
has been the play's sexual politics—a kind of crucifixion
my work tends to invite, I'm afraid. The central character
endures a sexual crisis in the course of the play, which
is only partially resolved at the end. First, I am of the
opinion that many people—straight and homosexual,
male and female—suffer sexual crises, so Francis's problem does not make him unique, or definitely homosexual.
Second, it has been my experience in life (but perhaps
I am alone) that problems of all sorts are only rarely con-
cretely resolved to the satisfaction of all concerned. If
there is a "hidden message" in *Gemini,* it is that if one
is to live at all, one must learn to endure a certain amount
of doubt and uncertainty—about many things, not only a
sexual preference.

Unfortunately, what I would identify as a mature and
sophisticated point of view tends to irritate people beyond reason. "Fag baiters," of whom there are many, including some of our most respected critics, hurl offal at
any hint of tolerance for homosexuality, one fool going so
far as to coin a term, "gayist," about *Gemini.* Even worse
are the open (and occasionally secret) homosexual critics
who are passionately offended that Francis does not at
the end of the play don leather chaps and keys and go off
to be fist-fucked by someone more butch than Randy.
Unfortunately, were I of a weaker mental constitution I'd
be schizophrenic by now, so contradictory and stupid has
been much of the so-called critical writing about my
work. For example, when one critic coined that ludicrous
word "gayist," calling *Gemini* and *Benno* pro-homosexual plays, the homophiliac magazine *The Advocate* attacked both plays and their author as rabidly anti-homosexual. When a newspaper critic attacked *Ulysses in
Traction* as pro-homosexual, *The Advocate* a month later
attacked it as rabidly anti-homosexual. One wishes these
people would make up their minds. "Gayness," in and of
itself, is of no interest to me whatever as a writer. I am

interested in the experiences of individual people in specific circumstances, and it would never occur to me to attack a work of fiction because I disagreed with the sexuality of a particular character—but these are the times in which we live.

A second attack on *Gemini,* and many of my other plays when they have been done, is that they are autobiographical. How this diminishes their value as art is unclear to me, but of even greater interest is how these critics—almost none of whom have exchanged more than a word or two with me—know so much about my life and background. It would be disingenuous of me to insist that there was absolutely no relation between plays like *Gemini, Benno Blimpie,* and *Ulysses in Traction* and actual experiences of mine; but all the same, the literal correlation between characters in these plays and actual people I have known, and between events in these plays and actual circumstances I have endured, is small. My family was very relieved that the people in *Gemini* bore such small similarity to them, or to mutual friends and neighbors. Meanwhile, about *Ulysses in Traction,* I have been accused of using particular drama departments and specific staff members of schools I never visited and knew nothing about.

A more serious criticism of *Gemini,* although one raised infrequently, is one I agree with, and one that haunts all the plays in this volume to one degree or another. It concerns the absence of a strong dramatic action. "Action" is one of those convenient words which is almost impossible to define in simple, objective, concrete terms, but which nonetheless expresses an important aspect in the structuring of drama along more or less conventional lines. In *Gemini,* the action ought to have been "to find the true sexual identity of the main character"; but instead of becoming the central action, this aspect becomes the author's excuse to bring together a number of characters who interest him. As a result, the play can seem diffuse and lacking in a strong central focus. As with many modern plays, the play has more to do with a specific atmosphere, projected by a carefully chosen series of minor events (the breakfast, the dinner, the mock-suicide of Bunny, the encounter in the tent of Randy and Francis, the accidental return of Judith, the farewells, and

so on), each of which becomes a pretext and a motivation
for the expression of conflicting attitudes by all the characters.

The style of *Gemini* can seem ramshackle and free-
associative, although in fact these events, the sequence
in which they occur, and the way they are fitted into the
larger texture of the play are all carefully chosen, and
entailed a lot of work before they came right. Still, this
lack of a central action—and for convenience I would
offer a simplistic definition of the action as the motor of
a play: that strong quest which beats under the surface
actions, which pulls the play inexorably from one moment to the next, and which gives the play its satisfying
sense of inevitability, overall coherence, and rightness—
involved me in *Gemini* in a sleight of hand, a juggling
act, where an action was indicated and seemed to be con-
stant, but where I was much more interested in other
things. It is probably true that the "sexual liberation" of
the seventies, however bogus and short-lived, had something to do with this. In an earlier age it would have been
essential to spend all the time in the play dealing with
Francis's problem, and it would have been almost impossible to take a comic tack in presenting the difficul-
ties—indeed, Francis might have had to commit suicide
to comfort a disturbed audience. In fact, there are many
actions in *Gemini* that could have resulted in a full-length
play: Bunny's search for affection and a good man, Herschel's search for a friend, and Fran's search for communication with his son. But I chose to stir these into a
stew, avoiding perhaps (though certainly flirting with) the
banality each of these situations might have invited, and
achieved in a small way, I hope, a sense of actual life,
where comings and goings, of course, have a random
quality and where it is usually impossible to perceive a
definite action.

In *Earth Worms*, similarly, I chose to digest a variety
of actions, each of which could have generated a full evening. My technique was not good for *Earth Worms*,
though, and that sleight of hand I achieved, in my opinion, in *Gemini* did not quite occur in *Earth Worms*.
There, too, the sexual confusion of the nominal hero provides a pretext for bringing together two people in whom

I was much more interested—the elderly Bernard and the maidenly Mary—to act out their peculiar, oddly parallel fantasies. There is even a peripheral character, the old, blind Edith, who is impossible to justify in terms of a central action, but who, in my opinion, is essential. *Earth Worms* was originally in three acts, and probably would have taken a week to perform. The current version (the original having disappeared, as have so many of my manuscripts) is really a series of linked excerpts from that overabundant original. Taken as a whole, it is probably not satisfactory, but I am proud of many aspects of this play, particularly the characters of Bernard and Edith. They demonstrate ways of coping with a number of problems that obsess me and have obsessed me since I can remember. They show ways of dealing with physical illness, physical ugliness, old age, and total neglect by the society at large, with courage and, in Bernard's case, flamboyance. These characters have a way of snatching joy, fantasy, and suspense from utterly barren and hopeless lives. There have been many years when it was impossible for me to get anyone to read my plays, let alone consider doing them, and thus I identify strongly with Bernard's total refusal to accept failure, and his continual and genuine hope—however hedged about it is with irony.

The most seriously harmed of these plays by the absence of a concrete action is *Ulysses in Traction*. This is a work about which I have mixed feelings. I asked to have it included here as a relief from so many nuns and wops. In *Ulysses* there is no action at all, and the pretext for the play—rehearsing an anti–Vietnam War play during a race riot—seems weak and hard to dramatize. In these days of movies and television, it is almost impossible to stage an offstage riot with verisimilitude. When we've all seen CinemaScope for years, we are all too aware that what is just offstage is a complex of speakers and tape machines, and not a horde of avenging blacks. Even forgetting that, though, the race riot is more a diversionary tactic than an action, and in the current version of the play (which has never been performed and probably never will be) there is not even an onstage link to the rioters. (In the first version, disastrously performed

at the Circle Rep, there was at least a black cleaning lady
to give a bathetic aria, which some thought a parody of
William Faulkner.)

Ulysses is about many things that concern me—the
emasculating of art by imprisoning it in an academic
framework, yet the probability that serious art will survive only there because the last twenty years have seen
a decline of serious professional art in the theater because
of a shrinking audience and immense costs; the hope-
lessness of serious artists forced to deal with academic
intrigue for their survival, and to do without the stimulus
of an audience with a spontaneous interest in the art they
practice. Put another way, the greatest theater artists,
starting with the Greeks and including Ibsen, have been
able to work as part of a larger community sharing their
interests. The community in which the artists in *Ulysses*
function is artificially created. In a play, it is not enough
to state these issues, they must be demonstrated; and it
is in the demonstration that *Ulysses* falls down, declining
into parody and bathos. Still, there are parts of this play
of which I am fond. I think the long scene in Act II between Lenny and the failed playwright is strong (it was
also strong in the first version but, alas, very long) and
there are passages of decent writing throughout. *Ulysses*
in the first version was a victim in New York of patterns
all too prevalent in the American theater. The author,
having in the eyes of some been overpraised for *Benno
Blimpie* and *Gemini*, was ripe for a fall. The theater, des-
perate for publicity, opened the play to a houseful—literally—of critics, before the cast had been able to absorb
last-minute changes. The result was a predictable mess.

Chronologically, *Ulysses* is the last play to have been
written; it is also a question mark. The first play is an
oddity called *Urlicht*. The title, which means "Primal
Light," is also that of a Mahler song (used in his second
symphony), and the character Gustav was named after
Mahler, a composer with whom I felt a strong identifi-
cation at the time of writing *Urlicht*. The play is a strange
mixture of adolescent whimsy overinfluenced by the
Theater of the Absurd, with a powerful personal vision
thrusting itself forth at the last minute. There are two
sections of which I am fond. One is Gustav's long speech
describing his opera. This is a parody of a style of the

later operas of Richard Strauss, when leitmotivs for every
conceivable and inconceivable action and emotion are
stated, then combined in every conceivable and inconceivable way. The second is the last part of the play,
when mother and son have revealed themselves and the
mother rejects her son, a passage, it seems to me, of considerable energy and impact. The play is in a dreamlike
locale—a subway terminal late at night, with the nun/
mother rising from below like a nightmare creature from
the unconscious. The idea of a creator who summons up
fantasy figures to destroy him is common to all my early
work, including a number of plays which, perhaps mer-
cifully, have been lost. Perhaps the play also demonstrates a confrontation between a creator (whose attempts
are sincere, however futile) and a woman who has abdi-
cated her creativity both as artist and mother in favor of
a rampaging destructiveness, thus acting out the inver-
sion and destruction of artistic values that has occurred
in the last thirty years. Needless to say, no one felt any
hurry to perform *Urlicht*. When I was at Yale, anxious to
perform this play in a Sunday workshop, every actress
and actor in the school refused to be in it—some insisting
it was shocking, filthy, and sick; others simply opining
that it was rubbish. A friend of a friend was imported
from Philadelphia to play Gustav, and the wife of a directing student bravely, and against everyone's advice,
volunteered for the nun. To my knowledge, the play has
not been done since.

A play called *The Life of Jacob Pindar* followed *Urlicht*. It ended with a suicide, as did so many plays of
that period, and has been lost. Then came *Wisdom Amok*,
by far the weirdest play in this collection. *Wisdom* went
through many versions, all much longer than the one included here, and I also wrote a large part of it as a novel,
though only after wrestling with the play version for at
least two years. I have no idea what to make of *Wisdom*.
I certainly identified with the failed artist, Augustine
Wisdom, who crams his unpublished manuscripts into
the wrong coffin in the first scene, and anyone can tell
that the play was written by a virulent ex-Catholic. Beyond that, who can say? Can it be that the madhouse for
nuns is a paradigm for the world, and that Rex, the triumphant Mother Superior, demonstrates that in this world

the only possible triumph is enjoyed by the most evil
and exploitative? One thing is certain: *Wisdom* is a sex-
obsessed play. But it is not pro-sex, it is anti-sex. Nor is it
selective about which aspects of sex it abjures. Everything connected with sex, from the very possession of
genitalia, is mocked and reviled in the play, and the given
is that love in a sexual context is not only a dirty joke, but
the cruelest illusion. Clearly the two main characters,
Augustine Wisdom and Mother Superior Eleanora Franklinus (called Rex), have invented one another for the pur-
poses of a fantasy duel. Wisdom needs to conjure up a
putatively female demon to destroy him, just as Rex is
forever on the lookout for a male maniac to devour (all
too literally). Nor are the lines of sympathy clear in the
play. When it comes to killing, Augustine is no slouch,
having murdered a goodly number of nuns before getting
his comeuppance and first tupping from Rex; while Rex
at times seems admirable, at least in her courage and
honesty.

Then there is *The Transfiguration of Benno Blimpie*,
the play that followed *Urlicht* and *Wisdom* and preceded
Earth Worms, Gemini, and *Ulysses.* Though I certainly
did not plan it that way, *Benno* became a turning point
of sorts. This is clear enough in retrospect, for in *Benno*
a more absurd and narrative kind of dramaturgy confronts
a pronounced realism. To my mind the play has never
entirely worked, because it is impossible to reconcile in
performance these two contradictory styles with their dis-
parate conventions. The long speeches of Benno to the
audience, framed in each case by rather puzzling speeches
of the girl (who is not clearly addressing anyone), interrupt the more effective and straightforward mimesis of
the girl and the old man, the mother and the father, and
their collective mistreatment of the boy Benno. Perhaps
the mistake of all the productions of *Benno* I've seen
(including one in London that I directed) has been in the
attempt to reconcile these warring forces. The dislocation
that would result from playing the contradictions straight
out is probably appropriate to the emotional life of the
play. I am not surprised at this discontinuity, for in fact
Benno was the result of a dream—a series of pregnant
images that I forced, upon waking, into a barely coherent

scenario. Perhaps it is for the best that I kept (not entirely willing it) the discontinuity of the dream; perhaps I should have struggled more to subdue these peculiarities. What was clearest and most disturbing about the dream was the way the adult Benno sat and passively watched his younger self tortured; both were actual and concrete, related yet separated. One was the other's dream, so to speak, but absolutely concrete for all that. This is virtually impossible to achieve on a stage, since there is no way that one can show two people who are different, in different time frames and separate bodies, who are nonetheless identical, one and the same. Those who have read Jung or the "Seth" books of Jane Roberts may be acquainted with the idea of synchronicity: that is, that the past, present, and future are all happening at once, and that all experience is simultaneous. Unconsciously, this idea, and perhaps an almost instinctive belief in it, ruled the form *Benno* would take.

In more technical terms, *Benno* pointed the way to my future work, which became more and more naturalistic on the surface, with the dislocations and rapid shifts in mood hidden, handled indirectly, or motivated by naturalistic inventions made to seem plausible by manipulation of plot and character. *Benno* also marked a return to South Philadelphia, which I had fled in my real life and avoided in most of my earlier plays. Although *Benno*, *Gemini*, and *Ulysses* are far from histories of my past and relationships, they are clearly much more anchored in situations and circumstances of which I have a certain firsthand knowledge. Obviously (and this shift was far from planned) it is this change that made it possible for at least some of my plays to reach a wider audience. But I am haunted by a fear that some of the freedom and spontaneity of the earlier plays, which can still be encountered in *Earth Worms* (like *Benno*, a transitional play), has swum away from me, recoiling from its imprisonment in a naturalistic framework.

As I enter my thirties and continue writing plays, this frankly schizophrenic aspect of my work has continued. A play called *Aggy*, like *Benno* and *Gemini*, occurs in South Philadelphia and despite a certain wildness is, at least on the surface, naturalistic. But another play called

Quartet: My Life, inspired by the composer Shostako-vich, is a return to the wilder and more free-associative world of *Wisdom Amok.*

If there is a likely emphasis in the continuation of my career as a playwright, it will probably be on the recon-ciliation of these contradictory impulses.

Albert Innaurato
December 1, 1979
New York City

GEMINI

Characters

FRAN GEMINIANI is forty-five, working-class, boisterous, and friendly. He is slightly overweight, coughs a lot from mild emphysema.

FRANCIS GEMINIANI, his son, is about to celebrate his twenty-first birthday. He is also plump, a little clumsy, is entering his senior year at Harvard.

LUCILLE POMPI is Fran's lady friend, very thin, early forties, working-class, but strives hard to act in accordance with her ideas of ladylike behavior and elegance.

BUNNY WEINBERGER, the Geminiani's next-door neighbor, is a heavyset, blowsy woman, about forty, once very beautiful and voluptuous, now rough-talking and inclined to drink too much.

HERSCHEL WEINBERGER, her son, is sixteen, very heavy, asthmatic, very bright, but eccentric. He is obsessed with public transportation in all its manifestations and is shy and a little backward socially.

JUDITH HASTINGS, Francis's classmate at Harvard, is a month or two younger than Francis. She is an exceedingly, perhaps even intimidatingly, beautiful Wasp. She is extremely intelligent, perhaps slightly more aggressive than she should be, but is basically well-meaning.

RANDY HASTINGS, her brother, has just finished his freshman year at Harvard. Like Judith, he is a quintessential, very handsome Wasp.

The play takes place on June 1 and 2, 1973. The latter marks Francis's twenty-first birthday.

Scenes

ACT I
Scene 1: June 1, 1973. Early morning.
Scene 2: That evening.

ACT II
Scene 1: June 2, 1973. Morning.
Scene 2: That evening.

The setting shows the backyards of two adjoining row houses in the Italian section of South Philadelphia. They are small, two-story, brick houses typical of the poorer sections of most big cities. In one house live the Geminianis, Fran and Francis, and in the other the Weinbergers, Bunny and Herschel. In the Geminiani yard is a fig tree, and along one side a high alley fence with a gate. The Weinberger yard contains an old ladder, a rusty old tricycle, garbage cans, and a certain amount of general debris, and is also bounded by an alley wall, behind which is a high utility or telephone pole.

ACT I

Scene 1

*The sound of garbage men emptying the garbage in the
alley. They are making an immense noise. It is just past
dawn and they are banging lids, overturning cans, and
yelling to one another.*

FRANCIS GEMINIANI *appears at his bedroom window. He
is dressed in a T-shirt, his hair is wild, his glasses are
awry. He has just been awakened and is in a rage.*

FRANCIS: Shut up! Will you please shut up! Why aren't
you men more civilized? Oh, Jesus Christ!
[*He sets a speaker on the windowsill, and turns on the
final portion full blast of Isolde's narrative and curse
from Act I of* Tristan und Isolde. BUNNY WEINBERGER
*appears at the second-floor window of her house. She
is in a torn nightgown and faded robe, and is also in
a rage.*]
BUNNY: Francis! Francis! Why are you playing that music
at six o' clock in the mornin'? You got somethin' against
my gettin' a good night's sleep?
FRANCIS: [*Leaning out his window.*] Do you hear the garbage men?
BUNNY: Sure. They're just doing their job. That's the trouble wit you college kids—got no respect for the working
man. Besides, I got an uncle out there. [*Shouts out to
alley behind fence.*] Hi ya, Uncle Jerry!
VOICE: [*From behind the fence*] Hi ya, Bun!
BUNNY: How's your hammer hanging? [*Then to* FRANCIS]
See, I got connections. You stick wit me, kid, I'll get
you a job. [*A knocking is heard at the front door of the*

5

Geminiani house.] And now you got them knockin' at your door. You woke everybody up. Ain't you gonna answer it?

FRANCIS: I'm going back to bed. [*He takes the speaker off the sill.*]

BUNNY: Good. Maybe we'll have some quiet.

[*She disappears inside her bedroom. The knocking continues. The garbage men fade away.* FRANCIS *has now put on a very quiet passage from Act IV of Verdi's* I Vespri Siciliani. *After a moment, a knocking is heard at the gate in the fence, the entrance to the Geminiani yard.* FRANCIS *does not come to his window. More knocking. A pause. Then a rolled-up sleeping bag comes sailing over the fence, followed by a small knapsack.* RANDY HASTINGS *appears at the top of the fence. He climbs over and jumps into the yard. He looks around. Suddenly a large knapsack, the kind that has an aluminum frame, appears at the top of the fence.* RANDY *takes it and puts it down on the ground. Next we see a rolled-up tent, a second sleeping bag on the fence, then a tennis racket, and then* JUDITH HASTINGS. *She perches on top of the fence, looks around, and then jumps into the yard.* RANDY *has piled everything neatly together in the middle of the yard. They are both in worn jeans and sneakers. They circle about the yard, peeking into* BUNNY's *part curiously.* JUDITH *notices the fig tree and smiles. She knocks at the back door. No answer.* RANDY *tries to open it, but it is latched from the inside. He then peeks into the window to the left of the door and sees* FRANCIS *sleeping in his room. He smiles at* JUDITH, *and they climb into* FRANCIS's *room.*]

JUDITH *and* RANDY: Surprise! Surprise!

[*The music stops.* FRANCIS *leaps out of bed.*]

JUDITH: [*Inside the room*] Put your glasses on, it's Judith. . . .

RANDY: . . . and Randy. What's the matter?

FRANCIS: What are you doing here?

JUDITH: Come to see you, of course—

FRANCIS: Why?

JUDITH: It's your birthday tomorrow, your twenty-first.

[*At this moment,* HERSCHEL *dashes out of the back door of his house and into the yard. He hurls himself*

*onto the rusty tricycle and, making subway engine
noises, careens about the yard.*]

RANDY: [*Looking through screen door*] Francis, who's
that?

FRANCIS: [*With* JUDITH *in kitchen window*] Herschel
next door.

RANDY: What's he doing?

FRANCIS: Hey, Herschel, what are you doing?

HERSCHEL: I'm pretending I'm a subway engine.

FRANCIS: Which one?

HERSCHEL: Three nineteen AA four six five AA BZ sub-
stratum two. Built in 1945, in April, first run on Memo-
rial Day.

FRANCIS: Herschel is into public transportation.

[BUNNY *comes out of her house, still in the same torn
and smudged nightgown and housecoat. She has a
quart beer bottle in one hand and a cigarette in the
other.*]

BUNNY: What the fuck's goin' on out here, hanh? Why
you up so early?

[HERSCHEL, *making engine noises, heads right for her.
She sidesteps the tricycle easily.*]

BUNNY: Jesus Christ, it's that engine you're goin' a see.

FRANCIS: [*From window, still with* JUDITH. RANDY *has
come out to get a better view.*] Bunny, these are friends
of mine from school. Judith Hastings and her brother,
Randy. [*Indicates* BUNNY.] This is my neighbor, Bunny
Weinberger.

BUNNY: I didn't know they had girls at Harvard.

FRANCIS: Judith is at Radcliffe.

BUNNY: This is my son, Herschel. He's a genius. He's
gotta IQ of 187 or 172, depending on which test you
use. [*To* HERSCHEL, *who is still careening about.*] Stop
that fuckin' noise! He's also got asthma, and he tends
to break out.

HERSCHEL: [*To* RANDY] You want to see my collection of
transfers?

RANDY: [*With a shrug*] Sure.

[HERSCHEL *dashes into his house.*]

BUNNY: [*Looking after him*] Well, all geniuses is a little
crazy. You kids look hungry, so damn skinny. [*She is
poking* RANDY *in the stomach.*]

RANDY: Do you think so?

BUNNY: I guess you're scholarship students at Harvard, hanh? Although Francis is on scholarship you wouldn't know it to look at him. You wan' some breakfast?

JUDITH: That would be very nice.

[BUNNY *starts for her door.*]

FRANCIS: Get the roaches out of the oven first, Bunny.

BUNNY: [*Good-naturedly*] Oh, go fuck yourself. I ain't had a live roach in here in a year, unless you count Herschel, I think he's part roach. Whatayas want? Fried eggs and bacon all right?

RANDY: Sure.

BUNNY: He's normal, at least. [*She goes inside.*]

FRANCIS: So . . . you're just here for the day?

JUDITH: For the day? Some people go away to the beach from the city, we have come away to the city from the beach.

RANDY: Can you say that in French?

JUDITH: [*Coming out of the house*] Il y a des gens qui vont . . .

FRANCIS: [*Interrupting*] How'd you get here?

JUDITH: We hitchhiked, of course.

FRANCIS: You rich people are crazy. It would never occur to me to hitchhike.

JUDITH: That's because you couldn't get picked up.

RANDY: Come on, Judith, you can help me set up the tent.

FRANCIS: [*From his room, putting on his pants*] Tent?

RANDY: Sure. We always sleep outside. We could put it up under this tree. What kind is it?

JUDITH: Fig, idiot.

RANDY: What's a fig tree doing in your yard?

FRANCIS: [*Coming out of house, pants on, but barefoot*] You'll have to ask my father, he planted it. But look, I don't want . . . I mean . . . well, you see, it's my father. I mean you can't stay here. He doesn't like company.

RANDY: But I thought wops loved company.

[JUDITH *hits him.*]

FRANCIS: Mafia.

JUDITH: The Mafia?

FRANCIS: You know, the Black Hand, Cosa Nostra, the Brotherhood. . . .

RANDY: Your father's in the . . .

FRANCIS: Hit man.

JUDITH: Oh, come on!

FRANCIS: He offs Wasps. It was bred into him at an early age, this raving hatred of white Anglo-Saxon Protestants, they call them white people.

RANDY: [*Looks worried.*] White people?

FRANCIS: He collects their ears after he murders them, he has a collection in his room. . . . [*Starts picking up their camping equipment and hands it to* JUDITH *and* RANDY.] I'll tell you what, let's go to the bus terminal, I'll finish getting dressed, we'll put your stuff in a locker, I'll show you around, we'll take a few pictures, then you can go back later tonight. I'll get my camera. [*He runs inside.*]

RANDY: You mean we have to carry this junk around some more?

JUDITH: [*At* FRANCIS's *window*] Why don't you come back with us—we've got plenty of room—Mother will love you—you can cook for us.

FRANCIS: [*Appears at window.*] I can't. I have a job.

RANDY: You can watch me work out.

JUDITH: Oh, Randy, grow up! I wanted to see you . . .

FRAN: [*Offstage*] Yo, Francis, you home!

FRANCIS: Oh, Jesus Christ!

[RANDY *is trying to escape for his life.* JUDITH *is holding him back.*]

FRAN: [*Offstage, yelling*] Yo, Francis, we're back!

[FRAN *unlocks the gate, which had a chain and padlock. He appears with an empty trashcan,* LUCILLE *right behind him, holding three freshly pressed shirts on hangers.* FRAN *sets the trashcan under his kitchen window, and then notices the visitors in his yard.*]

FRAN: [*Yelling into window*] You got company?

JUDITH: [*Hastily*] My name is Judith Hastings, and this is my brother Randy. We know Francis from Harvard.

FRAN: Oh yeah? I'm his dad. I didn't know Igor had friends. He just sits around all day, no job, nothin'. My name's Francis too. [*Turns to* RANDY.] But you can call me Franny, or Fran, or Frank. [*Turns to* JUDITH.] And you can call me honey, or sweetness and light, or darling, whatever you like. [*Indicates* LUCILLE, *who is trying to blend into the fence, because she has been surprised in a housecoat.*] This is Lucille.

LUCILLE: Oh dear.

JUDITH: Well, we were just leaving.

FRAN: Leavin'? But you just got here, you can't leave.

LUCILLE: [*Attempting elegance*] Well, Fran, thanks for comin' over. . . . [*She hands* FRAN *his shirts.*] Of course, I was rather surprised, its bein' so early, my dress.

BUNNY: [*Appears in her window.*] Hi ya, Fran.

FRAN: Yo, Bun.

BUNNY: [*Sees* LUCILLE.] I see you got the Holy Clam wit you. I'm cookin' breakfast.

LUCILLE: [*To* JUDITH *and* RANDY, *still explaining*] And then I have to wash my hair. . . .

BUNNY: Shut up, Lucille, you keep washin' it and it's gonna fall out, and not just your hair. Hey, you kids, you wan' some oregano in these eggs?

FRAN: Why? They're still gonna be Irish eggs.

BUNNY: I gotta Jew name, but I'm Irish. Real name's Murphy.

FRAN: You still got roaches in that oven? [*Coughs from emphysema, then laughs.*]

BUNNY: You still got rats up your ass?

LUCILLE: Bunny! [*Then to* FRAN] Stop smoking, hanh?

BUNNY: [*In her window, with a mixing bowl, singing*]
Oh, I got plenty of nothin'
and nothing's got plenty of me,
Got my ass,
Got my tits,
Got my cup of tea,
Ain't no use complainin',
Got my ass,
Got my ass,
Got my tits!"
[*Dialogue continues over* BUNNY's *song.*]

FRAN: [*To* RANDY *and* JUDITH] You just get here?

JUDITH: You're sure you want us to stay?

FRAN: Whataya mean am I sure?

RANDY: We're Wasps. . . .

FRAN: So? I'm broad-minded. Is that a tent?

RANDY: We like to sleep outside.

FRAN: You kids is all nuts, you know that? So put it up! [*Scratches.*]

LUCILLE: [*Setting up a lawn chair*] Stop scratching that rash.

FRAN: That's my fig tree, you know! I planted it.
[BUNNY *finishes her song and goes back to cooking.*

LUCILLE *sits down and talks to* RANDY.]

LUCILLE: So how do you do? My name is Lucille Pompi. I have a son at Yale and my daughter is a dental technician, she works at the Graduate Hospital, special shift, and my late husband ...

FRAN: *Sta'zit'*, Lucille, these kids look hungry. You must be on scholarship at Harvard, though Francis is on scholarship you'd never know it to look at him. We got lots of food in, only thing that keeps him from jumpin' out the window when he's home. [*Coughs.*]

LUCILLE: Turn away from people when you cough, hanh? [RANDY *and* JUDITH *are pitching the tent under the tree.*]

FRAN: We got brebalone and pepperoni, how 'bout some while horseshit finishes up thé eggs? We also got pizzel. Francis loves them but I got a whole box hid.

JUDITH: Oh, I'm sure breakfast will be more than enough.

FRAN: But you don't understand. That's gonna be a Irish breakfast—that's a half a egg, a quarter slice a bacon. ... [*Scratches.*]

LUCILLE: [*Genteel*] The Irish mean well but they don't know how to eat. [*To* FRAN, *genteel manner gone*] Don't scratch that rash!

FRAN: I'll get everything together.

JUDITH: I'll help you.

FRAN: Well, thank you, sweetheart. What's your name again?

JUDITH: Judith.
[*He lets her go in first and admires her figure. He shakes his head appreciatively and winks at* RANDY, *who winks back, laughing.* RANDY *continues pitching the tent.*]

LUCILLE: [*To* RANDY, *after* FRAN *and* JUDITH *have exited*] My son, Donny Pompi, is at Yale, he's a sophomore on the basketball team and in pre-med. He's on a Branford scholarship. Do you know him?

RANDY: I go to Harvard.

LUCILLE: But he's at Yale. Wouldn't you know him?

RANDY: No, I go to Harvard.

LUCILLE: Is there a difference?

FRAN: [*Coming out of the kitchen, yelling*] Yo, Francis! Where's your manners? Was you raised in the jungle? [FRAN *and* JUDITH *come into the yard; he is carrying a typing table with a tray of food on it, and she has a cake and napkins.*]

FRAN: Sometimes I wonder about him, his mother used to say when he was born he broke the mold, maybe she was right.

[LUCILLE *starts serving and repeating absentmindedly after* FRAN.]

FRAN: Now, we got here: Coffee cake . . .

LUCILLE: Coffee cake . . .

FRAN: Jelly doughnuts . . .

LUCILLE: Jelly doughnuts . . .

FRAN: Black olives, green olives, pitted black olives—they're easier to digest, chocolate-covered doughnuts—[*He holds one up.*]—they're Francis's favorites, so eat them first and save him some pimples—brebalone, pepperoni, pizzel, biscuits, a fiadone Lucille baked last week and some hot peppers. Don't be shy.

RANDY: Thanks.

FRAN: Yo, Francis! Where the hell are you?

BUNNY: [*Enters carrying a huge tray of food.*] Here's breakfast.

[*She is followed out by* HERSCHEL, *who is carrying a huge box.* BUNNY *notices that the Geminiani tray is on a typing table, so she sets her tray on a trash can that is under her kitchen window, and drags the whole thing to the center of the yard. She hands* RANDY *a plate with a fried egg on it.*]

HERSCHEL: [*To* RANDY] Here's my collection of transfers.

RANDY: Lot of them. [*Sits down in front of tent to eat.*]

HERSCHEL: [*Following* RANDY] Four thousand seven hundred and twenty-two. They start at eighteen seventy-three.

BUNNY: Biggest collection in the state outside of a museum. That's what my uncle works at the PTC told me.

HERSCHEL: [*Opening one of the albums*] These are from the old trolleys; they're my favorites, they're buried, you see.

FRAN: Yo, Francis!

FRANCIS: [*Inside, yelling*] Jesus Christ in heaven, I'm coming.

FRAN: That's my Ivy League son.

FRANCIS: [*Entering the yard*] Lot of food.

FRAN: These kids gotta eat. Looka how skinny they are.
You don' gotta eat, but that's all you do.

BUNNY: [*About* HERSCHEL, *who is gulping large quan-
tities of food*] This is another one. Looka him put that
food away. Slow down!

[HERSCHEL *chokes.*]

BUNNY: Oh, oh, he's gonna have a asthma attack. I think
he does it to punish me. You ever try to sleep with
someone havin' a asthma attack in the next room?
Drives you bananas. [*To* HERSCHEL, *still gulping*] Take
human bites, for Christ' sake! Jesus, it's like a threshing
machine: Varroom! Varroom!

FRAN: [*To* JUDITH] Don't be bashful, we got plenty.

JUDITH: I'm not bashful.

FRAN: Eat, then!

BUNNY: [*Lunges at* HERSCHEL *with the fly swatter.*] Slow
down! The end of the world ain't for another twenty
minutes.

[*He slows down.*]

BUNNY: That's right. [*She looks at his neck.*] Look at them
mosquito bites. You been pickin' them? I says, you
been pickin' them?

HERSCHEL: No.

BUNNY: I told you and I told you not to pick at them,
they'll get infected.

FRAN: [*To* RANDY] You got a appetite, at least.

JUDITH: [*Stands up; to* FRAN] Egli è casa dappertutto.

FRAN: [*Not having understood*] Hanh?

FRANCIS: She's an Italian major at Radcliffe.

JUDITH: [*Very conversationally*] Questo giardin mi piace
molto. Il nostro camino non furo facile, ma siamo gio-
vane e . . .

[*They all look at her, puzzled.*]

LUCILLE: You see, dear, that's Harvard Italian. We don't
speak that.

FRAN: What did you say?

JUDITH: [*Very embarrassed, sits down.*] Oh, nothing.

FRAN: You see, my people over there was the niggers.
The farmhands, they worked the land. We're Abruz-
zese; so we speak a kinda nigger Italian.

LUCILLE: Oh, Fran! He means it's a dialect.

BUNNY: [*Looking* FRAN *over mock-critically*] Niggers,

hanh? Let me look, let me look. Yeah, I thought so.
Suspicious complexion.

[*She grabs his crotch.* LUCILLE *scowls.*]

FRAN: [*To* BUNNY] You're not eatin' as much as usual,
Bun.

BUNNY: I'm eatin' light, got stage fright. Gotta go a court
today.

FRAN: Yeah, why?

LUCILLE: Oh, Bunny, please, not in front of the kids!

BUNNY: That bitch Mary O'Donnel attacked me. I was
lyin' there, mindin' my own business, and she walks
in, drops the groceries, screams, then throws herself on
top a me.

FRAN: Where was you lyin'?

BUNNY: In bed.

FRAN: Whose bed?

BUNNY: Whataya mean: Whose bed? Don' matter whose
bed. No matter where a person is, that person gotta
right to be treated wit courtesy. And her fuckin' husband was no use; he just says: Oh, Mary! turns over
and goes back to sleep. So's I hadda fend for myself.
She threw herself on top a me, see, so I broke her
fuckin' arm. Well, you woulda thought the whole world
was fuckin' endin'. She sat there and screamed. I didn't
know what to do. It was her house. I didn't know where
nothin' was and she's a shitty housekeeper. So I shook
her fuckin' husband's arm and said get the fuck up, I
just broke your fuckin' wife's arm. But he shook me off,
you know how these men are, afta, so's I put on my
slip, and I put on my dress and got the hell out of there.
I'll tell you my ears was burnin'. That witch has gotta
tongue like the murders in the Rue Morgue. Then, of
all the face, she's got the guts to go to the cops and say
I assaulted her. Well, I was real ashamed to have to
admit I did go after Mary O'Donnel. She smells like
old peanuts. Ever smell her, Lucille?

[LUCILLE *shudders and turns away.*]

BUNNY: So's I gotta go to court and stand trial. But I ain't
worried. I gotta uncle on the force, he's a captain. Come
on, Herschel. Sam the Jew wan's a see his kid today.

[*She picks up her tray.*]

LUCILLE: [*Not moving*] I'll help clean up.

JUDITH: [*Jumping up*] So will I.

BUNNY: Good, 'cause I gotta get ready to meet my judge. I'll show youse where everything is.

HERSCHEL: [*To* RANDY] Do you want to see my collection of subway posters?

RANDY: [*After some hesitation*] Well, all right.

HERSCHEL: [*Following* RANDY *into house, with his transfers*] I have eight hundred . . .

BUNNY: [*Holding door for* LUCILLE] Right this way, the palace is open.

[FRAN *and* FRANCIS *are left alone.*]

FRAN: I didn't know your friends was comin'.

FRANCIS: I didn't either.

FRAN: They are your friends, ain't they?

FRANCIS: It isn't that simple.

FRAN: You kids is all nuts, you know that? It was that simple when I was growin' up. You hung out on the corner, see, and the guys you hung out wit was your friends, see? Never stopped to think about it.

FRANCIS: Those guys you hung out with were pretty quick to drop you when you had all the trouble with the bookies, and when Mother left. You might say they deserted you.

FRAN: Yeah, yeah, you might say that.

FRANCIS: So then, they weren't friends.

FRAN: Course they was. People desert other people, don' make no difference if they're friends or not. I mean, if they wasn't friends to begin wit, you couldn't say they deserted me, could you?

FRANCIS: I guess not.

FRAN: Francis, this Judith, she's really somethin'. I didn't know you had the eye, you know?

FRANCIS: How was your trip to Wildwood?

FRAN: Well, Lucille had a fight wit Aunt Emma. That's why we came back. It was over water bugs. I didn't see no water bugs. But Lucille said they was everywhere. Aunt Emma thought she was accusin' her of bein' dirty. So we came back.

FRANCIS: Lucille is quite a phenomenon.

FRAN: She's good people, she means well. There ain't nothin' like a woman's company, remember that, my son, there ain't nothin' like a woman. You can think there is. I thought the horses was just as good; hell, I thought the horses was better. But I was wrong. But you gotta be careful of white women. I guess us dagos go afta them; hell, I went afta you mother, and she was as white as this Judith, though not near as pretty. But you gotta be careful of them kinda women. A white woman's like a big hole, you can never be sure what's in there. So you be careful, even if she is a Italian major. What do you want for your birthday tomorrow?

[*They start clearing the yard, folding the chairs, putting trashcans back in place, typing table back in the house.*]

FRANCIS: Not to be reminded of it.

FRAN: C'mon, we gotta do somethin'. That's a big occasion: Twenty-one! I know what! You and your guests can have a big dinner out wit Lucille and me to celebrate.

FRANCIS: Oh, I think they'll have left by then.

FRAN: They just got here!

FRANCIS: Well, you know how these kids are nowadays, all nuts. They can't stand to be in one place more than a few hours.

FRAN: But they just pitched their tent under the fig tree, even. No, no, I think you're wrong. I think we're in for a visit. And I hope so, they seem like nice kids.

FRANCIS: Well, they're a little crazy; you know, speed, it twists the mind.

FRAN: Speed?

FRANCIS: Yeah, they're both what we call speed freaks. That's why they're so skinny.

FRAN: You mean they ain't on scholarship?

FRANCIS: They're on speed.

FRAN: Oh, my God, them poor kids. They need some help. I'm gonna call Doc Pollicarpo, maybe he could help them.

[RANDY *comes out of* BUNNY'*s house, carrying heavy books.*]

RANDY: Herschel lent me his books on subways.... [*He sets them down in front of the tent.*]

FRAN: You poor kid.

RANDY: [*Misunderstanding*] Well ...

FRAN: No wonder you're so skinny.

RANDY: I'm not that skinny.

FRAN: Some other kid started you on it? Somebody tie you down and force it into your veins?

RANDY: What?

FRAN: Looka his eyes—that's a real strange color. I guess that proves it. You got holes in your arms too?

RANDY: What—why?

FRAN: Come here and sit down, you need rest, you need good food, have a black olive, that's good for speed.

RANDY: [*Shocked*] Speed?

FRAN: And your sister too? That beautiful young girl on speed? It's a heartbreaker. That stuff it works fast, that's why they call it speed.

[FRANCIS *nods in agreement.*]

FRAN: You can see it rot the brain.

RANDY: But I'm not on . . . [*Looks at* FRANCIS, *understanding.*]

FRANCIS: [*Shrugs.*] My father got it in his head you were on speed.

RANDY: I never touch it.

FRAN: [*Understanding*] Oh, yeah, let's make a fool of the old man. [*Yelling*] Yo, Lucille, get the hell out here. [*To* RANDY] I'm sorry, young man, my son is a little twisted. His mother used to say when he came along he—

FRANCIS: [*Has heard this many times.*] —when he came along he broke the mold.

FRAN: [*Yelling*] Lucille! I'm not gonna call you again.

LUCILLE: [*Coming out*] I'm here. And don't scratch that rash, makes it worse.

FRAN: [*Yelling*] Yo, Bun, gook luck wit the judge! [*To* LUCILLE] Come on. [*Heads toward the kitchen, turns back.*] Randy, if you're gonna smoke pot out here, do it quiet.

LUCILLE: Oh, I'm sure he's too nice a boy to—

FRAN: Lucille, get inna house!

[FRAN, *with* LUCILLE, *enters house.*]

RANDY: What's all this about speed? That's what I call a sixties mentality.

FRANCIS: Where's Judith?

RANDY: Still cleaning up, I guess. [*Pulls out a box of joints.*] Want some pot?

FRANCIS: Why'd you come? You could have given me some warning.

RANDY: We're not an atomic attack. [*He starts boxing with* FRANCIS.]

FRANCIS: You dropped in like one.

[RANDY *starts doing push-ups.*]

FRANCIS: What are you doing?

RANDY: I've been working out every day and taking tiger's milk and nutriment. . . .

FRANCIS: What about Wate-On?

RANDY: Overrated. [*Rolls over on his back.*] Hey, hold my legs.

FRANCIS: You want to play *Sunrise at Campobello?*

RANDY: Smart ass, I want to do sit-ups.

[FRANCIS *kneels and gets a hold of* RANDY's *feet.* RANDY *starts doing sit-ups.*]

FRANCIS: [*Grunts.*] One . . . three . . . You weren't this bad last spring. Even though you did drag me to the gym once—I even had to take a shower—I stumbled around without my glasses, I couldn't see anything, my arms were out like Frankenstein's—they thought I was very strange. [*He looks down at his arms.*] My arms are getting tired—and what is this supposed to do?

RANDY: [*Still lying on the ground*] I'm tired of being skinny.

FRANCIS: You aren't that skinny.

RANDY: I'm grotesque-looking. Look at my chest. [*Lifts shirt.*] I look like a newborn duck. I want pectorals, I want biceps, I want shoulders. I want people to stop sniggering when they look at me.

FRANCIS: I don't snigger when I look at you.

RANDY: [*Seriously*] You're my friend.

[FRANCIS *rises, uncomfortable.* RANDY *lights up a joint.*]

RANDY: Is there a pool around here? I'd like to go swimming.

FRANCIS: That's a good way to get spinal meningitis. Look, Randy, don't you think I'm an unlikely choice for a jock buddy?

[JUDITH *comes out of the house and joins them on the stoop.*]

JUDITH: Sorry that took so long, but Lucille didn't do anything, she just stood there and insisted I had to know her son. Hey, Francis, how are you going to entertain me? Is there a museum in walking distance of Philadelphia?

RANDY: That's low-priority; we're going to the boat races.

JUDITH: Randy, why don't you simply realize you're pathetic, and stop boring intelligent people?

RANDY: And why don't you treat your hemorrhoids and stop acting like somebody out of Picasso's blue period. . . .

[BUNNY *comes out of her house. She is wearing a very tight white crocheted suit and carrying a plastic flowered shopping bag. She is dressed for court.*]

BUNNY: [*Strikes a "stunning" pose.*] How do I look?

RANDY: Like you can win the case.

BUNNY: You're sweet. Give me a kiss for luck. [*Grabs and kisses him. Then yells.*] Herschel! [*Back to* RANDY] Look at his skin, look at his eyes; ain't anybody around here looks like you, honey. Like a fuckin' white sheik! [HERSCHEL *enters from his house. He is dressed for a visit with his father, in an enormous, ill-fitting brown suit.*]

BUNNY: Oh, Herschel. Come on. [*Brushes his suit roughly.*] And look you, don't you go havin' no asthma attacks wit your father, he blames me.

JUDITH: [*Suddenly*] Herschel, Randy'll go with you; he wants to go to the park and study your subway books. [*She grabs one of the big books and drops it in* RANDY'*s hands.* RANDY *looks shocked.*]

HERSCHEL: [*Astounded and delighted*] Really?

JUDITH: [*Before* RANDY *can speak*] And do you happen to have, by any chance, a map of the subway system? Randy was just saying how much he wanted to study one.

HERSCHEL: Yes! [*Digs in his pockets.*] I have three. This one is the most up-to-date. You're interested—really interested?

RANDY: Well—I . . .

HERSCHEL: [*Grabbing* RANDY'*s arm*] Come on, I'll walk you to the park! [*Drags* RANDY *off down the alley.*] I know the way and everything. . . .

BUNNY: [*Yelling after them*] Don't fall down, Herschel, that suit costs a fortune to clean. [*To* JUDITH *and* FRANCIS] Well, I'm off. Wish me luck.

JUDITH and FRANCIS: [*Smoking a joint*] Good luck.

BUNNY: [*Crosses to the gate.*] I'll see youse later. I mean I hope I see youse later.

[*She exits, crossing her fingers for luck.* JUDITH *passes the joint to* FRANCIS. *She goes as if to kiss him, but instead blows smoke in his mouth. He chokes.*]

FRANCIS: Did you come here to humiliate me?

JUDITH: What?

FRANCIS: What do you call coming here with your brother, climbing over the back fence, walking in on me, half-naked, unannounced? And then, Bunny, Herschel—the house is a mess—

JUDITH: That doesn't bother me, really. You oughtn't to be ashamed.

FRANCIS: Oh, I wish you hadn't come, that's all, I wish you hadn't come, you or Randy. . . .

JUDITH: But why? I took you seriously, I took—everything seriously and then I hadn't heard—

FRANCIS: I didn't want any more of either of you.

JUDITH: Francis!

FRANCIS: Have you looked at me? I'm fat!

JUDITH: You're not fat!

FRANCIS: Then what do you call this? [*Makes two rolls of fat with his hands.*] If I try I can make three—

JUDITH: You're crazy! What does that have to do with anything?

FRANCIS: No attractive person has ever been interested in me. . . .

JUDITH: Well, maybe they thought you were a bore.

FRANCIS: "Love enters through the eyes," that's Dante. . . .

JUDITH: And he liked little girls.

FRANCIS: Look, I don't know what you see when you look at me. I've made myself a monster—and tomorrow I'm to be twenty-one and all I can feel is myself sinking.

JUDITH: But, Francis . . .

FRANCIS: Look, I don't want to discuss it now, now here, not with my father around the corner. Now I'm going into my room and play some music. Then I'm going for a walk. I would appreciate it if you'd strike your tent and gather up your things and your brother and leave before I return.

[*He goes into his room and puts on some quiet music.* JUDITH *is left alone. Suddenly* RANDY *appears over the fence.*]

RANDY: This is very mysterious.

BLACKOUT

Scene 2

Scene the same. Later that day. It is early evening. During the scene, night falls.

FRAN *is cooking spaghetti in his kitchen. He is singing "Strangers in the Night."*

RANDY *is inside the tent.*

FRANCIS *enters through the gate. Sees the tent. He slams the gate.*

FRANCIS: They're still here.
FRAN: [*From inside house*] Yo, Francis, is that you?
FRANCIS: Yes.
FRAN: I'm in the kitchen.
  [FRANCIS *goes inside.*]
FRAN: Where have you been?
FRANCIS: Where is she now?
FRAN: In your room. Why don't you go in to see her?
FRANCIS: Didn't it ever occur to you that I don' want you to interfere . . . ?
FRAN: [*Smiles.*] "Strangers in the night . . ."
  [FRANCIS *goes into his room.* HERSCHEL *comes bounding in from the alley.*]
HERSCHEL: [*To* FRAN] Hi. Where's Randy?
FRAN: In his tent. [*Yells.*] Yo, Randy! You got company.
  [RANDY *peeks out of the tent.* HERSCHEL *sits down by the tent.*]
HERSCHEL: Hi. I just got back from my father's. He wanted me to stay over but I faked a petit mal and he let me go.
RANDY: A petit mal?
HERSCHEL: You know, a fit. A little one. I stumbled around and I slobbered and I told him everything was black. He got worried. I told him I left my medicine back here, so he gave me money for a cab. I took the bus.
  [FRANCIS *and* JUDITH *appear in window.*]

HERSCHEL: Like, I was wondering, would you like to come with me to, like, see the engine? It's not far from here. It's all right if you don't want to come, like, I mean, I understand, you know? Everybody can't be interested in public transportation, it's not that interesting, you know? So, like, I understand if you aren't interested but would you like to come?

RANDY: [*Who has gotten a towel and toilet case out of his knapsack*] Can we have dinner first?

HERSCHEL: You mean you'll come? How about that! I'll go and change—I'll be right back. [*He starts to run, trips over his own feet, falls, picks himself up, and runs into his house.*]

JUDITH: [*From window*] I see you're about to be broadened.

RANDY: What could I do? [*To* FRAN *in kitchen*] Mr. Geminiani!

FRAN: [*Appears in kitchen window.*] Fran, it's Fran!

RANDY: Fran. Can I take a shower?

FRAN: Be my guest. You got a towel?

RANDY: Yes. [*He goes into the house.*]

FRAN: [*Comes out, yelling.*] Yo, Francis!

FRANCIS: [*He and* JUDITH *are right behind him.*] Jesus Christ, I'm right here.

FRAN: That's my Ivy League son. Look, once in a while when your lips get tired, go in and stir the spaghettis, hanh? I'm going to get Lucille.

FRANCIS: She lives around the corner, why can't she come over herself?

FRAN: Don' get smart, and show some respect. She believes in the boogie man. [*He throws the kitchen towel in through the window, as if he were making a jump shot.*] Yes! Two points! [*Holds up two fingers like cuckold's horns.*] "Strangers in the night . . ." [*He exits through the gate.*]

JUDITH: Lucille and your father are—well, you know, aren't they?

FRANCIS: I don't know, they drink an awful lot of coffee.

JUDITH: Stimulates the gonads—[*She embraces* FRANCIS *and kisses him. He looks uncomfortable.*] What's the matter?

FRANCIS: I'm sorry.

JUDITH: Sorry about what?

[*He looks away.*]

JUDITH: You know, I think you are an eternal adolescent, a German Adolescent, a German Romantic Adolescent. You were born out of context, you'd have been much happier in the forties of the last century when it was eternally twilight.

FRANCIS: Do I detect a veiled reference to *Zwielicht* by Eichendorff?

JUDITH: I took Basic European Literature also, and did better than you did.

FRANCIS: You did not.

JUDITH: I got the highest mark on the objective test: 98! What did you get? [*She laughs.*]

FRANCIS: [*Bantering with her*] My SAT verbal and achievement tests were higher than yours.

JUDITH: How do you know?

FRANCIS: I looked them up in the office. I pretended to go faint, and while the registrar ran for water, I looked at your file.

JUDITH: [*Entering into his game*] I find that hard to believe; I had the highest score in the verbal at St. Paul's and also in the English Achievement Test.

FRANCIS: That's what it said alongside your IQ.

JUDITH: [*Taken aback in spite of herself*] My IQ?

FRANCIS: Very interesting, that IQ. It was recorded in bright red ink. There was also a parenthesis, in which someone had written: "Poor girl, but she has great determination."

JUDITH: I find jokes about IQ's in poor taste.

FRANCIS: Then you are an adolescent, a German Adolescent, a German Romantic Adolescent.

JUDITH: And before this edifying discussion you were about to say, "Fuck you, Judith."

FRANCIS: Don't put it that way. . . .

JUDITH: But more or less it was get lost, see you later, oh yes, have a nice summer—and maybe, just maybe, I'll tell you why later. You seem to want to skip that part, the why. [*She picks up the end of a garden hose, and points it at* FRANCIS *like a machine gun, and with a Humphrey Bogart voice, says:*] Look, I came to see you, that's ballsy, now you've got to reciprocate and tell me why. . . . [*She puts down the hose, and the accent.*] Do I bore you? Do you think I'm ugly? Do I have bad breath?

FRANCIS: Oh, come on!

JUDITH: Hey, Francis, we're just alike, can't you see that?

FRANCIS: [*Indicates the house and yard.*] Oh yeah.

JUDITH: Two overachievers. Really. I know my family is better off than yours; but we're just alike, and there was something last winter and now you're telling me . . .

FRANCIS: Look, I'm going to be twenty-one tomorrow. Well . . . I don't know what to say.

JUDITH: Is there a reason?

FRANCIS: I don't think I can say.

JUDITH: That doesn't make any sense.

FRANCIS: I think I'm queer.

JUDITH: Why don't we back up a bit. I said, "We're just alike et cetera," and you said you were going to be twenty-one tomorrow, and I looked at you with deep-set, sea-blue eyes, and you said . . .

FRANCIS: I think I'm queer.

JUDITH: [*Laughs.*] Well, I guess we can't get around it. Do you want to amplify? I mean this seems like quite a leap from what I remember of those long, sweet, ec-static nights, naked in each other's young arms, cling-ing to . . .

FRANCIS: We fucked. Big deal. That's what kids are sup-posed to do. And be serious.

JUDITH: I am serious. Is there a particular boy?

FRANCIS: Yes.

JUDITH: An adolescent, a German Adolescent . . .

FRANCIS: Not German, no.

JUDITH: Do I know him?

[FRANCIS *doesn't answer.*]

JUDITH: Reciprocal?

FRANCIS: It was just this spring. He began to haunt me. We became friends. We talked a lot—late in my room when you were studying. Well, I don't know, and you see—I've had, well, crushes before. I dreamed of him. It's not reciprocal, no, he doesn't know, but it became more and more obvious to me. I mean, I'd look at him, and then some other boy would catch my eye and I'd think—you see?

JUDITH: Well. I suppose I could start teaching you the

secrets of makeup.

[FRANCIS *turns away, annoyed.*]

JUDITH: Well, how do you expect me to react? You seem to think I ought to leap out the window because of it. But it's like you're suddenly turning to me and saying you are from Mars. Well, you might be, but I don't see much evidence and I can't see what difference it makes. I'm talking about you and me, I and thou and all that. All right, maybe you do have an eye for the boys, well, so do I, but you . . . you are special to me. I wouldn't throw you over just because a hockey player looked good, why do you have to give me up?

FRANCIS: I don't think that makes any sense, Judith. I mean, if I were from Mars, it would make a difference, I'd have seven legs and talk a different language and that's how I feel now.

[JUDITH *embraces him.*]

FRANCIS: Don't touch me so much, Judith, and don't look at me. . . .

JUDITH: Then you're afraid. That explains that fat and ugly nonsense and this sudden homosexual panic. You're afraid that anyone who responds to you will make demands you can't meet. You're afraid you'll fail. . . .

FRANCIS: Good Evening, Ladies and Gentlemen, Texaco Presents: "Banality on Parade!"

JUDITH: You're afraid to venture. That's why you've enshrined someone who doesn't respond to you, probably doesn't even know you're interested. If the relationship never happens, you are never put to the test and can't fail. The Overachiever's Great Nightmare!

FRANCIS: That's crazy!

JUDITH: I bet this boy who draws you is some Harvard sprite, a dew-touched freshman. . . .

FRANCIS: He was a freshman.

JUDITH: In Randy's class and that proves it. Look at Randy—what kind of response could someone like that have but the giggles? And you know that. You're afraid of commitment. And remember what Dante says about those who refuse to make commitments. They're not even in hell, but are condemned to run about the outskirts for eternity.

[FRANCIS, *who has heard enough, has stuck his head*

inside BUNNY's *kitchen window and brought it down
over his neck like a guillotine.* JUDITH *now runs over
to the fence and starts climbing to the top.*]

JUDITH: *Ed io che reguardai vidi una insegna che gir-
ando correva tanta ratta, che d'ogni posa me parea
indegna ...!*

[*She leaps off the fence.* FRANCIS *runs to her aid.*]

FRANCIS: Judith! Jesus Christ!

JUDITH: [*As he helps her up*] You see? I ventured, I made
the great leap and remained unscathed.

[HERSCHEL *runs out of his house, dressed in his old
pants and torn sweat shirt, carrying one sneaker.*]

HERSCHEL: I heard a noise. Is Randy all right?

FRANCIS: Judith, you're all right?

JUDITH: Good as nude! [*Limps over to stoop and sits.*]

FRANCIS: Oh, shit! I forgot to stir the spaghetti. Now
they'll all stick together.... [*Runs into the kitchen,
runs out again.*] You're sure you're all right?

JUDITH: Stir the spaghetti. We don't want them sticking
together.

[FRANCIS *goes into the kitchen.*]

HERSCHEL: You're the one who fell?

JUDITH: You might put it that way.

HERSCHEL: [*Sits down beside* JUDITH. *Puts on his other
sneaker.*] I do that. One time I fell while I was having
an asthma attack. My mother called the ambulance. She
has, like, an uncle who's a driver. They rushed me to
the hospital. Like, you know, the siren screaming? That
was two years ago, right before I went to high school.
It was St. Agnes Hospital over Track Thirty-seven on
the A, the AA, the AA one through seven and the B
express lines, maybe you passed it? I didn't get, like,
hurt falling, you know. Still, my mother asked me what
I wanted most in the whole world, you know? I told
her and she let me ride the subway for twelve whole
hours. Like, she rode them with me. She had to stay
home from work for two days.

JUDITH: [*Crosses to tent, and gets a bandanna out of her
knapsack. She sits down and starts cleaning her knee,
which she'd hurt in leaping off the fence.*] Why are you
so interested in the subways?

HERSCHEL: [*Joins her on the ground.*] Oh, not just the
subways. I love buses too, you know? And my favorites

are, well, you won't laugh? The trolleys. They are very
beautiful. There's a trolley graveyard about two blocks
from here. I was thinking, like maybe Randy would
like to see that, you know? I could go see the engine
anytime. The trolley graveyard is well, like, I guess,
beautiful, you know? Really. They're just there, like
old creatures everyone's forgotten, some of them rusted
out, and some of them on their sides, and one, the old
thirty-two, is like standing straight up as though sayin',
like, I'm going to stand here and be myself, no matter
what. I talk to them. Oh, I shouldn't have said that.
Don't tell my mother, please? It's, you know, like people who go to castles and look for, for, well, like,
knights in shining armor, you know? That past was
beautiful and somehow, like, pure. The same is true of
the trolleys. I follow the old thirty-two route all the
time. It leads right to the graveyard where the thirty-
two is buried, you know? It's like, well, fate. The tracks
are half-covered with filth and pitch, new pitch like the
city pours on. It oozes in the summer and people walk
on it, but you can see the tracks and you see, like, it's
true, like, old things last, good things last, like, you
know? The trolleys are all filthy and half-covered and
rusted out and laughed at, and even though they're not
much use to anybody and kind of ugly like, by most
standards, they're, like, they're, well, I guess, beautiful,
you know?

[RANDY *enters, having finished his shower. He flicks
his towel at* HERSCHEL.]

RANDY: Hey, that shower is a trip. I should have taken
my surfboard.

HERSCHEL: Like, you should have used our shower, it's
in much better shape, you know? Next time you want
to take a shower, let me know.

JUDITH: Well, there's one cosmic issue settled.

RANDY: [*Crosses to kitchen window.*] Mmmmm. That
sauce smells good.

FRANCIS: [*Appears in kitchen window.*] We call it gravy.

RANDY: When will it be ready?

FRANCIS: Soon. [*Disappears inside house.*]

HERSCHEL: [*To* RANDY] Then we can go to the graveyard.
[RANDY *looks surprised.*]

HERSCHEL: See, like, I decided it might be, well, more

fun, if we saw all the dead trolleys, you know, and leave the engine for later.

RANDY: Whatever you say. [*Back to the window.*] Francis look—is there something wrong?

FRAN: [*Offstage, yelling*] Yo, Francis! We're here. [*Come in from gate.*] Hi, kids. [*Going into house*] You stir that stuff?

FRANCIS: [*From inside*] Yeah.
  [RANDY *gets a shirt out of his knapsack and crawls into the tent.* HERSCHEL *starts crawling into the tent.*]

RANDY: Herschel . . . careful!

HERSCHEL: [*Inside the tent*] I'm careful.

LUCILLE: [*Offstage*] Judith!

RANDY: Well, sit over there.
  [HERSCHEL *plops down, blocking the entire entrance with his back.* LUCILLE *comes into the yard with a sweater and jacket. She approaches* JUDITH.]

LUCILLE: Judy, I brought you a sweater. I thought you might be chilly later tonight and I didn't know if you brought one with you.

JUDITH: Thank you.

LUCILLE: [*Puts sweater around* JUDITH'S *shoulders.*] It's real sheep's wool. My friend Diane gave it to me. Her daughter, Joann, is a model for KYZ-TV in Center City—special shift. She's a Cancer, so am I, that's why Fran says I'm a disease. My son, Donny, he's at Yale in pre-med, Branford scholarship, I think he'll make a wonderful doctor, don't Yale make wonderful doctors?

JUDITH: I'm sure I don't know.
  [FRAN *comes out with* FRANCIS. *He is carrying a large fold-up metal table.*]

FRAN: Make yourself useful, Lucille. I got the table, get the plates.

RANDY: [*Getting away from* HERSCHEL, *who is hovering around him*] I'll help set up.
  [LUCILLE *goes into the house, and returns with a tray with plates, napkins, cutlery, glasses, bug spray, and a "plastic lace" tablecloth.*]

FRAN: How was your shower?

RANDY: I expected to see seals and Eskimos any minute.

FRAN: At least you got out of the bathroom alive. There are beach chairs in the cellar, why don't you get them?

Francis, show this young man where the beach chairs
is in the cellar.

[FRAN *goes back into house,* FRANCIS, RANDY, *and* HER-
SCHEL *go past the house to the cellar, and* LUCILLE
starts setting the table.]

LUCILLE: You know Judy, my daughter, she's a dental
technician at the Graduate Hospital—special shift. She
wanted to go to Yale, but she couldn't get in. She
thought it was her teeth. They're buck. She said the
woman looked at her funny the whole time at the in-
terview. Now I told her she should just carry herself
with poise and forget her teeth. Y'know what she said
to me: How can I forget my teeth; they're in my mouth!
Not a very poised thing to say. That's why she didn't
get into Yale: No poise. That's why she ain't got no
husband, either. Do the people at Yale think teeth are
important?

JUDITH: I don't know anything about Yale.

LUCILLE: But what do you think?

JUDITH: Yes, I think teeth are very important for success
in life. [*She is setting out cutlery.*] At the prep school
I attended they had us practice our bite three times a
day.

LUCILLE: [*Politely, taken in*] Oh?

JUDITH: We would bite off a poised bite, and chew with
poise, and then sing a C major scale whilst we swilled
the food in our mouths. I could even sing songs whilst
swilling food with poise. In fact, I once sang the first
aria of the Queen of the Night while swilling half a
hamburger and a bucket of french fries. . . . Of course,
remaining utterly poised, or "pwased," as we say at
Harvard.

LUCILLE: Oh. [*She walks around the table spraying insect repellant.*] It kills them very quickly.

[FRANCIS, RANDY, *and* HERSCHEL *enter the yard with
beach chairs and old kitchen chairs, which they proceed to set up.*]

RANDY: [*To* FRANCIS, *continuing a conversation*] C'mon,
Francis, what's going on?

FRAN: [*From the kitchen*] Yo, Lucille, give me a hand!

JUDITH: I'll be glad to help. [*Runs into the kitchen.*]

RANDY: Come on, Francis, I mean I'm three years younger
than you—so tell me . . .

[*Simultaneously,* LUCILLE *and* HERSCHEL *approach* RANDY.]

HERSCHEL: Would you like to see my models of the trol ley fleet of 1926?

LUCILLE: [*Giving* RANDY *a jacket*] I brought you one o my son's jackets, because I thought you might get col later and I didn't know if you brought one wit you. M son's girl friend bought it for him at Wanamaker's.

[FRAN *and* JUDITH *come back out.*]

BUNNY: [*Calling from inside her house*] Yo! Where i everybody?

FRAN: Yo, Bun! We're out here.

[BUNNY *comes stumbling out of her house. She ha been drinking. She never stops moving, constantl dancing and leaping about, she cries out in wa whoops and screams of victory.*]

BUNNY: I won! I won! I wanna kiss from everybody bu Lucille! [*She goes around kissing everyone, except* LU CILLE. *She gets to* RANDY.] Oh, you're such a hone bun, I could eat you. [*She kisses him, then grabs hi crotch.*] I'll skip Francis, too.

RANDY: Wanna smoke, Herschel?

HERSCHEL: Sure.

[*They sit down by the tent,* HERSCHEL *sitting as fa away from* BUNNY *as possible.*]

BUNNY: Break out the horse piss, Fran!

[FRAN *goes into the kitchen for liquor.*]

BUNNY: Jesus Christ in Heaven, I won!

FRAN: [*Returns with a bottle of scotch.*] How do yo want it?

BUNNY: Straight up the dark and narrow path, honey. [*Sh takes a swig from the bottle.*] You shoulda seen me i that courtroom, I told them all about it, that bitch didn' even have the decency to fart before throwin' herse on top a me. I coulda been ruptured for life, I says, an she's a Catholic, I couldn't believe it. Catholics got self control.

LUCILLE: [*To* JUDITH] Well, good Catholics have self control. Sister Mary Emaryd, my friend, she used t work at Wanamaker's before she married Christ She . . .

BUNNY: [*To* RANDY] That judge looked at me, let me tel you.

LUCILLE: She would allow herself to go to the bathroom only twice a day.

BUNNY: [*To* FRAN] I felt twenty again.

LUCILLE: [*To* JUDITH] She said: Urgency is all in the mind.

BUNNY: [*To* RANDY] I felt like a fuckin' young filly in heat. Look, honey, you ever see my boobies swayin'? [*She sways them for* RANDY. *He giggles.*]

LUCILLE: [*To* FRANCIS] I go to the bathroom more than that, yet I go to Mass every Sunday....

BUNNY: [*To* RANDY] You smokin' that killer weed, hon?

RANDY: Sure. You want some?

BUNNY: Don' need that shit. Don' need nothin' to get high, I'm high naturally. I was born floatin'. [*She leans on table, almost knocking everything over.*] Come and dance with me, baby. [*She grabs a very reluctant* RANDY.] C'mon! "Flat foot floozie with the floy, floy ..." [*They start doing the jitterbug, and* RANDY *bumps into* BUNNY, *knocking the breath out of her.*]

BUNNY: Fuck you, world! Fuck you, Mary O'Donnel! Fuck you, Sam the Jew! Fuck you, Catholic Church! Fuck you, Mom! I won! You shoulda seen them look at me, I felt like a fuckin' starlit. My boobies swayin', and when I walked to the stand I did my strut, my fuckin' bitch-in-heat strut. Come on, Lucille, can you strut like this? [*She comes up behind* LUCILLE *and "bumps" her.* LUCILLE *starts swearing in Italian.* BUNNY *turns to* JUDITH.] Come on, honey, what's your name, can you strut like this? I can fuckin' strut up a storm. My hips have made many a wave in their time, honey, many a wave! I sent out hurricanes, I sent out earthquakes, I sent out tidal waves from my fuckin' hips. Yo, Fran!

FRAN: Yo, Bun!

BUNNY: Remember when I was in that fuckin' community theater down at Gruen Recreation Center?

FRAN: Seventeenth Street.

LUCILLE: Sixteenth and Wolf!

BUNNY: I played Sadie Thompson in that play. I let my hair grow down long. It was real long then, not dyed shit yellow like it is now. I fuckin' got hair like hepatitis now. I played that part! I hadda sheer slip on and my legs, Jesus Christ, my legs! I fuckin' felt the earth trem-

ble when I walked, I played that bitch like Mount Ve-
suvius and the clappin', honey, the clappin'!

FRAN: You were a big hit, yep.

BUNNY: At the curtain call, I held my boobs out like this:
[*She sticks out her chest.*] ... and they screamed,
honey, those fuckin' grown men screamed! [*To* RANDY]
Feel 'em, honey, feel these grapes of mine. [*She puts*
RANDY's *hand on her boobs.*]

RANDY: Mrs. Weinberger!

BUNNY: They're still nice, hanh? I fuckin' won that case!
[*She has to sit down.*] Then I married Sam the Jew and
bore Herschel. Look at the fruit of my loins, look, this
is one of the earthquakes I sent out of my hips. Boom!
Boom! When he walks you can hear him around the
corner, but he's a fuckin' genius at least. He's got an
IQ of 187 or 172, dependin' on which test you use,
despite his father!

LUCILLE: [*This has been building up.*] *Che disgraziat'!*
[*She runs into the house, followed by* FRAN.]

BUNNY: [*Looking after* FRAN] I coulda had ... well, almost anybody, more or less. I coulda been a chorus girl,
then I met Sam the Kike and that was that. He had the
evil eye, that Hebe, them little pointy eyes. He'd screw
them up like he was lookin' for blackheads, then, suddenly, they'd go real soft and get big. I was a sucker
for them fuckin' eyes. He's a jeweler, called me his
jewel. Sam the Jew. I smell like old peanuts!

RANDY: [*Offering her the joint*] Sure you don't want
some?

BUNNY: No, honey, I got me some coke for a giddy sniff.
I get it from my uncle on the force; he gives me a
discount, he's a captain. [*She suddenly sees* HERSCHEL
smoking behind the tent.] Hey, wait a minute! You
been smokin' that shit? Herschel! Have you been
smokin' that shit?

HERSCHEL: [*Butts the joint quickly.*] No ...

BUNNY: Don' you lie to me. Didn't I tell you never to
smoke that shit? It'll fuckin' rot your brain and you'll
be more of a vegetable than you already are. God damn
you, I'll beat the shit outa you! [*She lunges for him.*]

HERSCHEL: [*Scurrying out of her way*] Come on!

BUNNY: Come on?? Come on??? I'll come on, you fuckin'
four-eyed fat-assed creep, I'll come on!

[*She grabs the bottle of scotch and chases* HERSCHEL *into the house. We see them in their kitchen window. She is beating the shit out of* HERSCHEL.]

BUNNY: Twelve fuckin' hours! Twelve fuckin' hours I was in labor wit you, screamin' on that table, and for what? To fuckin' find you smokin' dope? [*His asthma attack is starting.*] That's right! Go ahead! Have a fuckin' asthma attack, cough your fuckin' head off! See if I care! [*She disappears inside the house.* HERSCHEL *is at the window, gasping for air, until he realizes that she has gone. His asthma attack miraculously stops. He disappears. During* HERSCHEL's *attack everyone onstage stares at him, horrified.* RANDY *passes* JUDITH *the joint. She refuses it.* FRANCIS *takes a toke, and passes it back to* RANDY. BUNNY, *inside her house, is heard singing at the out-of-tune piano, offstage.*]

BUNNY: "Moon river, wider than a mile,
      I'm screwing up in style someday. . . ."

[FRAN *and* LUCILLE *come in from the house. He has a big bowl of spaghetti, and she is carrying a very elaborate antipasto.*]

FRAN: [*Sitting down at the head of the table*] Well, I hope everybody's gotta appetite, 'cause there's enough to feed the Chinee army and ain't no room to keep it either.

LUCILLE: [*Sniffing the air*] I think the Delassandros down the alley are burning their children's clothing again. That smell!

[RANDY *and* FRANCIS *break up, and put out the joint.*]

FRAN: You all got plates, I'll serve. Francis, you get the gravy pot, I'll pass the macs, we also got antipast'; made special by Lucille Pompi . . . [LUCILLE *simpers.*] . . . and Lucille Pompi's antipast' is a delicacy.

[*He gives* LUCILLE *a hug.* FRANCIS *arrives with the gravy pot.* FRAN *is serving.*]

FRAN: And here we got the gravy meat: veal, sausage, lamb, meatballs, and braciole. [*He passes plate to* JUDITH.]

JUDITH: Oh, that's too much!

FRAN: Your stomach's bigger than your eyes. We also got wine. Francis!

[RANDY *snaps his fingers at* FRANCIS, *as if to say: Hop*

to it. FRANCIS *goes into house for wine.* FRAN *passes plate to* LUCILLE.]

FRAN: Lucille?

LUCILLE: No thank you, Fran, I'll just pick.

FRAN: [*Passes the plate to* RANDY.] Randy?

[LUCILLE *is busy making sure everyone is taken care of.* FRANCIS *has returned and is going around the table pouring wine.* FRAN *serves a plate to* FRANCIS.]

FRAN: Francis?

FRANCIS: I'm not so hungry tonight.

FRAN: [*Keeping the plate for himself*] Oh, we better get down on our knees, we've just witnessed a miracle.

LUCILLE: Oh, Fran, don't blaspheme.

FRAN: [*Everyone is eating but* LUCILLE.] Sure you don' wan' none, Lucille?

LUCILLE: I'll just pick out of your plate. [*She then proceeds to pick a large piece of lettuce from* FRAN'S *plate and stuffs it in her mouth.*]

FRAN: [*To* RANDY *and* JUDITH] You kids enjoying your stay?

[LUCILLE *now gets a forkful of spaghetti from* FRAN'S *plate and proceeds to eat that.*]

FRAN: This is your first time in South Philly, I bet. You ought to get Francis to take you around tomorrow and see the sights. Them sights'll make you nearsighted, that's how pretty South Philly is.

[LUCILLE *has speared more lettuce from* FRAN, *and he grabs her wrist.*]

FRAN: Yo, Lucille, I'll get you a plate.

LUCILLE: [*She frees her hand, stuffs the lettuce in her mouth, and says:*] No, thank you, Fran, I'm not hungry. [*She notices something on* JUDITH'S *plate, picks it, and eats it.* JUDITH *and* RANDY *are amazed.*]

FRAN: Lucille! Let that kid alone and fill your own plate.

LUCILLE: [*With a full mouth*] Fran, I'm not hungry! [*She sees a tomato wedge on* RANDY'S *plate. She picks up her fork, and pounces on the tomato.*]

FRAN: Lucille!

LUCILLE: He wasn't going to eat that.

FRAN: How do you know?

LUCILLE: Look how skinny he is.

[HERSCHEL *appears in his doorway.*]

FRAN: Hi ya, Herschel.

[*Everyone greets him.*]

FRAN: You feel better?

HERSCHEL: I guess.

FRAN: Well, get a plate and sit down!

HERSCHEL: You don't mind?

FRAN: You're the guest of honor.

[HERSCHEL *comes down to the table, to the empty chair, and starts pulling it around the table, making* FRANCIS *get out of the way, until he is next to* RANDY. RANDY, JUDITH, *and* LUCILLE, *who are all sitting on the long side of the table, have to scoot over to make room for* HERSCHEL. *He sits down next to* RANDY.]

HERSCHEL: [*To* RANDY] Can we still . . .

RANDY: Yeah, yeah, sure.

[FRAN *has piled spaghetti and sauce for* HERSCHEL. *He is trying to pass the plate down to* HERSCHEL, *but* LU-CILLE *snatches it, gets a forkful of pasta, and then passes the plate on. Everyone except* FRANCIS *is eating.*]

FRAN: Gonna be night soon. And tomorrow's my son's birthday. Seems like yesterday he was my little buddy, on the chubby side, but cute all the same, and tomorrow he's gonna be—what? Six? Gonna be a man tomorrow. Looka him squirm. Everybody hits twenty-one sooner or later, 'cept me, I'm still nineteen. *Salute!*

[*They all lift their glasses in a toast and drink, except* HERSCHEL, *who keeps shoveling it down.*]

FRAN: Judith, look, you can see that fig tree wave in the wind if you squint. Francis, remember the day I planted it? I got the sledgehammer out of the cellar, people that was here before us left it, and I broke that concrete. His mother, she'd had enough of both of us, and took off, headin' down South. She was like a bird had too much of winter. Met a nice southern man.

LUCILLE: Protestant.

FRAN: They're married. Can't have kids, though; she had a hysterectomy just before she left. It's a shame. She's good people and so's this man, she should had kids wit him. He's real normal, nice-lookin', don' cough like I do, don' get rashes neither, and to him, horses is for ridin'!

[*He breaks himself up. Then starts to cough.* LUCILLE *is picking out of* JUDITH's *plate. Big forkful of spaghetti.*]

FRAN: They'd have had nice kids. The kind that woulda made her happy. She's one of them people that like to fade inna the air. Don' wanna stand out. Francis and me, well, we stand out. Don' wanna, understand, but we talk too loud, cough, scratch ourselves, get rashes, are kinda big. You have to notice us. Don' have to like us but you gotta see us.

[LUCILLE *pats* FRAN's *cheek lovingly.*]

FRAN: Well, his mother, she was good people and meant well, but she wasn't too easy wit us, she wanted a home in the suburbs, all the Sears and Roebuck catalogs lined up against the wall, and two white kids, just like her, white like the fog, kids you hadda squint to see. Well, this one day, she packed her bags, see, rented a big truck and took everything, even my portable TV. [*He laughs at the "joke."*] I guess it'll be cool tonight. She left me, you see, she left me. So I come out here and smash that concrete. Next day I planted the fig tree. I went to the one guy in the neighborhood would give me the time of day, borrowed thirty dollars, and bought this tree, the dirt, some fertilizer. . . .

[LUCILLE's *hand is in his plate again.*]

FRAN: Jesus Christ in Heaven! Lucille! Would you fill your own plate and stop actin' like the poor relative?!

LUCILLE: [*Quickly stuffs food in her mouth.*] Stop pickin' on me! I ain't actin' like the poor relative!

FRAN: Whataya call pickin' at his plate, then pickin' at my plate, then pickin' at his plate, then pickin' at her plate, for Christ' sake, hanh? Stop pickin'! Take! Take wit both hands, it's there, why you act like there ain't plenty when there is, hanh? What's the matter you???!!!! [*He has taken two enormous handfuls of spaghetti out of the bowl and dropped them into* LUCILLE's *plate.*]

LUCILLE: [*Screaming*] Eh! Sta'zit'!

FRAN: [*Shaking her plate under her nose*] Mangi taci' o—

LUCILLE: [*Stands up and screams at him.*] Fongoul! [*She runs out of the yard.*]

FRAN: Jesus Christ! See you kids later. [*Yells.*] Lucille, I was only kidding! [*Runs off after her.*]

HERSCHEL: [*Rising, to* RANDY] I'm finished.

RANDY: [*With a sigh*] All right. [*To* JUDITH *and* FRANCIS] See you later.

[HERSCHEL *and* RANDY *exit through the alley.*]

JUDITH: [*Rises, starts stacking.*] I'll put the dishes in the sink. [*She suddenly drops the plates on the table.*] It's Randy, isn't it?

BUNNY: [*Stumbles out of her house. She is in her robe and nightgown again.*] Hi, you two. You got some more horse piss? I'm out.

FRANCIS: I'll look, Bunny. [*Runs into his kitchen.*]

BUNNY: You look sort of peaked, hon, upset over somethin'? A man, maybe?

JUDITH: Maybe.

BUNNY: Well, take my advice and heat up the coke bottle; men ain't worth shit, not shit.

FRANCIS [*Coming out with a bottle*] Here, Bunny,

BUNNY: [*Takes a slug of whiskey.*] You're a saint, just a fuckin' saint.

[*She collapses in a heap, completely out.* FRANCIS *gets her under each arm, and* JUDITH *holds the door open.* FRANCIS *starts dragging her back in.*]

BUNNY: [*Coming to for a moment*] Shit! Why am I such a whale? Why ain't I a porpoise or a dolphin? Why do I gotta be a whale wit hepatitis hair?

FRANCIS: Come on, Bunny, I'll help you inside. . . .

BUNNY: You're a saint, a fuckin' saint.

[*They disappear inside* BUNNY's *house.* FRANCIS *returns immediately.*]

JUDITH: You and Randy. . . !

FRANCIS: Me and Randy nothing. He doesn't know a thing about it. He's been following me around all day asking why I won't look at him. What can I say? We were friends, and he can't understand. . . .

[RANDY *and* HERSCHEL *have reentered from the alley.*]

FRANCIS: Well, who can understand. . . .

JUDITH: What about the trolleys?

HERSCHEL: A different guard was there. We can go tomorrow though, my friend'll be there.

RANDY: [*To* JUDITH] What's the matter?

JUDITH: [*To* FRANCIS, *indicating* RANDY] Just look at him. [*Peals of laughter.*] And look at you.

HERSCHEL: [*To* RANDY] It's early yet, would you like to see my books on ornamental tiles. . . .

RANDY: Good night, Herschel.

HERSCHEL: I guess everybody can't be interested in . . .

RANDY: [*Pushes him inside, and closes the door behind him.*] Good night, Herschel!

HERSCHEL: Good night, Randy. [*Disappears inside his house.*]

RANDY: [*To* FRANCIS *and* JUDITH] Now, what's going on? [JUDITH *continues laughing.*]

RANDY: Francis?

FRANCIS: All right, Judith, why don't you just tell him?

JUDITH: And you don't want him told? What future is there for you if he doesn't even know? Happiness begins with knowledge, doesn't it?

FRANCIS: If it does, you are in a lot of trouble! [*Runs into his house, slamming the door.*]

RANDY: Hey, look, this is unfair. What's going on?

JUDITH: I have discovered this fine day that I have a rival for the affections of one Francis Geminiani.

RANDY: Oh yeah? I'm not surprised.

JUDITH: What?

RANDY: Well, Judy, you're kind of a bitch, you know. I mean, talking in Italian to his father and Lucille—nothing personal, I mean. . . .

JUDITH: Well, you are a creep, aren't you?

RANDY: And I mean like forcing me to look at those subway books with Herschel, just so you could be alone with Francis. So who's this rival? Somebody from the neighborhood who can make good gravy? [*He is laughing, and crawling inside the tent.*]

JUDITH: [*Starts rubbing her hands together gleefully.*] Well, the person in question is in the yard right now, under the fig tree, and it isn't me.

RANDY: [*Pops his head out.*] What?

BLACKOUT

ACT II

Scene 1

Scene the same. The next morning, about nine o'clock.

As the lights come up, FRANCIS *is seen in his window, staring at the tent.* JUDITH *is asleep in a sleeping bag outside the tent, and* RANDY *is inside.*

BUNNY comes out of her house, dressed in her ragged housecoat; she is disoriented and mumbles to herself. FRANCIS *sees her but says nothing.*

She is carrying a brown paper bag. She disappears into the alley, and is next seen climbing up the telephone pole behind the alley wall. She has to stop every few rungs and almost falls off once or twice. Finally she gets to the top of the alley wall, still clutching the bag, shakes her fist at the heavens, and prepares to jump.

A dog is heard barking in the distance.

FRANCIS: [*Yelling from his window*] Hey, Bunny! What are you doing?
BUNNY: [*Peering in his direction, trying to bring him into focus*] Hanh?
FRANCIS: What are you doing?
BUNNY: Who's 'at?
FRANCIS: Francis next door. Come down, you'll hurt yourself.
BUNNY: What are ya, blind? You go to Harvard and can't tell I'm gonna jump?
FRANCIS: Bunny!
BUNNY: Shut up, Francis, I'm gonna splatter my fuckin'

39

body on the concrete down there and don' wan' no
interference. I thought it all out. My uncle's an under-
taker, he'll do it cheap.

[HERSCHEL *sticks his head out the second-story window of* BUNNY'S *house.*]

HERSCHEL: Mom! What are you doing?

BUNNY: Herschel, don' look, it'll give you asthma.

HERSCHEL: Don't jump, Mom!

BUNNY: Herschel, I gotta favor to ask of you. If I don' die
in jumpin', I want you to finish me off wit this. [*Waves
the bag.*] It's rat poison. Was Uncle Eddie's Christmas
present.

HERSCHEL: Mom, please!

BUNNY: You didn't scratch them new mosquito bites, did
you?

HERSCHEL: No. And I took my medicine and I used my
atomizer and brushed my teeth, please don't jump.

BUNNY: Good, you keep it up. Don' wan' to be a mess at
my funeral.

HERSCHEL: Funeral!

[*Pulls his head in, and runs out into the yard.* JUDITH
is awake and getting dressed. RANDY *comes out of the
tent, a little confused by the noise.* FRANCIS *has come
out and is trying to coax her down.*]

RANDY: What's going on?

HERSCHEL: [*Arrives, puffing, in the yard. His pajamas
are disgracefully dirty, as is his robe, which is much
too small for him.*] Please, Mom, I'm sorry, I didn't
mean to do it. . . .

BUNNY: What?

HERSCHEL: I don't know, it must be something I did. I'll
never have asthma again, I'll stop having seizures, I'll
take gym class. Don't jump!

BUNNY: [*Starts climbing higher, until she is about the
height of the second-story window.*] Herschel, is that
any way to act, hanh? Was you raised in the jungle?
Show some dignity, you want the neighbors to talk?

HERSCHEL: I'll burn my transfer collection, I'll give up
the subways. . . .

BUNNY: Nah, that's all right, Herschel. You'll be better
off in a home.

HERSCHEL: A home??!!! [*He can hardly get the word out.
He starts having an asthma attack.*]

BUNNY: Jesus Christ in heaven, he's havin' an attack! Can't I even commit suicide in peace?

JUDITH: Should I call the police?

FRANCIS: Call Lucille. DE 6-1567.

JUDITH: DE 6-1567. [*She runs into* FRANCIS's *house.*]

RANDY: What about Herschel?

BUNNY: Get his fuckin' atomizer—it's in the third room on the second floor.

[RANDY *runs into* BUNNY's *house.*]

BUNNY: Jesus Christ in heaven! And it's all for attention.

FRANCIS: What is, Bunny?

BUNNY: His fuckin' attacks! I read them books! It's all for attention, that all these kids want nowadays. I didn't get no attention when I was a kid and look at me! Am I weird? Nah! I didn't get no asthma, I didn't even get pimples.

JUDITH: [*Appears in the kitchen window.*] I get a busy signal.

FRANCIS: Busy? This time of day?

BUNNY: They think because they can fart and blink at the same time they got the world conquered.

FRANCIS: Did you get the number right?

BUNNY: That's all they want: attention!

JUDITH: DE 6-1567.

FRANCIS: Jesus! That's our number. It's DE 6-1656.

[JUDITH *disappears inside the house.* RANDY *appears in the second-story window of* BUNNY's *house.*]

RANDY: I can't find the atomizer!

HERSCHEL: [*Gasping, on the ground at the foot of the wall*] By the bed, under all the Kleenex!

[RANDY *continues looking for it.*]

FRANCIS: Come on, Bunny, climb down!

BUNNY: [*Climbing down to the top of the wall*] Education! That's these kids' problems! Look at him—a fuckin' genius; and he looks like some live turd some fuckin' giant laid. Huff some more, Herschel. . . .

RANDY: [*Running out of house*] I got it! I got it!

[HERSCHEL *grabs the atomizer. His attack subsides.*]

BUNNY: They all oughtta be put to work! That's what happened to me. Yeah! My mom put me to work when I was ten, singin' songs for pennies in the Franciscan monastery on Wolf Street!

[JUDITH *comes back into the yard.*]

BUNNY: I hadda sing for everybody—them bums, them old ladies. Once some crazy old lady made me sing "Mein Yiddische Mama" six times—then gave me a five-dollar bill. Well, even though it's a Catholic place I figured, shit, make the money. So I learned "Bei Mir Bist Du Shoen" for the next week and sang it—and they beat the shit outa me. If that wasn't a birth trauma, what was! I read them books, know all about it. I've hadda shit-filled life; feel like some turd stuck in the pipe so Herschel get your fat ass outa the way, you too, hon, or I'll crush youse!

FRAN: [*Offstage, yelling*] What's goin' on out here?

BUNNY: Yo, Fran!

FRAN: Yo, Bun!

BUNNY: I'm gonna jump!

LUCILLE: [*Running into the yard from gate, in hair curlers*] *Che disgraziat'!* Who's gonna clean it up, hanh?

FRAN: [*Follows* LUCILLE *in.*] Whataya mean you're gonna jump?

BUNNY: Whataya mean, whataya mean? I'm gonna leap off this fuckin' wall and if that don' finish me I'm takin' this rat poison and Herschel better move or I'm takin' him with me. Jesus Christ, can't even die without his havin' a attack.

[FRAN *and* FRANCIS *half-carry, half-drag* HERSCHEL *away from the wall and lay him down on the stoop. He is screaming and kicking.*]

BUNNY: You mean I gotta listen to that in heaven?

LUCILLE: You ain't going to heaven!

FRAN: Come on, be good and get down. You don't got no reason to jump!

BUNNY: I got reason, I got reason!

FRAN: Yeah, what?

BUNNY: Got nobody in the whole fuckin' world, I turned ugly, I got no money, I ain't got no prospects. . . .

FRAN: That's been true of my whole life and you don' see me jumpin' off alley walls and takin' rat poison. Besides, it's Francis's twenty-first birthday today.

BUNNY: You mean there's gonna be a party?

FRAN: A big one!

BUNNY: Why didn't you say so, hanh? Get that friggin' ladder, I'm comin' down!

[FRANCIS *and* RANDY *run to get the ladder that has*

been leaning against the fence. They set it up under
the wall and help BUNNY *climb down.*]

BUNNY: [*To* RANDY] You're so strong, hon, give me a kiss!
[*Kisses him. Then she turns on* HERSCHEL, *who is still*
wheezing and crying.] You! Get in that fuckin' house!
Makin' a spectacle of yourself wit them pajamas!
[*She chases* HERSCHEL *into their house. Much shaking*
of heads from the others. Everyone is very tense. FRAN-
CIS *takes the ladder back to the fence.*]

HERSCHEL: [*As he is running inside*] What the fuck do
you want me to do?

BUNNY: [*In her house, continuing a diatribe against* HER-
SCHEL] And what's this I hear from your no-good
father? You had a fuckin' petit mal yesterday?!

HERSCHEL: [*In the house*] No I didn't!

BUNNY: Liar! Didn't I tell you to behave wit him?
[*Sounds of her beating him.*] I told you to act normal.

HERSCHEL: Who could act normal with you for a mother?
[*A sound like a piano falling over is heard from*
BUNNY'*s house. A silence. Then suddenly, long sur-*
prised screams of pain from HERSCHEL. FRAN *tries to*
hug FRANCIS. FRANCIS *gets away.* BUNNY *comes run-*
ning out of her house to the stoop.]

BUNNY: You guys wanna get a piano offa Herschel?

FRAN: What's the piano doin' on Herschel?

BUNNY: He gave me some lip and I threw it on him.

FRAN: Oh, all right. [*Kisses* FRANCIS.] Happy birthday,
my son.

[FRAN *and* FRANCIS *run into* BUNNY'*s house.*]

BUNNY: Do you think I ruptured him for life?

[BUNNY *and* RANDY *run into the house.* JUDITH *begins*
to follow, but LUCILLE *stops her.*]

LUCILLE: Ain't ladylike to go in there.

JUDITH: Herschel might be hurt.

LUCILLE: If that kid ain't dead yet, he's indestructible.
[*From inside the house, noises of the piano being*
lifted.] He's always fallin' down stairs, gettin' hit by
cars, gettin' beat up, havin' fits, gettin' asthma, throwin'
up, comin' down with pneumonia. A piano ain't gonna
hurt him. [*She sets a garden chair next to the tent.*]
Besides, that piano's out of tune, how much damage
could it do?

JUDITH: This is crazy! All that noise and Bunny on the wall . . .

LUCILLE: [*Sits in chair.*] Happens alla the time. That's why no neighbors stuck their heads out. We're used to it around here. Tessie across the street come back from the shore last Sunday and found this burglar in her cellar.

[JUDITH *has gone in the tent to finish dressing.*]

LUCILLE: Judy, she ties him to an old sofa, then, wit her sister, she shoves it down the front steps. Then she sets it on fire. We come back from church and there is this sofa on the front steps wit a screamin' man on it and flames everywhere. We call the fire engine. They hose the poor bastard down and rush him to the hospital. So this mornin' was mild, believe me.

[JUDITH *is now sitting by the tent, putting on her sneakers.*]

LUCILLE: Do you wanna come wit me to Wanamaker's and buy Francis a present? I have a employee's discount so you can buy him somethin' real nice for less. Or did you get somethin' already?

JUDITH: Not really—a few joke things. I don't think he's gonna think they're funny.

[*She gets a brush and mirror out of her knapsack. Music is heard from* BUNNY'S *house.* BUNNY *appears in her window, brushing her hair.*]

BUNNY: Yo, Lucille! We got the piano up. You wanna come in and sing?

LUCILLE: No, Bunny.

BUNNY: Well, I'm cookin' breakfast. You wan' some?

LUCILLE and JUDITH: No thanks.

JUDITH: How is Herschel?

BUNNY: A little purple about the shins, but he'll survive. You sure you don' wan' some breakfast?

JUDITH: No thank you!

BUNNY: You should take some lessons from your brother. [*She disappears inside her house.*]

LUCILLE: What did she mean about your brother?

JUDITH: Everybody loves Randy—EVERYBODY it seems!

LUCILLE: Well, he's nice-lookin', that's for sure. But I'm not crazy about him. I never warm up to white people much. You're an exception. You got poise. You have lovely teeth.

[*From inside the house we hear:*]
"I want a girl
Just like the girl
That married dear old Dad,
She was a pearl
And the only girl
That Daddy ever had. . . ."
[*Dialogue continues over this.*]

JUDITH: They got Francis to play the piano, all those wrong notes.

LUCILLE: Why are you interested in Francis when you're so beautiful?

JUDITH: If I hear that once more, I'm going to stick my face in acid!

LUCILLE: But why? *Perchè*? What do you see in him?

JUDITH: Why are you interested in his father?

LUCILLE: I ain't got much choice. I'm not pretty. I'm a widow. Nobody wants a widow. It's like bein' an old sheet. I might be clean and kept nice, but people can't help noticin' it's been used.

[BUNNY *is heard singing "When Irish eyes are smilin'."*]

LUCILLE: [*Continues over song.*] So I put up with Fran. He's good people, he means well. But you know, he coughs alla the time, eats too much, makes noises, you know he's got the colitis, and them rashes! Between coughin', scratchin', and runnin' to the bathroom, I'm surprised he's got so much weight on him. Oh, well, that's my life.

[JUDITH *offers her the brush. She is about to use it, then discreetly pulls* JUDITH's *hair out of the bristles.*]

LUCILLE: But, Francis? Like father like son, remember.

JUDITH: Oh, I don't know. We talked yesterday and I was up most of the night, thinking: why? All the possible bad reasons started cramming themselves into my head. Perhaps I have sensed it all along and I was attracted to Francis because he was . . . [*Stops herself.*] Well, just because he's the way he is.

[*From inside the house we hear:*]
"For it was Mary, Mary,
Plain as any name can be,
For in society, propriety
Will say, Marie."

LUCILLE: [*Speaks over this.*] You mean queer? Don't be

shocked, I know what queer is. [*She turns her chair toward* JUDITH.] I had a long talk wit my son, Donny, about it before he went off. He's at Yale, pre-med, Branford scholarship. I warned him to be careful. My friend Diane's husband, he's a foot doctor, they met in a singles bar, then got married because he had corns real bad, well, he told me, Yale puts out a lot of queers along wit the doctors and the lawyers. But Donny's got a girl friend, and though I think she's a pig, I guess it proves he's got some interest in the girls. But Francis? Well, Fran and me had a long talk. He's afraid for Francis. Well, I think Francis is. There ain't been no girls around here except to sell cookies. That's why Fran was so happy to see you, and wanted you to stay, even though you wanted to go. It's hard on a man to have a queer for a son. I mean, I guess Fran would rather he was queer than humpbacked or dead, still it's hard.

JUDITH: Well, I thought that might be why I was interested. He'd be safe then. But I don't think so. He and I are really alike, you see. Neither of us makes contact with people. We both goof a lot, but most of the time, that's all there is.

BUNNY: [*From inside her house*] All right, I'm slingin' this shit on the table!

JUDITH: And there are other reasons. Just where I am, you know? I'm a romantic, I guess, and I assume there is something worth doing, that active is better than passive. But I feel on the edge of falling, or freezing.

LUCILLE: [*Shakes her head.*] When I was your age— madone . . . !

JUDITH: Maybe it's harder for us, now. The war's over, no one much is ethnic anymore, there aren't many jobs. When there were marches and strikes and moratoriums, people didn't think much about the future, they were distracted, sort of a hippie bread and circuses idea.

LUCILLE: [*Nods her head, but she doesn't understand one word.*] Yeah.

JUDITH: No one had time to worry about how they'd live five years from now—it was all now. Everybody could be a hero, occupy a dean's office, publish his memoirs, have them serialized in *The New York Times*—

LUCILLE: Wit the small print!

JUDITH: And you have to wonder, all that energy, and that

courage, was it just adolescence? Sometimes I'm afraid.
Just afraid. Maybe we're at the end of the spiral which
people once thought endless. Maybe it's running out.
I don't want it to be over. Francis is afraid too. But
together ... I'm sorry, I'm not making any sense, I
didn't sleep much.

LUCILLE: But you didn't buy him a birthday present.

JUDITH: Is that important?

LUCILLE: Vital. It's the gesture. Don' matter what it is
but you got to make the gesture. It shows respect. It
shows you're serious. No birthday present and he's
gotta right to wonder if you mean it. It's like an outward
sign. You just can't go around sayin', I need you, or I
love you, and then ignorin' them on special occasions.
That don' make no sense. So you buy them the birthday
present, you send them the card, you go visit them inna
hospital, you bake them the cake—you show them respect. *Cabisce?* Respect!

JUDITH: *Sì.*

LUCILLE: *Bene.* All you can do is try and hope. That's
how I got my husband, may God forgive him, and may
he rest in peace. You really like Francis? Come on, you
come wit me to Wanamaker's we buy Francis a present
we cheer ourselves up.

[FRAN *comes out of* BUNNY's *house.*]

FRAN: Yo, Lucille!

LUCILLE: Judith and me's goin' ta Wanamaker's to buy
Francis a present.

FRAN: See youse later, be good and be careful.

[LUCILLE *and* JUDITH *exit through the gate.* FRANCIS
comes racing out of BUNNY's *house.*]

FRAN: Yo, where you goin'?

FRANCIS: Nowhere.

FRAN: You got company.

FRANCIS: I didn't invite them.

FRAN: [*Embraces* FRANCIS.] Happy birthday, son.

FRANCIS: Don't hang on me so much.

FRAN: What are you afraid of? You got somewhere to go
you take some coin. [*Offers him some money.*]

FRANCIS: I don't need any money.

FRAN: Well, take some more.

FRANCIS: I don't need any more.

FRAN: Take!

FRANCIS: I don't need it!!

FRAN: Look, my son, I'm gonna give you a piece of advice I learned from the army, from dealin' wit your mother, and from twenty years in the printers' union: Take! Take wit both hands, both feet, and your mouth too. If your ass is flexible enough take wit that, use your knees and your elbows, train your balls and take! *Prend'—cabisce?* Somebody offers you somethin', you take it, then run . . . [*Puts the money in* FRANCIS's *shirt pocket.*] . . . but always say thank you first. And look, if there's ever anything, well, that conventional people, not like us Geminiani Italians—but other people might be ashamed of, don't ever be afraid to come to me, no matter how hard it is, I'll understand—understand?

FRANCIS: I don't understand. [*Suddenly embraces his father.*] But I understand, okay? [*Runs out through the gate.*]

FRAN: Where you goin'?

FRANCIS: To buy some diet soda.

FRAN: That diet crap is gonna kill ya.

[RANDY *comes out of* BUNNY's *house, trailed by* HERSCHEL.]

RANDY: Where's Francis?

FRAN: He went to buy diet crap.

HERSCHEL: [*Grabs* RANDY's *arm and starts pulling him toward the alley.*] Maybe we'll pass him, you know, like on our way to the trolleys. . . .

RANDY: [*Freeing himself*] Is there a pool around here? I'd like to go swimming.

FRAN: Yeah.

HERSCHEL: You promised!

FRAN: There's a community center about four blocks from here, Herschel can go with you. You can change here.

RANDY: Great.

[RANDY *crawls into the tent to change.* BUNNY *comes out of her house, eating a sandwich.*]

BUNNY: Hey, Herschel, I thought you was draggin' Beau Brummel to the trolleys—

HERSCHEL: He wants to go swimming.

BUNNY: Why don't you go wit him?

HERSCHEL: [*Under his breath*] Fuck!

BUNNY: Where's the birthday boy?

FRAN: He took off.

BUNNY: Helluva way to treat company. Prob'ly went to buy a opera record.

RANDY: [*Still inside the tent*] He already has thousands.

FRAN: [*To* BUNNY] Look, I got stuff to do, gotta buy Francis a birthday cake. Bun, you wanna come?

BUNNY: Sure, I could use a doughnut or two.

[*They exit through the gate.* HERSCHEL *picks up his tricycle.*]

HERSCHEL: Randy, Randy!

RANDY: [*From inside the tent*] What?

HERSCHEL: Would you like to play trolley?

RANDY: How?

HERSCHEL: Just call ding, when I ask you to. Like ... [*Pipes out.*] Ding!

RANDY: Okay.

HERSCHEL: [*Careening around the yard like a trolley, making a lot of noise*] Ritner! ... Now.

RANDY: Ding!

HERSCHEL: Good. [*Careens.*] Tasker! ... Now.

RANDY: Ding!

HERSCHEL: Dickinson! ... Now. [*Silence.*] Now. Oh, you missed that one.

RANDY: [*Comes out of the tent, in a T-shirt and shorts.*] Ding!

[HERSCHEL *is gaping at him.*]

RANDY: Do you think I look weird?

[HERSCHEL *shakes his head "no."*]

RANDY: I mean, skinny.

HERSCHEL: I think you look, like, you know—

RANDY: Yeah, yeah. But do you think my legs are too thin?

HERSCHEL: Oh no!

RANDY: Boy, it's rough being this thin, you know, I've tried to put on at least ten pounds. I bought two quarts of this stuff called Wate-On.

HERSCHEL: [*Points to his stomach.*] Oh yeah, like "weight on"—

RANDY: Putrid stuff. I drank a quart of it, tastes like milk of magnesia, I got sick for a week and lost ten pounds.

HERSCHEL: I tried to kill myself by drinking a quart of milk of magnesia once; but I didn't lose any weight.

[FRANCIS *enters through the gate, drinking a diet soda. A tense moment between* FRANCIS *and* RANDY.]

RANDY: We're going swimming.

FRANCIS: I'll stay here.

RANDY: Okay, Herschel, let's go. . . .

[*They start off; suddenly* RANDY *staggers, clutches the air, twists about, acts dizzy, and falls to the ground. He is faking a petit mal.*]

HERSCHEL: [*Very alarmed*] Randy, what is it?

FRANCIS: [*Catching on*] Looks like a petit mal, Herschel.

HERSCHEL: No, no, that's epilepsy. Take your belt off!

FRANCIS: Why?

HERSCHEL: So he won't bite his tongue off. Give it to me! [*Sticks belt in* RANDY's *mouth.*] I'll go get my medicine! [*Rushes into his house.*]

RANDY: [*Who has been writhing on the ground until now, suddenly sits up.*] Are you a faggot?

[HERSCHEL *comes running out with a bottle of medicine.* RANDY *starts writhing again.*]

HERSCHEL: Here—you have to shake it first!

FRANCIS: [*Shaking the bottle*] I think he'll need some Valium too—

HERSCHEL: Good idea! [*Runs into house and reappears almost instantly.*] Fives or tens?

FRANCIS: Fives should do it.

[HERSCHEL *races into house.*]

RANDY: [*Sits up, dropping the fit.*] I mean homosexual— I mean, gay person—

HERSCHEL: [*Racing back out*] We're out!

[RANDY *fakes the fit again.*]

FRANCIS: Do you have any aspirin?

RANDY: [*Mumbling unintelligibly*] Aspirin upsets my stomach!

FRANCIS: Aspirin upsets his stomach.

HERSCHEL: Tylenol?

FRANCIS: Tylenol?

RANDY: Tylenol!

HERSCHEL and FRANCIS: Tylenol!

HERSCHEL: I'll go get some! [*Races off through the alley.*]

RANDY: [*He stands, dusts himself off, awkward pause.*] When we talked and all that, you know in your room, were you just trying to make me?

FRANCIS: I don't know.

RANDY: I don't care that much, but it's worse being treated like you were laying a trap for me. And I didn't think you were gay—odd maybe. Have there . . . [*He realizes how silly this is going to sound.*] . . . been many before me?

FRANCIS: Well, starting in high school, there was Max. He was a poet, a Libra, on the fencing team, short and dark, compact you might say, very dashing with his épées. Then there were George and Eliot, they were twins. Then, Sheldon Gold, briefly.

RANDY: How many did you sleep with?

FRANCIS: Sleep with? They didn't even talk to me.

RANDY: You never told them how you felt?

FRANCIS: Well, that's it, you see. I'm never sure how I feel, really.

RANDY: Have you ever had sex with a man?

[FRANCIS *shakes his head "no."*]

RANDY: Were there girls before Judith?

FRANCIS: Well, there was Elaine Hoffenburg. She had braces.

RANDY: Braces on her teeth?

FRANCIS: Legs. I took her to the senior prom. [RANDY *looks incredulous.*] Well, I was no catch, either. I was very fat then. It wasn't too bad. Once she got enough momentum going, she could do a passable waltz. Then there was Luise Morely. Slightly pockmarked but pretty in a plain sort of way. We held hands through *The Sandpiper*, then we did it afterward. It was my first time. Elaine had been willing, but it was a little hard getting her legs apart.

RANDY: Gross! I worked for months to get Nancy Simmons to go to the prom with me, then I got car-sick on the way and threw up all over her; and you remember Roberta Hasserfluth, I broke up with her just as you and Judith got together, well, we decided we would do it, so we went to the drive-in movie in Waltham. It was *The Four Stewardesses*—

FRANCIS: Wasn't that in 3-D?

RANDY: Oh, was it ever, we had to wear goggles and everything. Well, I bought this bottle of Mateus, see, and since I'd never bought wine before I forgot you needed a corkscrew. So I couldn't get it open, so there we are watching this dirty movie in the dead of winter, with this bottle of Mateus between my legs, trying to get it open with my car key—

FRANCIS: Well, did you ever do it?

RANDY: Too cold! I'm sort of a jerk with girls, but I like them. I like you too, you're my friend. But I don't think I'm in love with you. Does that mean you were in love with me? [FRANCIS *shrugs.*] I mean, Francis, has it ever occurred to you you might be suffering from homosexual panic?

FRANCIS: [*Snaps his fingers.*] I knew I should have taken Psych. 101.

RANDY: I mean, it's true. It's really common in a competitive society. My father was suffering from homosexual panic last year. He took his secretary Betsy to Europe to cure it. He got in trouble with the IRS over it. He said anything that cures him of homosexuality ought to be deductible.

FRANCIS: [*Shakes his head, irritated at being put on.*] Oh, really.

RANDY: I'm serious. I mean, if you've never slept with a man, never laid a hand on me . . .

FRANCIS: Are you saying that if you were to strip right now and lie down inside that tent, I couldn't—well, do anything?

RANDY: Well, there's only one way to find out. [*Starts to strip.*]

FRANCIS: What are you doing? Randy, what are you doing?

RANDY: I'm stripping.

FRANCIS: Are you crazy? In front of me? Here?

[FRANCIS *makes a dash for his door, but* RANDY *intercepts him.* RANDY *stands in front of the door, blocking it. He looks around the yard, up at the windows, then unzips his fly.*]

FRANCIS: Jesus Christ!

RANDY: [*Walks over to the tent.*] I'll save the rest for inside the tent. [*Crawls inside.*] [*Peeks out*] When you think of this, and you will, be kind! [*Disappears*]

FRANCIS: Randy! [*Anxious*] Randy? Jesus Christ! Oh, Jesus—

FRANCIS: Jesus Christ! Oh, Jesus . . . [*Holding his chin*] I didn't shave this morning.

[FRANCIS *is about to crawl into the tent as* HERSCHEL *comes bounding in from the alley.*]

HERSCHEL: How's Randy?

FRANCIS: [*Exasperated*] Jesus Christ, Herschel, he's dead!

HERSCHEL: [*Horror-struck*] He is??!!

FRANCIS: Ten minutes ago; heart failure.

HERSCHEL: Are you sure? I mean, I faked a heart attack in gym class last month. Maybe he's faking. Call an ambulance!

FRANCIS: Damn it, Herschel, he's dead, now go away!

HERSCHEL: Can I see the body?

RANDY: [*Sticks his head out of the tent.*] Hello, Herschel.

HERSCHEL: Randy! He said . . .

RANDY: I heard. Look, Herschel, Francis and I—

FRANCIS: [*Trying to stop him*] Randy!

RANDY: —are involved in a very serious ritual. We will both be drummed out of our exclusive clubs at Harvard if we don't do this.

HERSCHEL: Oh, heavy.

RANDY: Very. So, Herschel, would you please go away and come back a little later?

HERSCHEL: Sure.

[*He sets a little bottle of Tylenol in front of the tent and starts for the alley.* RANDY *throws the shorts out at* FRANCIS. HERSCHEL *turns back.*]

HERSCHEL: Like five minutes?

FRANCIS: [*Grabs the shorts, hides them behind his back.*] Herschel, take a long walk!

[HERSCHEL, *dejected, exits out the alley.* FRANCIS *hesitates, peers into the tent, and finally crawls inside. There is no movement for a few seconds, then* RANDY, *wrapped in the sleeping bag, comes bounding out of the tent, followed by* FRANCIS.]

FRANCIS: Randy, what's the matter? What's the matter? Why did you strip if you didn't mean it? Were you bringing me on?

RANDY: No! [*Runs back into the tent.*]

FRANCIS: Is that what was going on this spring? Perhaps somewhere in some subconscious avenue of that boy-man mind of yours you sensed I had a vulnerable point and decided to make the most of it?

RANDY: [*From inside the tent*] I was seventeen fucking years old this spring—what's your excuse?

FRANCIS: Well, you're eighteen now.

RANDY: [*Coming out of tent, wearing jeans*] I liked you!

FRANCIS: [*Sarcastic*] Thanks!

RANDY: I really did.

FRANCIS: It's vicious of you.

RANDY: How?

FRANCIS: Because you did it all just to humiliate me—

RANDY: I really do like you. I mean, liking does exist, doesn't it? It doesn't have to include sex, or love, or deep need, does it?

FRANCIS: I don't know.

RANDY: I don't know either.

FRANCIS: I don't know either.

RANDY: Boy . . . you are really fucked up. [*He embraces* FRANCIS.]

FRANCIS: I know.

[*He puts his arms around* RANDY. JUDITH *enters the yard from the gate carrying a large gaily wrapped box. She sees this embrace and lets out a surprised yell. The two jump apart, confused, and looking guilty.*]

RANDY: Judith!

JUDITH: You're disgusting!

RANDY: It's not my fault, he's older than I am!

JUDITH: He's younger than you are!

FRANCIS: Judith . . .

JUDITH: [*Turns on him.*] And you!

FRANCIS: Now, look, Judith, it didn't have anything to do with sex!

JUDITH: Oh no! I'm sure! Nothing you do has anything to do with sex! It's all a bring-on, isn't it? You get to that point, and then you're ugly, or you're fat, or you're gay! What did you use on him? That you were ugly, fat, and straight? Well, I'm on to you! Happy birthday! [*She throws the box at* FRANCIS.]

FRANCIS: Act your age, Judith!

JUDITH: Oh ho, act my age, act my age says this paragon of maturity, this pristine sage now come of age!

FRANCIS: It's hard to explain. . . .

RANDY: That's right!

JUDITH: Hard? Hard to explain? What is? You're going to fuck my brother, that's very simple, that's the birds and the bees, that's Biology 1A. I thought I loved you. I

thought I loved you! [*Starts hitting* RANDY.] I thought
I loved him!

FRANCIS: Judith, will you please calm down.

JUDITH: And my mother told me never to trust fatties,
they're self-indulgent. Go have a banana split!

RANDY: For Christ' sake, calm down!

JUDITH: I knew there was something suspicious in your
wanting to come along. I bet the two of you were laughing at me, comparing notes, carrying on behind my
back the whole time. Why, Francis, why would you do
this to me?

FRANCIS: He was bringing me on, standing here with no
clothes on, hanging on to me, what would you do?

JUDITH: Puke!

RANDY: Do you think I enjoyed it? Huh, tubby?

JUDITH: [*To* RANDY] So you're a faggot too—won't the
sophomore class be surprised?

RANDY: Why are you screaming at me, it's his fault!

FRANCIS: [*Shaking his finger at* RANDY] It's your fault!

JUDITH: Oh, my God, it's love! M and M—mutual mas-
turbation!

RANDY: [*Angry*] I thought I could help him, I should have
known better, I can't help you—
[*Shoves* FRANCIS. HERSCHEL *comes bounding in from
alley.*]

HERSCHEL: Randy, your ceremony seems to be over, we
can go see the . . .

RANDY: [*Screaming, runs into tent.*] And I can't help you
either, Herschel!

HERSCHEL: Francis . . .

FRANCIS: God damn it, Herschel, go away!

HERSCHEL: Oh, no, I did it again!
[JUDITH *is on one side of the stage, talking to* FRANCIS,
and HERSCHEL *is on the other side, talking to the tent.*]

JUDITH: And I was even out buying you a present!

HERSCHEL: I tried to be your friend, I don't know how . . .

JUDITH: And I was willing to be understanding.

HERSCHEL: I'm just stupid.

JUDITH: All those Callas records, and I hate her voice and
her wobble!

FRANCIS: She only wobbles on the late recordings!

HERSCHEL: What did I do?

JUDITH: And that "Toti dal Monte," for Christ' sake, she sounds like a broken steam engine!

FRANCIS: Her mad scene is still the best on records!

HERSCHEL: It's just me!

JUDITH: And what about my mad scene?

HERSCHEL: I'm just retarded like they all say! [*He runs into his house.*]

RANDY: [*From inside the tent*] Shut up, Judith!

JUDITH: Oh, God, and I even came here bringing your beloved! And you kissed me, and you stroked me, and we held hands along the Charles River, and I thought: He's weird, he's pudgy, he likes Maria Callas, but he responds to me! What a laugh! That's funnier than *The Barber of Seville*, that's funnier than *The Girl of the Golden West*—

FRANCIS: Shut up, shut up, Judith, God damn it, act your age! You're like a fucking six-year-old!

JUDITH: And you? How old are you?!

[*They are right in front of the Geminiani door.* BUNNY, FRAN, *and* LUCILLE *enter grandly from* FRAN's *house, carrying a huge birthday cake and singing. They are wearing party hats.* BUNNY *is running around, putting hats on* JUDITH *and* FRANCIS, *and* RANDY, *as he emerges from the tent.* FRAN *has the cake on the same typing table that was used for breakfast. He also has a camera.*]

BUNNY, FRAN, *and* LUCILLE:
   Happy birthday to you,
   Happy birthday to you,
   Happy birthday, dear Francis,
   Happy birthday to you!

FRAN: Happy birthday, my son! [*Snaps a picture.*]

LUCILLE: Come on, blow out the candles and cut the cake, it's too hot to wait.

BUNNY: There's only six candles, all we could find.

   [FRANCIS *is about to blow them out.*]

LUCILLE: Come on, make a wish.

   [*He does.* FRAN *takes another picture, and* FRANCIS *blows out the candles. They all cheer and applaud.* JUDITH *and* RANDY *are still stunned.*]

FRANCIS: Thank you. I would first like to thank my father, now that I am officially an adult, for teaching me how to dance and sing and cough and fart and scratch and

above all how to treat a rash once it becomes visible to
the general public, then I would like to thank my next-
door neighbor Bunny . . .

[FRAN *snaps a photo of* BUNNY.]

FRANCIS: . . . for demonstrating once and for all that motherhood ought to be abolished, along with drunks and
  whores; Lucille, for teaching me how to ruin the happiest occasion with one glance and the cheapest insect
  spray; and Randy, for providing us with living proof of
  the vacuity of American Higher Education; and then
  Judith, our brilliant, bubbly, and, let's not forget, mature Italian major from Radcliffe will recite to us in her
  Main Line Italian all the nonsense syllables of her upbringing and her recent reading. And I want you all to
  know precisely what I think of all this: this neighborhood, Bunny and Lucille, Randy and Judith!

[*He rips into the cake with his hands and tears it apart,
hurling pieces at* JUDITH *and the others. All duck away.
After* FRANCIS *has destroyed the cake, ke runs off
through the gate.* HERSCHEL *stumbles out of his house,
holding the bag of rat poison, powder all over his
mouth.*]

HERSCHEL: I swallowed Uncle Eddie's rat poison!

BUNNY: My baby!

FRAN: Holy shit!

BUNNY: [*On her knees by* HERSCHEL] My baby!

LUCILLE: Who's gonna clean it up, hanh?

BLACKOUT

Scene 2

Evening. FRAN *has a huge trash bag and is cleaning up
the yard.* LUCILLE *is sitting on the divider between the
two houses.* RANDY *is finishing packing. Their tent has
been struck and is rolled up again.*

LUCILLE: Rum and chocolate sauce everywhere—did he
  know how much it cost?

FRAN: Well, it was his birthday cake, if he wanted a throw it around, it's his right I guess.

LUCILLE: But it ain't his right to clean it up, hanh? [*She points to a piece of cake.*] Over there. Jesus, I'm sick and tired of cleanin' up afta people. [*Points again.*] Over here. Cleanin' up afta my brothers . . .

FRAN: [*Under his breath, still picking up*] Your brothers . . .

LUCILLE: Afta Pop . . .

FRAN: Afta Pop . . .

LUCILLE: Then my mom got senile . . .

FRAN: Then Mom . . .

LUCILLE: Then my husband . . .

FRAN: Your husband . . .

LUCILLE: Then Donny . . .

FRAN: [*Joking*] Ain't he at Yale?

LUCILLE: Hanh? Of course he's at Yale, that's a stupid question, *ma stupidezza. . . .*

RANDY: I'll see if Judith is ready. [*Runs into* BUNNY's *house.*]

FRAN: I hope Francis gets back soon—I think his guests are gonna leave any minute—

LUCILLE: Well, I'm surprised they stayed as long as they did. Well, at least he didn't play so much opera music this weekend—all that screamin'—that's what I got against opera, Fran, ain't like real life.

[*She tries to clean up some whipped cream with a Kleenex.* BUNNY *enters from her house, depressed.*]

BUNNY: Yo, Fran.

FRAN: Yo, Bun. How's Herschel?

BUNNY: Better and better, just ate all my leftovers.

FRAN: I guess they're gettin' ready to leave.

BUNNY: Yep.

LUCILLE: [*About* BUNNY, *mean*] *E questa si chiama una madre?*

FRAN: Lucille, take this bag in the house—tape up the top so nothin' gets in. . . .

[LUCILLE *takes the bag and goes into* FRAN's *house. He calls after her.*]

FRAN: And put on the coffee!

BUNNY: [*Sits down on her stoop.*] She could use a enema, lye and hot pepper! [*Looks at* FRAN.] Remember way back when, when we did it?

FRAN: Oh, Bun.

BUNNY: Oh, Fran! 'Sbeen a long time. I think it's time we did it again. Don't say it, you got Lucille! What's Lucille? Shit, she gotta get on the subway to get her hips movin'.

FRAN: You don' need me, Bun.

BUNNY: We was good together.

FRAN: How often? Five times the most? I remember the first time. [*He sits down beside her.*] You remember? We forced Francis to take Herschel to the movies; it was *Lady and the Tramp.* They was that young, we could force them. Can you see the two of them together?

BUNNY: They was both so fat they probably took up a whole row between them.

FRAN: Didn't they have rashes too?

BUNNY: Nah, that was the third time. We forced Francis to take Herschel into Center City to buy calamine lotion.

[*She puts her head on his shoulder. He looks up to his window, checking for* LUCILLE.]

FRAN: Why don't you give Sam a call?

BUNNY: He ain't interested.

FRAN: I bet you still like him.

BUNNY: You still like your wife?

FRAN: Sure, I married her, didn't I? We went together two years and were pretty happy until Francis came along. She wasn't the same after that. Oh well, she's gone. And now there's Lucille—at least she bakes good fiadone. And she's good people, even if she schives too much. I mean, what kinda choice I got? Hanh? Women today, they look at you, they see a man wheezin', coughin', goin' to the bathroom, scratchin', gettin' rashes, they take off. But Sam ain't attached yet—give him a call, fix yourself up, grow up a little—

BUNNY: Grow up a little? Like that was easy. Jesus, if only I didn't still act and feel nineteen. I look in the mirror and I know there's fat and wrinkles there, Jesus Christ do I know there's fat and wrinkles! Yet I'll be damned if I don't still, somewhere in there, see this nineteen-year-old filly hot to trot and on fire for some kind of success in life! [*Looks at house, tricycle.*] And look what I got—

FRAN: So Herschel's a little crazy, but he's gonna do wonders—

BUNNY: He's a fuckin' genius! Grow up a little. And what
about Francis?

FRAN: Don' know, this Judith girl—

BUNNY: She seems to like him, hard as that is to believe,
but I don't see much evidence of his liking her.

FRAN: No, I guess not, but kids nowadays, maybe they
act different when they're goin' together—and maybe
she isn't his last chance.

BUNNY: Don't kid yourself. Look, why don't you just ask
him and save yourself years of wonderin' and never
bein' sure . . . ?

FRAN: It's the hardest thing for a father to ask his son.
Don' know why it should be, I know guys who . . . like
. . . other guys who are regular, you know, in every
other way. But you know, it's his life now, he's gonna
pay the consequences for whatever he does . . . but still,
I hope.

BUNNY: Well, I worry about Herschel too. But Jesus, I
figure we're lucky if he lives to be twenty-one—

LUCILLE: [Appears in the doorway.] Yo, Fran!

FRAN: [Gets away from BUNNY.] Yo, Lucille!

LUCILLE: I see the monster comin' down the street—[She
goes back in.]

FRAN: Bunny, let's go inside, he won't want to see us
right off—

[They go into BUNNY's house. FRANCIS enters from the
gate. He sees the packed knapsacks under the fig tree.
After a moment, JUDITH enters from BUNNY's house.
She is wearing a skirt and blouse.]

JUDITH: Well . . . Azazel has returned.

FRANCIS: Who?

JUDITH: Who else? The Prodigal!

[LUCILLE comes out of FRAN's house, carrying a coffee
pot and a new robe for HERSCHEL. She sees FRANCIS.]

LUCILLE: Ma Sporcaccione! [She slams the door, and
goes into BUNNY's house.]

FRANCIS: Is everyone furious at me?

JUDITH: We have Bunny's uncle on the force waiting inside with handcuffs.

FRANCIS: Oh, Jesus, you're at it again—

JUDITH: Well, to be serious, Lucille is making a novena

to Saint Jude the Obscure, Patron Saint of the Hopeless and Pudgy who spoil their own birthday parties. [*She gets a sweater out of her knapsack.*] Herschel took rat poison.

FRANCIS: Is he dead?

JUDITH: No more than ever. Bunny called her uncle on the ambulance squad and he was rushed to St. Agnes Hospital, across Track Thirty-seven on the A, the AA one through seven, and the B express lines, perhaps you've passed it? They cleaned up the yard as best they could, but you'll probably be finding birthday cake here and there for the next few months. Still, the fall rains and the march of time should wash away all stains from your yard, your life, and these, the Days of our Youth! Thank you.

FRANCIS: And you're leaving.

JUDITH: You noticed! Maybe you aren't autistic. Yes, we're walking over to Broad Street, where we will get a cab to Thirtieth Street Station, where we will take the nine oh five train to Boston, from there we're going to our summer home. We are not hitching, you'll notice, we've lost the stomach for it. Oh, by the way, happy birthday.

FRANCIS: Thank you.

JUDITH: I'm sorry.

FRANCIS: So am I.

[*They are about to go to each other, when* RANDY *comes out of* BUNNY'*s house.*]

RANDY: C'mon, Judith. We have nineteen minutes to catch that train.

[FRAN *and* LUCILLE *come out of* BUNNY'*s house.*]

FRAN: So, Igor's back, hanh? I guess you kids is off.

[RANDY *and* JUDITH *are putting on their knapsacks and collecting their belongings.*]

RANDY: We're off!

LUCILLE: Good-bye!

FRAN: The way I see it, life is made up of hellos and good-byes and forgivin' and forgettin'. So you two forgive and forget and come back, hanh? Even if Frankenstein ain't here, you're always welcome.

[BUNNY *comes out of her house with* HERSCHEL. *He is wearing clean pajamas and a new bathrobe.*]

BUNNY: [*Sees* FRANCIS.] So, Igor's back, hanh? [*To* RANDY

and JUDITH] We wanted to see youse off, you're good people, you kids.

LUCILLE: [*To* JUDITH] If I give you Donny's number at Yale, maybe you could get in touch with him this fall, he's nice, real good-looking, and athletic, and he ain't no party pooper neither. [*She gives* JUDITH *a slip of paper.*] I have somethin' in the house for you. [*She goes inside.*]

HERSCHEL: [*To* RANDY, *shyly*] Like, if I promise to lose weight and get less weird, can we be friends?

RANDY: Sure, even if you gain and get weirder.

HERSCHEL: Like, don't lie to me, you know? Like, I understand if you aren't interested. But can I, like, you know, write you letters?

RANDY: Oh sure. I'll give you our summer address, otherwise, just write me at Harvard.

[*He writes address on a little piece of paper that* HERSCHEL *had ready.* LUCILLE *returns with a plate wrapped in tin foil. The following three lines are said at about the same time.*]

JUDITH: C'mon, Randy, let's go!

LUCILLE: C'mon, Randy, you're gonna miss the train.

RANDY: See you, Herschel.

[JUDITH, FRAN, *and* LUCILLE *go out through the gate. They stand in the entrance saying final good-byes.* RANDY, *about to say good-bye to Francis, is grabbed by* BUNNY.]

BUNNY: Oh, honey bun, I feel like I've known you for years. Maybe I'm gettin' funny in the head, but I know a promising hunk when I see one.

RANDY: Thank you.

BUNNY: I'm gonna miss you.

[RANDY *smiles and tries to get away, but she hangs on.*]

JUDITH: [*Calling from the gate*] C'mon, Randy!

BUNNY: Be careful when you sit down on toilets, put paper there, you hear? And see that some people may be pretty, even if they got strange faces, and mean well, even if they act weird, and think of me once in a while, hanh? [*She kisses him.*] Goodbye!

[*She goes into her house.* HERSCHEL *and* RANDY *shake hands, then* HERSCHEL, *looking back sadly, blinking back tears, follows his mother into the house.*]

RANDY: [*Goes to* FRANCIS.] In the fall, right?

FRANCIS: Right.

[*They shake hands.*]

JUDITH: Randy!

RANDY: Listen, I was just trying to help, okay?

[RANDY *leaves. The good-byes are heard from behind the fence.* FRANCIS *is left alone.*]

FRAN: Come back soon! Please!

[FRANCIS *goes into his room and puts on a quiet, sad piece of music.* FRAN *and* LUCILLE *come back into the yard.*]

FRAN: Let's go to your place, hanh? Need some coffee.

LUCILLE: I got some nice cheesecake for you, Fran.

FRAN: Yeah? Sounds good. [*Yells to* FRANCIS.] Yo, Francis! We're goin' a Lucille's for coffee and cake. Wanna come? [*There is no answer.*] Yo, Francis!

FRANCIS: [*From his room*] God damn it, no!

FRAN: That's my Ivy League son.

[FRAN *and* LUCILLE *exit through the gate.* FRANCIS *appears in his window. He is very agitated. The music is playing.*]

FRANCIS: Jesus Christ, what am I doing? [*Calls out.*] Dad! Dad! Yo, Dad! [*He runs out of the house to the gate.*]

FRAN: [*Heard from offstage*] What is it?

FRANCIS: Give me some coin, I'm going to Boston! [*Runs back into his room.*]

FRAN: [*Running into yard*] Jesus Christ in heaven! Yo, Bun!

[BUNNY's *lights go on.* FRANCIS *turns off the music.*]

BUNNY: [*At her window*] Yo, Fran!

FRAN: Call your uncle on the ambulance service. We gotta get Francis to the train!

BUNNY: Holy shit! [*She goes to her telephone in the kitchen.*]

LUCILLE: [*Running into house*] I'll help you pack.

BUNNY: [*On the phone*] Hello, Uncle Marty, bring your fuckin' ambulance down, we gotta make a train!

HERSCHEL: [*Coming out of his house*] What's going on?

FRAN: Francis is going to Boston.

HERSCHEL: To see Randy?

BUNNY: [*Still on the phone*] Hello, Uncle Jimmy, send a fuckin' squad car down, we gotta make a train.

FRAN: Hey, Herschel! Catch them kids. [*Pushes him to the gate.*]

HERSCHEL: This way's quicker! [*Runs out through alley behind his house.*]

FRAN: [*Yelling after him*] And bring them back! I'm fuckin' outa money. Lucille!

LUCILLE: [*In* FRANCIS's *room, with a large laundry bag*] There ain't no clean clothes in here!

FRAN: You got some money? I'm out.

LUCILLE: [*Hurling coin purse out the window*] Look!

FRANCIS: Oh, I want to take my new records—Callas in *Parsifal*, 1950, and the 1955 *Norma*! [*Runs into his room.*]

FRAN: [*Going through change purse*] Jesus Christ, Lucille, all these pennies!

LUCILLE: For the tax!

FRAN: Yo, Bun!

BUNNY: Yo, Fran!

FRAN: We need some more money!
[BUNNY *comes out of her house, reaches into her bosom, and removes wad.*]

BUNNY: Here's the house money, take what you need. [*Sirens are heard in the distance, getting closer.*] They're comin'!
[FRANCIS *runs out of the house, holding record albums.*]

BUNNY: You stick wit me, kid, I got connections! [*Hugs* FRANCIS, *as* FRAN *counts money.*] Where's Gargantua!

FRAN: He went to get the kids. [*To* FRANCIS] I think this is enough— [*Gives him money.*]

BUNNY: I hope he doesn't frighten them away!

LUCILLE: [*Runs out of the house with the laundry bag.*] This is the best I could do—go to a laundromat when you get there!

FRANCIS: [*Takes bag, hugs her.*] Thanks everybody, I mean, thanks....

FRAN: Well, it's your birthday.
[*Sirens increase.* HERSCHEL *comes running in from the alley with* JUDITH *and* RANDY.]

HERSCHEL: I got 'em! I got 'em!

FRAN: They're back!
[FRANCIS *embraces* JUDITH. *Sirens much louder.*]

BUNNY: [*At gate.*] My uncles is here!
 [*The kids run out. The others watch at the gate.*]
FRAN: [*Checks his watch, then puts his arms around*
 LUCILLE *and* BUNNY.] I think they're gonna make it!

BLACKOUT

THE TRANSFIGURATION
OF BENNO BLIMPIE

The stage is divided as follows:

BENNO'S ROOM

BENNO, an enormously fat young man of twenty, sits on a stool from which he can survey the action comfortably. This is in an area somewhat removed from the rest of the stage. The area represents BENNO's current room, in which he has barricaded himself. He sits on his stool for the entire length of the play.

When BENNO is involved in a scene he acts as if he were present, and the others act the same. In these scenes he is playing a young boy, and he makes this plain by changing his voice slightly so that it is higher.

His clothes are very large on him, and tentlike. They look as if they haven't been washed or changed in weeks. His complexion is blotchy and pockmarked. His hair is greasy and full of tangles.

THE PARK

This is another area, where trash and dead leaves are scattered about. It is inhabited by the GIRL and the OLD MAN—all their scenes take place here.

The OLD MAN is BENNO's grandfather, an Italian immigrant, about seventy. The GIRL is from the neighborhood, thirteen, tough, Irish parents.

THE KITCHEN

A third area, this represents the kitchen in the home of

BENNO'S PARENTS, and of the young BENNO. Once again, this is an area somewhat isolated, and it should reflect an urban working-class home.

Benno's parents are seen as they were when he was a young boy. His father is in his early thirties or very late twenties, good-looking, a former athlete. His mother is older than the father, less attractive.

It should be kept in mind that Benno is remembering the scenes that are acted out on stage. Thus he is controlling them. He watches these scenes with great intensity and concentration.

Scene 1

Lights up on BENNO, *eating.*

In dim light, one by one, MOTHER, FATHER, GIRL, OLD
MAN *in characteristic poses.*

They freeze. BENNO *finishes eating and speaks to the
audience.*

BENNO: I am Benno. I am eating myself to death.

BLACKOUT

Scene 2

Lights up on Benno. He speaks to the audience.

BENNO: And there were weeds, feet, and bugs. There
were black ants and red ants and giant ants and worms.
There were worms and spiders and snails. One day I
crushed one hundred eighteen snails with my bare feet.
I was very fat even then. It was after a rainstorm. I ran
in the grass and took off my shoes and socks. The snails
inched out and I smashed every one I saw for an hour.
I had snail blood all over my feet. My grandfather asked
me what it was.

OLD MAN: [*The Park. He speaks as though* BENNO *were
a little boy standing beside him.*] Eh, Benno, what you
got all over your feet, hanh? You mother gonna give me

71

hell. Why can't you look afta yourself, hanh? What is
that shit on you feet?

BENNO: [*High voice, playing little boy, acting as though
he were beside the* OLD MAN] Snail wine.

OLD MAN: You crazy, crazy!

[*Hits where* BENNO *would be standing.* BENNO *reacts
to the blow in place. The lights go down on the* OLD
MAN, *but stay up on* BENNO. *Ice cream truck jingle
heard.*]

BENNO: I have eaten seventeen chocolate cones today.
Soft ice cream, the kind they sell in trucks. Those trucks
announce themselves with tinkling, mechanical tunes
played over and over. I heard the neighborhood truck
making its rounds and I ran out and bought seventeen
cones. Chocolate. I was out of breath from running
down the stairs.

[*A light up on* BENNO's MOTHER *in Kitchen.* BENNO
changes his voice to a high whine. MOTHER *reacts as
though he were beside her and busies herself in the
Kitchen.*]

BENNO: [*high voice*] Momma, I wanna chocolate cone.

MOTHER: You're too fat as it is, Benno.

BENNO: I'm hungry. I wanna chocolate cone.

MOTHER: Shut up, fatsy. Why are you so fat? Tell me that.
Hanh? Why are you so fat? Well, at least fat men got
big ones.

BENNO: Ma, I want one.

MOTHER: I remember old Joey Fercanti around the corner in the old neighborhood. We was growin' up together. He was fatter even than you. He took my sister
and me inna the alley one day and took it out and
stuffed it inna his shirt pocket. He said: God provides
for fat guys. An' I turned him down. I hadda go out an'
marry that father of yours, the bastid. Joey was a looker
even if he was fat. Better than you, God knows. Not all
them blotches in the face and he didn't fall down every
ten minutes. Well . . . maybe God'll give you a big one,
but sure as hell, I doubt it.

BENNO: Ma, please, I want one.

MOTHER: Shut your face, fat jerk!

[*Lights dim out on* MOTHER.]

BENNO: [*To audience*] Mother. I used to think my father
dropped roaches down her slit and that's why I heard

her high giggle at night. There was no door between their room and mine; just a curtain with a rip in it. I heard her high giggle and I thought my father must have collected a lot of cockroaches that night in the cellar and was dropping them down her drain. A lot of them twisting in her tubes; suffocating, fornicating, giving birth; you know, whatever cockroaches do in cunts. And when she went into the bathroom and washed afterward, you see, I thought she was flooding them out and down the toilet. Then one night I watched through the rip in the curtain. I preferred the cockroaches. Father.

[FATHER *enters tossing a football.*]

FATHER: And now, playing center quarterback and primary receiver for Bishop Neumann, Number 64, Dominick Vertucci! [*He plays wildly, pantomiming a frenzied football game. He plays as though he were the star of the team and is driving them to victory. He pantomimes hearing cheers for himself and raises his hands over his head in victory.*] Geez, geez, thanks, I couldna done it without the guys—thanks, geez.... [*Catches himself, becomes flustered and shamefaced.*] Aw, shit, was only pretendin', Benno. Even I pretend sometimes. Gotta go home anyways. You bitch mother raise hell if we're late. Come on, Benno. [*Leaves sadly. As though taking* BENNO'S *hand*] Don't trip over this curb....

[BENNO *trips.*]

FATHER: Aw shit, Benno!

[FATHER *exits. Lights come up on the Park. The* GIRL *plays. Out of the corner of her eye she watches the* OLD MAN, *who watches her intently. She allows her game to take her close to him.*]

GIRL: [*To the* OLD MAN] Hey you! Buy me a chocolate cone.

OLD MAN: You mother, what she say?

GIRL: Who's gonna tell her?

[*A pause. She plays her game again.*]

OLD MAN: I seen you. I seen you playin' in the street. You tough. How old?

GIRL: Buy me a cone.

OLD MAN: Can't. My Social Security check ain't come this month. Down to my last dime.

GIRL: The man'll trust you. C'mon. Buy me a chocolate
    cone.
    [*A pause.*]
OLD MAN: Come on. Benno, come on.
    [*They walk off hand in hand.*]
BENNO: I was in an oven. A fat roast burning in the oven.
    There was a glass door to my oven and they came to it
    and laughed and pointed. Fat roasts are funny burning
    in ovens. I couldn't move. If I moved, I burned my
    back. If I moved, I burned my side. If I turned, old
    burns were given to the heat. I was trapped, you see.
    Once I thought, wait until you're older, Benno, wait
    until you're older. Strength then, and force enough to
    burst through the oven door into the sun, into freedom.
    One day I did break through the glass door. But on the
    other side all there was was another oven with another
    glass door and laughing people pointing at me. And
    there was no sun. Has there even been a sun? I am still
    in the oven, I am still in the oven, I am still in the oven.
    And I am burning up, trapped and pierced, burning up!
    That's why I am eating myself to death.

BLACKOUT

Scene 3

Lights up on the Park and on BENNO. BENNO *has a flashlight with which he plays for a moment before the scene
begins.*

*The Park is lit to suggest a very shady area. The light
fades into heavy darkness.*

The GIRL *enters barefoot. She walks slowly through the
mud, humming to herself, occasionally she stops and
wanders a step or two backwards.*

Very slowly, the OLD MAN *enters. He is obviously following her, and has been. The* GIRL *realizes this but doesn't
show it. As she approaches the dark area she stops and*

*plays in place. He watches her, rapt for a moment, then
decides to speak.*

BENNO *pays intense attention to the scene.*

OLD MAN: What you doin' playin' inna mud?

GIRL: Walkin' barefoot.

OLD MAN: Dummy, you cut you feet.

GIRL: I want it.

OLD MAN: There are snakes and rats in here. They eat
little girls, startin' down there. And swallow them,
whole. Be careful.

GIRL: Ain't a little girl. An' I want to.

OLD MAN: You wanna cut you feet?

GIRL: I dunno. [*A pause. She walks a bit toward the dark
area.*] Maybe a man'll come by and pick the glass outa
the cut. Maybe a man'll hold my foot and lick it and cry
over it.

OLD MAN: You're crazy! [*A pause.*] Men hide around here.
Under them heavy trees. They hide, you hear? And
they wait. For little girls to come by, barefoot. Little
girls don't fight hard. [*A pause.*] Little girls, they got
soft feet. Men wait with rope, to tie them, hard. Be
careful!

GIRL: [*After a moment*] Take your shoes and socks off.

OLD MAN: What? Why?

GIRL: I want it. C'mon. Walk with me. Over here, in the
shade, under these trees.

[*She walks into the dark area and vanishes. The* OLD
MAN *waits an instant, then takes his shoes and socks
off. The socks are white with a pronounced yellow
tinge. He walks in after the* GIRL. BENNO *has watched
and listened to this scene intently. The light brightens
on him. He shines his flashlight around the area the*
OLD MAN *and* GIRL *have just left—the area which isn't
dark. Then shines the flashlight into his own eyes. He
squints and shudders.*]

BENNO: [*Quickly, passionately*] Cimabue, Giotto, Donatello, Pico della Mirandola, Bellini, Michelangelo,
Rafaello, Botticelli, Brunelleschi, I want, I want, want,
want, want, Brunelleschi, Botticelli, Raffaello, Michelangelo, Bellini, Pico della Mirandola, Donatello, Giotto,
Cimabue. I want, please, please, I want—wantwant-

wantwantwantwant! Give me ... give me ... [*He is panting, his eyes are shut tightly. He has begun to cry.*] No one, no one, no one ... no ... one ...

[*He shines the flashlight slowly into the dark area. The* OLD MAN *is caressing and kissing the* GIRL's *feet. She moans. Hold a moment.*]

BLACKOUT

Scene 4

Lights up on the Kitchen, and on BENNO.

BENNO *doesn't change position, but takes part intently in the scene.* MOTHER *and* FATHER *act as though he were present. They talk to him as though he were sitting in the third place set at the table.* BENNO *uses his high voice.*

MOTHER: [*To* FATHER] Eh, Dominick! Where's your old man?

FATHER: How the hell should I know?

MOTHER: He's your father!

[*She busies herself.* FATHER *consults a racing sheet with great interest. He has a pencil in hand and figures numbers along the side of the sheet. After a while, the* MOTHER *glares at him.*]

MOTHER: Look! What is your father, the star boarder? Hanh? Tell me that, what is your father? I tell him and tell him we have supper at six on the dot and does he show? Hanh? Hanh? He don't show. What am I supposed to do with the food—Benno, don't smack your lips like a pig, PIG! Oink, oink, oink—leave it out for the rats? I asked you, Dominick, what am I supposed to do with the food?

[FATHER *ignores her.*]

MOTHER: That's right, Mary, slave for them and let them ignore you. Gotta cook twice, gotta clean up twice, and I work too. What is this, a hotel? Hanh? Your no-good, free-loadin' father come up to the table afta we finish, like a big rat!

FATHER: Look, fry the steak, I'm hungry. And I want it rare.

MOTHER: Awwww! Eat it raw, you creep!

FATHER: I wanna see the blood. That's how you know it's rare, you can see the blood.

BENNO: [*High voice. Trying to make friends with his* FATHER] That's how you know it's rare, you can see the blood.

MOTHER: [*To* BENNO] You shut up, fatty. What the hell do you know? [*To* FATHER] Looka him bustin' outa those pants and looka those blotches on his face. He's enough to break mirrors, God forbid! And don't get me off the topic of the star boarder. T'resa was sayin' . . .

FATHER: You got red peppers in them potatoes?

MOTHER: We run out.

FATHER: [*Suddenly angry*] God damn it to hell, you know I want red peppers in the fried potatoes! That's when they're good. They burn when they go down.

BENNO: [*As before*] They burn when they go down.

MOTHER: [*To* BENNO] Shut up, you fat creep! [*To* FATHER] And you! Who the hell are you to start screaming at me like you own the place? Hanh? What the hell are you? Nothin', that's what! Up to your ass in debt, a lousy gambler. Who works their ass off? Who slaves? I do—Mary, that's who. I get up and work myself to the bone for you and your monster kid and your free-loading old man. I go to work at six and then have to come home to look after you and this *disgraziato* freak! How much did you give me for the house last week, hanh? Tell me that, big man, big horse player, how much did you give me for the house? A big fat fifteen dollars, that's how much! That's supposed to pay the mortgage, buy food, pay this cripple's doctor bills and keep your no-good, smelly father in stogies! How far's fifteen dollars supposed to go, hanh? What's it supposed to buy— the Taj Mahal? You wanna good meal, you go to the bookie, go to the Pooch! You love him more than you love me!

FATHER: [*Retreating behind the racing form*] All right, all right.

MOTHER: You was always out bettin' them nags. This nag,

this nag, Mary, you never bet on. You want red pepper!
Who the hell are you to want red pepper? You can't
even get it up.

FATHER: You stupid bitch! In front of the kid!

MOTHER: Kid? What kid? Where's the kid? You ever see
a kid that looked like that? He's just like you—nothin'.
A ton of nothin'!

FATHER: [*Angry again*] Whose fault? Hanh? Whose fault?
Without red pepper he can't digest. Red peppers eat
up the fat. You eat red peppers, you can eat anything,
even the shit you cook, and still stay thin and healthy.
The shit you cook! How do you cook it, hanh? By sittin'
on it? It smells of your ass! It smells of your friggin'
cunt!

MOTHER: How would you know? You ain't been in it for
years—all you smell is the Pooch!

FATHER: And another thing, you friggin' Napolitan bitch,
you never, never put enough oregano in the gravy. And
you never put enough oil. It's dry, like your tits! Not
enough red pepper, not enough oregano, not enough
oil, no wonder you got a freak for a son! That's why he
ain't normal!

MOTHER: He ain't normal because he takes after you! He
got no balls either. Your father is ball-less, you is ball-
less. And your kid is ball-less. It runs in the family. I
looked at him last night. There ain't nothin' down
there, only flab. And your father's screwin' a thirteen-
year-old girl. Everybody knows.

FATHER: You shut that big, ugly Napolitan mouth!

MOTHER: *Madonna me'!* The whole neighborhood knows.
Your father's a sex fiend and he's livin' in my house.
And she's a Irish girl, the slut, the *putana!*

FATHER: Shut up! Shut up!

MOTHER: [*Screaming*] Your father's a bum, you're a ball-
less bum with no cock, and your son's a good-for-
nothin' ball-less bum!

FATHER: Cunt!
[*He slaps her. She throws herself to the floor as though
the blow had sent her reeling.*]

BENNO: [*High voice*] Daddy!

MOTHER: [*On the floor, hysterical*] That's right! Run off
to the Pooch! You love him more than you ever loved
me!

BENNO: [*High voice, crying*] Mommy!

MOTHER: Get away from me, you good-for-nothin' fatty, you! You louse, you good-for-nothin'—you—fruit! [*Crawls off, weeping.*]

BENNO: My steak is rare, I can see the blood.

BLACKOUT

Scene 5

Lights up on BENNO *and the* GIRL.

The GIRL *is alone. She is dancing to a very ugly, fifties rock-and-roll tune. She sings along for a moment.* BENNO *stares out, abstracted.*

GIRL: Last night I dreamed I was eating a boiled chicken leg. I started by licking it. I made my tongue all wet and slobbered all over it, up and down, up and down, all around. Then, with my front teeth, I tore off the leg's tip. It was a piece of skin, yellow. I rolled the skin under my teeth, sucking all the juice out of it. Then, I spit it out. Then, suddenly, I stuck all my teeth into the middle of the leg and let it dangle in my mouth. Not biting, not chewing, just letting it dangle.

[*She freezes in place. The light on her dims but does not go out. A tape of the ugly rock tune is heard. On the tape, the* GIRL *is singing very softly into a closely held microphone. The sound is breathy and wet. Then the tape fades very slowly under the following.*]

BENNO: [*He starts slowly, with little expression.*] Benno loved to draw. And he loved drawings. As soon as he was old enough he stole carfare from his mother's purse and went to the big museum. He snuck in. He ran to the Renaissance paintings. And he stared at them. He stared at their designs, most particularly at their designs. And at their colors. But the designs, to begin with, were the most significant to him. The circle, for instance, fascinated him; and the right angle as used in a painting like *The Last Supper* thrilled him. He would

trace the angles and the circles in these paintings with
his fingers when the guards weren't looking. Then, on
paper napkins and the dirty lined paper from the Catholic school, he would make designs like those. He drew
arcs and circles, and angles and lines, trying to vary
them with the deception and subtlety of the masters.
He wasn't interested in drawing people. He knew what
they looked like. Think of the structure of the foot. The
lines bend, then they curve. The arch juts up, then juts
down; two angles, like a roof. Underneath there is the
inverse. The sole is like a barreled vault. Then, at the
front, five straight lines—but with rounded tips. Benno
drew idealized feet, or distorted them in his own way.
He was not interested in the imperfections of real feet.
Benno's make-believe feet were curved or gracefully
inclined. Real feet are crooked and crushed. One day,
out of guilt, Benno's Pop-pop bought him a paint set
with a Social Security check that bounced or something
and caused some discomfort. Benno painted—he col-
ored in his designs. He painted hour upon hour upon
hour. He lulled himself asleep planning paintings as
though they were battle campaigns. He dreamed col-
ored designs and designs of colors and waking, tried to
copy these. Once, once when he had finished painting
six straight lines carefully, he stared at his painting and
heard . . . heard music played up the back of his spine.
It made no difference. When he had finished a painting, Benno was still fat, ugly, and alone. Nothing makes
a difference, nothing alters anything. It took Benno a
very long time to learn this. And Benno wasn't sure he
had learned it, really, until he started eating himself to
death. Then Benno knew he had learned. For all that
matters is the taste of our own flesh. It tastes horrible,
particularly if we are fat and sweat a lot. But there are
no disappointments there; and those feelings of horror
and disgust at chewing ourselves are the only feelings
we can be sure of. Benno will put his eyes out soon.
Then there will be no seductive angles or circles.
Benno will be left to stumble about his filthy room, the
windows nailed shut, biting at himself. Thank you.
[*The lights go out on* BENNO. *They intensify on the*
GIRL, *who starts singing and dancing again.*]
GIRL: So anyway, then I dreamed that I tore off the bite

in my mouth. Just then I was woke up by my brother
screaming. He sleeps in the bed next to mine. His un-
derpants were covered in jit. He'd had a wet dream.
[*She sniggers.*] He didn't know what it was. I did. I
didn't tell him what it was. He started crying. He
thought he was gonna die. I let him think so. I'm hungry. I hope Mom serves chicken soon.

BLACKOUT

Scene 6

The lights come up on BENNO *and on the Park.*

The GIRL *and* OLD MAN *are lying down. The light is heavy
and shadowy.*

OLD MAN: [*Looks off, nervous.*] Damn kids! Make a lotta
noise. Benno, why you no play wit them?

BENNO: [*High voice*] What, Pop-pop?

OLD MAN: Why you no have friends, Benno? Why you
always around me?

BENNO: [*High voice*] I love you, Pop-pop.
[*The* GIRL *laughs, mocking.*]

BENNO: I do love you, Pop-pop.

OLD MAN: [*To* BENNO] Shut up, you crazy, you. If you
gonna stay around be quiet. Stay over there.

BENNO: [*High voice*] I'm drawing, Pop-pop. I'll be quiet.
[*The* OLD MAN *draws closer to the* GIRL *and whispers
in her ear.*]

OLD MAN: You very pretty for an Irish girl. I like you hair,
it is so long and thick. And you thighs, they very soft.
When I touch them, I feel them long time after.

GIRL: You have bumps on your feet. And there's somethin' strange on your heels. It's like moss.

OLD MAN: You fingers is beautiful. You toes is beautiful.
[*Sucks on her fingers.*]

BENNO: [*High voice*] Pop-pop . . .

OLD MAN: [*Very annoyed*] Benno, go 'way! I'm tellin' you,

go 'way. Go over to them boys in the trees over there. Go play wit them. You hear me, Benno? Go on!
[*Gets up and mimes chasing* BENNO *away.* BENNO *reacts facially in place. The* OLD MAN, *looking off as though following* BENNO *with his eyes.*]

OLD MAN: Maybe they be friends for him.

GIRL: Benno's so fat.

OLD MAN: He's my oldest grandchild.

GIRL: He's a monster. Ooooo! He's so ugly. Benno Blimpie, we call him.

OLD MAN: Lemme get on top a you.

GIRL: No, use your fingers like you did yesterday.

OLD MAN: I wanna do somethin' different.

GIRL: Somethin' different? [*Caresses his thigh.*] What? I don't wanna do nothin' different. [*Sticks her tongue in his mouth.*]

OLD MAN: I gotta do somethin' different.

GIRL: What?

OLD MAN: Somethin'. You like it.

GIRL: What'll you give me?

OLD MAN: My Social Security check comes next week. I give you if you let me.

GIRL: How much?

OLD MAN: Sixty-two twenty.

GIRL: Bring it next week. We'll see then. Use your fingers today.

OLD MAN: [*Reaches under her dress.*] Like this?

GIRL: [*Spreads her legs.*] Yes.

OLD MAN: Touch me.
[*The* GIRL *starts to unzip him.* BENNO *screams.*]

OLD MAN: Damn it to hell! That's Benno.
[*They both look off and the* OLD MAN *rises.*]

GIRL: It's them boys. They got him.

OLD MAN: Shit! [*Starts to go off.*]

GIRL: [*Holds him back.*] Don't go. They're just playin'. That's how boys play nowadays. Come on. Use your fingers today. Next week bring me the check. Kiss me.

OLD MAN: Like this? [*Kisses her.*]

GIRL: Use your fingers.

OLD MAN: [*Reaches under her dress*] Like this?

GIRL: [*Unzipping him*] Yes . . . yes . . .

BENNO: [*Screaming as though terrified and in pain*] Pop-pop! Pop-pop! Pop-pop!

[*Blackout.* BENNO *continues screaming for a beat in the dark. Then silence.*]

Scene 7

Lights up on the Kitchen and on BENNO.

FATHER *hovers about the stove.*

FATHER: Goddammit, Benno, quit followin' me. Where did she keep things, Benno? You know where that bitch, God forgive me, kept everything? Aw—how would you know? Sit down. How many eggs you want, Benno? Six enough? Benno, I make seven, that should fill us both. I hope she dies in that filthy Napolitan shack livin' with her virgin sister. Get the black pepper, Benno—don't spill it—watch out, don't spill it. Be careful, or you'll spill it; watch out . . . shit fire, you spilled it! Why are you so clumsy, my son? [*Stoops down as though picking black pepper up off the floor.*] Hey! I know what. I'll put pepperoni in the eggs. That's always good! [*Sings as he mimes adding the ingredients.*] "Pepperoni hits the spot, helps you shit because it's hot." Why didn't you fight back, Benno, hanh? Why didn't you fight back? I heard, I heard, Benno, what them kids did to you. Why did you lay there like some queer? Hanh! I'll turn the heat up just a tidge. And maybe we better put some milk. Is there somethin' wrong with you, my son? Are you a pansy, my son? Why ain't you out there in the street, playin' ball, roughin' up like I did? Why you always in here with you mama, like a girl? Shit, the eggs is stickin' to the pan, I'll stir them. We better put a tidge of sugar in. There. Why are you so fat, my son? Why don't you exercise? I'd never of let them kids near me when I was your age. I'll put some oregano in. Never. I'll tell you, I was a holy terror, a holy terror, geez. I'd have kicked them inna balls, like this. I'd have beat them with my fists, like this. I was no fatty, no pansy. I'd have punched them, I'd have beaten them senseless.

[*Dances around as though in a boxing ring.*] Left, right, left, right and kick to the balls. [*Mimes a fight.*] Take that, motherfucker, take that and that! A right to the side of the head—pow! A left to the jaw and boop!—a knee between the legs! And another left and another right—he's down, he's bleedin'—my God!—he's out! Hey! Hey! [*Runs to the stove.*] Shit! Shit fire and save the matches! The eggs is burned.

BLACKOUT

Scene 8

Lights up on BENNO *and on the* GIRL. *Near her is a small night table with stained and sticky-looking bottles and jars on it.*

When the light hits her she sprays a large amount of very smelly hair spray on her hair, then teases her hair violently. Then she smears an enormous amount of purple lipstick on sensuously puffed-out lips. During this she sings a very ugly rock tune and occasionally does a dance step to it.

GIRL: Last night I spilled spaghetti all over me. The sauce went over my white blouse and my blue dress; and it was thick sauce with peppers and bits of meat in it. It was a big mess. And Donny, my cousin, wiped it off. He's spiffy. Twenty and in the Navy. He took his napkin, it had red stains from his mouth on it, and wiped my blouse off. Wiped and wiped, not too hard but strong. Then he took another napkin, my brother's, and wiped my dress off. Wiped and wiped, makin' a small circle in my lap. Donny has big hands, a lotta hair on them around the knuckles and the veins is very thick. His fingers is thick, too, and the middle one is long and heavy. I dream about Donny's hand makin' circles in my lap.
[*Freezes in place. The light on her dims.*]

BENNO: Benno grew up thinking that talent and sensitivity were things people took seriously. At least that important people took seriously—artists, for instance, and teachers. Benno grew up hoping that looks and sex didn't matter. That paintings would satisfy any longing he'd ever have. And when that longing got too strong, a quick pulling with the palm would be enough. Benno was wrong. Benno has been heard to say that nothing matters save the taste of his own flesh. But since then, time has passed. For your benefit he has conjured up scenes better not remembered. And Benno realizes that he was guilty of oversimplification. There are things that matter: looks matter, sex matters. These are all that matter. Benno feels that those who deny this are participating in a huge joke. Benno has learned his lesson. Paintings, you see, aren't enough. When loneliness and emptiness and longing congeal like a jelly, nothing assuages the ache. Nothing, nothing, nothing. It was the end of spring, the traditional season of youth, renewal, and young love. Benno returned to his old neighborhood, having celebrated his twentieth birthday. He found the poorest side street in his old neighborhood. Fitzgerald Street, by name. And he rented a room on the third floor of a row house on Fitzgerald Street. Benno nailed shut all the windows in that room, even though it was summer. Something about imbibing his own smell. Benno is not as isolated as you might think. He hears the horrible street noises. He hears the monster children screaming. He even allows himself to have his shade up one-half hour a day. Today at 1 P.M., Benno had his shade up. He stared out his nailed window, stared through the caked dirt that streaks the window's glass. He saw a wild circle flashing red across the street. He stared at that circle and was tempted to . . . never mind. He was tempted and stared and was tempted some more. And then he saw the agent of that circle. It was a little girl. A beautiful girl. Oh yes, Benno knows beauty. He knows if he tell you. Once, when he saw something beautiful, it would flash across his eyes like a hot knife and he would peer, eyes stuck there until they ached. Once, he tells you, no longer. For beauty has lost his power over me, it has lost its power, no more beauty, no more longing to grasp it within me and smother it with my bulk, please God, no more beauty. [*He is almost weeping. He eats passionately and slowly pulls himself together.*]

GIRL: [*Unfreezes and continues with her makeup.*] When Donny finished wiping me off, I smiled up at him and his eyes, they're black, got very big. When Ma wasn't looking, I let my fingers take a walk along his thigh. I saw the big bump in the middle of his thigh get bigger. Then, when Ma was clearin' the table, I spilled the plate of meatballs all over me. While she was in the kitchen, Donny licked them off with his tongue. Ma caught him and gave him hell. Pop laughed. Donny ran into the bathroom and puked all over, like a sissy. I changed my mind about Donny. I think Donny is a jerk-off.

[*Lights out on* GIRL.]

BENNO: Benno has decided: he will no longer lift the shade, he will no longer look out into the street. Benno stayed in this tiny room. He left every two days to buy food. Otherwise he never went out. Except in cases of emergency such as when the ice cream truck came along. He did nothing. He ate continually from when he awoke until he fell asleep. He did nothing save remember. When I become so fat I cannot get into his clothes and can barely move, I will nail the door shut. I will put his eyes out with a long nail and I will bite at himself until he dies. In the middle of this filthy hole on the third floor of a row house in the poorest side street of my old neighborhood there will I be: a mountain of flesh. There are rats in this room. I see them slithering along the sides of the wall. They will eat me. These rats will find Benno beautiful. They will long for him. He will be a sexual object to them. They will make the devouring of Benno's body an erotic act. They will gnaw hollows into his face, into his belly. And in those hollows, they will fornicate. Then they will perish. The instant before he is ready to die, Benno will swallow a hugh draft of poison. These rats in eating Benno will be eating poisoned meat. The poison will cause a fearful splitting of stomachs, vital rat organs will swell up and burst even while the rats are making love. Even while they are eating. Posthumously, Benno will have been loved.

BLACKOUT

Scene 9

Lights up on Park and on BENNO.

The GIRL *and the* OLD MAN *are seated together on the ground. The* OLD MAN *has a wine bottle in a paper bag with him and takes swigs from it. The* GIRL *is in a Catholic schoolgirl's uniform—white blouse; blue, rather long skirt; and white ankle socks with blue oxfords. She has a school satchel nearby.*

OLD MAN: Benno, you stay over there and draw. Don' bother me. You old enough to go pee-pee by yourself.
GIRL: He's funny, retarded.
OLD MAN: You hear me, Benno?
BENNO: [*High voice*] Yes, Pop-pop.
GIRL: [*Mimicking*] Yes, Pop-pop.
OLD MAN: Just be sure you stay away! An' don' you go tellin' you bitch mother, either.
BENNO: [*High voice*] I won't, Pop-pop.
GIRL: Queerie!
OLD MAN: You hear me good, Benno. Leave me alone today.
BENNO: [*High voice*] Yes, Pop-pop. [*Quietly to himself, high voice*] I love you, Pop-pop. [*Normal voice, to the audience*] And Benno wept. He didn't realize at that time that there is nothing funnier than a fat boy weeping. Nothing funnier. Nothing. [*A pause. He laughs dryly. The light dims somewhat on* BENNO. *But he stares at the scene intently.*]
OLD MAN: [*Takes a drink, offers the bottle to the* GIRL.] Drink this!
GIRL: Don' wan' none.
OLD MAN: Drink.

GIRL: Don' wan' none, I said! [*Takes a long swig and grimaces.*] Oooooooh! What is it?

OLD MAN: *La vita, carina, la vita.*

GIRL: Don' know Eyetalian. You bring the check?

OLD MAN: Sixty-two twenty.

GIRL: Lemme see.

OLD MAN: Later.

GIRL: Lemme see.

[*He reaches into his back pocket and presents her with the check. She scrutinizes it.*]

GIRL: Yeah . . . yeah . . . sixty-two twenty. Sign it over to me.

OLD MAN: What do you mean?

GIRL: You know what I mean. Sign it over.

OLD MAN: Can't write.

GIRL: Make yer sign.

OLD MAN: Got no pencil.

GIRL: Got one in my school bag. [*Reaches into her school bag and removes a pencil.*] New point. Come on.

OLD MAN: All right.

[*Makes his mark on the check. The* GIRL *reaches for the wine and takes a long pull.*]

GIRL: [*As he notices her drinking*] Didn't have no lunch today. On a diet. Give it to me.

OLD MAN: Afta. [*Puts check in his back pocket.*]

GIRL: Benno hangs around you a lot. Why? He ain't normal.

OLD MAN: Kiss me.

GIRL: My brother beat him up, broke his glasses. Said he wanted to crush his nose against his face like a pimple.

OLD MAN: Touch me.

GIRL: You love Benno?

OLD MAN: Let me do it now, I be gentle.

GIRL: Do you love him?

OLD MAN: I take you top off.

GIRL: [*Twists away.*] Yesterday my brother told me he gonna beat Benno up afta school on Monday. You gonna try and stop him?

OLD MAN: Help me wit you buttons.

GIRL: Not yet. Use your fingers.

OLD MAN: Want more today. Help me wit the buttons.

GIRL: [*He tries to start undressing the* GIRL. *She resists, but in a lazy, teasing way. The* OLD MAN *sometimes stops trying to remove her top and caresses her.*] Why is Benno so weird? Drawing all the time. Never playin' in the street? In school on Tuesday—c'mon, cut it out—he started talkin' about this Eyetalian painter. Just started talking; sister didn't call on him or nothing. Cut that out. Then Benno showed us his drawings. They was weird. One was supposed to be a old man. He was long and thin with these blurry features. Looked like my brother's dickie floatin' in the bathtub. Stop it! I don't like you slobbering on me!

OLD MAN: Drink some more. [*Takes a long swig and passes her the bottle.*]

GIRL: Lick my feet like you did before. [*Drinks.*]

OLD MAN: I want more—I want more. [*Gets on top of her.*]

BENNO: [*High voice, loudly*] Pop-pop, look what I drew. Look, see the circles. . . .

OLD MAN: [*Jumping off the* GIRL] God damn it to hell, Benno! Get away from here, go on! [*Acts as though chasing* BENNO *off.*] Damn kid, always around, always in the way. [*Lies down beside the* GIRL.]

GIRL: [*Giggles.*] Benno couldn't genuflect at mass on Wednesday. He couldn't get that far down. And when he did get down on his knees, he couldn't get up. Even sister laughed. Then we all had to go to confession for laughing at mass. Even sister. I smelled the priest in the confessional. All sweaty and underarmy. But nice. Do you love Benno?

OLD MAN: [*Caressing her, kissing her hair*] You, *carina*, you I love; all of you. Fine Irish hair and the little hairs down there. I wanna scoop you up with my mouth. You hear me, with my mouth! I wanna bury my teeth, bury them, in there, in and in and in. Come to me, *cara*, I ready. I wan' . . .

GIRL: [*Squirming away*] You wanna, you wanna, you wanna! You're drunk, you're a slob!

OLD MAN: I wan' more from you this time, this time more!

GIRL: Hey, hey!

[*He reaches under her dress.*]

GIRL: I'm not in the mood! [*She reaches for the bottle and takes a long swig.*]

OLD MAN: [*Lies back and strokes her.*] In the *paese*, over there, over the seas, I took a little girl inna wood. I was how old? Nineteen maybe, who knows? I take her inna the wood and swallow her whole. You hear, swallow her whole?! I start at her feet. [*Grabs the* GIRL'S *foot. She utters an annoyed cry.*] Took her toes inna my mouth and bite them off, one by one. Then I bite inna her leg . . . [*Grabs her leg and holds it tight while she struggles.*] . . . and chew onna the bone. It was hard that bone, but then, then I have good teeth and chew hard. I ate all of her, and today, today I wan' more. . . . [*The* GIRL *finally pushes him away with all her strength.*]

GIRL: No! I'm sick of you and your yellow skin and your sores and your smell!

OLD MAN: [*Trying to get on top of her*] Bella mia, mia bella, ti voglio! I wanna dig inna you skin!

GIRL: [*Twisting away*] Dago shit! Smelly!

BENNO: [*High voice*] Pop-pop! Pop-pop!

[*The* OLD MAN *has begun to chase the* GIRL, *reaching out for her. This has started slowly but becomes wild. The* OLD MAN *starts gasping for breath and getting dizzy.*]

BENNO: [*High voice*] Why are you running like that, Pop-pop? Stop it, I'm scared!

GIRL: [*Dodging the* OLD MAN *as though it were a game*] Grandson's a queerie, granddad's a smelly!

OLD MAN: [*Still chasing her, panting*] I wan' more, more!

BENNO: [*High voice*] Please, Pop-pop!

GIRL: Smelly!

BENNO: [*High voice*] Leave her alone, Pop-pop!

OLD MAN: [*Gasping*] Mia! Bella mia, ti voglio! Fermati! T'amo!

GIRL: Wop bastard!

[*The* OLD MAN *lunges and catches the* GIRL. *She utters a cry and fights him. Neither is playful. The* OLD MAN *throws her to the ground. She screams. He tries to hurl himself on top of her but she moves at the last minute and he hits the ground with a thud and a cry. He is stunned briefly.*]

BENNO: [*High voice*] Oh! Oh, Pop-pop . . .

[*The* GIRL *runs to the wine bottle and breaks it.*]

GIRL: [*Waving the broken bottle*] Come on, dago shit, come on!

OLD MAN: [*Laughs.*] Tigra, tigra, come on, *tigra!*
[*They circle each other slowly. Occasionally the* GIRL *strikes out at the* OLD MAN. *He is playful but she is very serious. From his stool* BENNO *watches in terror.*]

BENNO: Pop-pop, should I run for the police?

OLD MAN: [*To the* GIRL, *still circling*] I wanna chew you up!

GIRL: Asshole! [*Lunges again and cuts him on the arm.*]

OLD MAN: [*Yells but chases her more violently.*] Mia, *vieni!*

BENNO: Leave her alone, Pop-pop, she's crazy!
[*The* OLD MAN *acts as though* BENNO *is tugging at him and turns to push him away.*]

OLD MAN: Go home, queerie, go home! Today I wan' more. . . .
[*With a scream the* GIRL *lunges and stabs the* OLD MAN *in the back with the broken bottle. He screams and falls.*]

OLD MAN: [*Screaming*] Aiuto, aiuto, Benno, help me!
[*He twists desperately in the mud as though trying to stop the pain in his back.* BENNO *gasps, then stares. The* GIRL *also stares wide-eyed. The* OLD MAN *continues to scream and throws up in the mud.*]

GIRL: [*In a stunned whisper*] Go 'head, puke, you wop bastard!

OLD MAN: [*Almost voiceless*] I . . . I . . . I . . .
[*Dies. There is a pause. The* GIRL *becomes suddenly hysterical.*]

GIRL: Bastard! Bastard! Filthy wop bastard! Oh, my God, my God, I've . . . I've . . . he's . . . [*With a cry she throws the bottle down. It shatters. She looks at it frightened, then bends over the corpse, screaming.*] Dago, dago, wop, filthy, dago bastard, bastard, bitch, dago, jerk-off, bitch, motherfucker, filthy . . . mother . . . [*She is gasping. She pulls herself together suddenly and looks around.*] Geez . . . the check! [*She searches the body for the check and finds it. She removes it from the back pocket.*] Muddy. [*Wipes the check on her skirt.*] Hey . . . hey . . . you kiddin'? [*Kicks the body.*] Oh . . . oh, Caarist! Hey, Benno, your Pop-pop's dead. Don't you tell nobody or my brother'll get you good. Oh . . . [*Looks at the body.*] Oh . . . Caarist! [*Runs off.*]

BENNO: [*A pause. Then he whispers, normal voice*] Pop-pop.

BLACKOUT

Scene 10

Lights up on BENNO *and the Kitchen. The* FATHER *is pacing tensely.*

FATHER: Where the hell is your mother, Benno? Hanh? Mary! Mary! Where the hell are you! We should be there! Mary!

MOTHER: [*Offstage*] All right, for Christ's sake, I'm comin'!

FATHER; Jesus Christ—let me make sure everythin' is ready, Benno. [*Opens ice box.*] Yep, got the spareribs for the gravy—Uncle Fonse likes them—Benno—don't eat the cake, it's for the relatives, afta. [*Calling*] Mary, for Christ's sake, hurry.

MOTHER: [*Off*] Jesus Christ in heaven shove that friggin' racin' form in that big mouth, I'm comin'!
[*A pause. She enters. She seems ashamed. The dress she is wearing is too small for her. He looks at her.*]

FATHER: Jesus—is that all you had to wear?

MOTHER: Ain't had no money to buy a dress in years—

FATHER: Well, at least they'll know you was Benno's mother and you eat well—wear a shawl or somethin'. Come on.

MOTHER: Not yet.

FATHER: Oh, Jesus!

MOTHER: I ain't ready yet! Gotta get inna the mood. I don't like wakes. You go on, I'll come later. Not ready, I tell you.

FATHER: And the kid?

MOTHER: Why can't you take him, you ashamed? You think they'll think he's my fault if he comes in wit me? Hanh? Is that what you think? Oh, their little Dominick could never commit somethin' like this flabby monster.

He could never cause such ugliness to come inna the world. It's Mary's fault.

FATHER: Look you, none of your shit tonight. You keep that big ugly Napolitan mouth shut. And you bring the kid. It's my father's wake and I want you to show some respect, or so help me God, I'll take the strap to you right there.

MOTHER: All right, all right, get the hell out.

FATHER: Make sure that kid keeps decent too. [*Exits.*]

MOTHER: Let's have some coffee, Benno. I need it. [*Heats coffee.*] Oh, Jesus, Jesus, how'm I gonna face it? All them relatives of his: his sister Edith, that witch of a prune face, *faccia brutt', Virgine, ti conosci'*, Benno stop slobberin', and his brother, Basil—face like a rhinoceros' ass—how'm I gonna face them? They hate me. They look down on me—Mary the peasant, they call me. But it was me, the Virgin knows, me, Mary the horse, put the old man up. Me! I hadda see him come and spit inna the sink every day. Me! And I hadda run the vacuum cleaner to get the scales from his sores. Those damn scales were everywhere, like fairy dust. I even found 'em on the windowsill. How did they get on the windowsill? What did he do, scratch them while watchin' some broad walk down the street? And do they thank me for cleanin' up afta him week afta friggin' week? Nah! Benno, why you puttin' five teaspoons of sugar in you coffee, hanh? Why can't you put two like a human being? Three, even three I could see, God knows, but five? Who do you take afta? Hanh? [*Gets up and pours coffee for herself.*] Take some coffee, Mary. Weep into them grounds. And them goddamned lousy shits look down at me. My father, my friggin' father, God rest his soul, was eight times, nah, nine times the man theirs was! Nine times, you hear me? The day before he died I went a see him. Couldn't find him. Where was he, where? Then, suddenly, I hear this clang, this loud clang. CLANG! It come from the cellar. I run down. There he is, seventy-six, at least, chasin' rats with the shovel. He screamed: *Ecco! Ecco!* And then he smashes one with the shovel. CLANG!! It splattered all over the cellar. That was a real man. Not a ball-less bum like you no-good bastard father. Well, have a cookie, Mary, you deserve it. [*To* BENNO] No

more for you, dinosaur, you've had seven. No more, I
said. You shit, you!

[*Pantomimes reaching over and slapping his hand.*
BENNO *winces in place, as though fighting back tears.*]

MOTHER: Cry baby! Looka him hold back the tears. No-
good sissy! Men don't cry. And looka! Just a big lump
of lard. Jesus, I could store you up and cook with you.
What did I do, oh Virgin, to deserve all this suffering?
Hanh? Looka them pimples. Don't scratch them you
no-good! If only you wasn't so flabby. If only you had
some muscle on them monster arms and legs. But all
you is is a huge, flabby rat. You hear me? A rat; with
them big, black dartin' eyes. I'm sick a you; and sick
a that creep you no-good bastard father. Who goes out
and works like a dog? Me! Who comes home and cleans
like a horse? Hanh? I do! And who put that no-good
bum, your Pop-pop, God rest his soul, up for years and
years and then he has to go out and let some nigger
stab him with his own wine bottle and we don't even
get his last check, god damn it all to hell, *I* did and *I*
do, that's who! Mary! Mary the horse! Mary the horse,
they call me—don't take another cookie, you pig—Mary
the horse. [*She is becoming hysterical.*] They used a
call me Bella, beautiful, you know that? Beautiful and
I had red hair, flaming, and big boobs, almost as big as
yours, you little queer, and a shape, *Madone'*, what a
shape! Old Joey Fercanti, I coulda married him, said
my lips should be on the silver screen, that's how big
they were and thick and red. Bella, Bella they called
me. And when I danced they look at me, and when I
walked home from the market even with a dozen other
girls, they looked at me, and when I got married all the
guys in the neighborhood got drunk. Bella! And look
at me now—I'm almost as ugly as you, I'm a hag, a
bitch! Got no shape no more and my hair's gray and
fallin' out and your father, your father that no-good
lousy son of a bitch did this to me, worked at me and
worked at me, a rat, chewin' at me, with big dartin'
eyes and tearin' me to pieces! Look at me good. Oh,
my God, my God, how did I wind up like this, with the
peelin' wallpaper and nothin' else, no furniture, no
money, not a decent dress. What am I gonna wear to
that wake? They'll laugh, you hear me, they'll laugh.

[*She has reached a frenzy. And sobs for a moment and then slowly begins to calm down. Occasionally her chest heaves from sobbing.* BENNO *stares wide-eyed. She has calmed down. Slowly she rises and pours herself another cup of coffee.*]

MOTHER: Have some more coffee, Mary. That's all you got, caffeine, that's all you got in the whole world. [*To* BENNO] And you, monster, you with them big eyes, them big black eyes, what do you want now?

BENNO: [*High voice, soft*] A cookie.

[MOTHER *sobs. Lights dim on* MOTHER.]

Scene 11

BENNO *speaks urgently to the audience.*

BENNO: And what about love? Specifically, what about sexual love? Did or did not this fat one ever have congress with anything other than his palm? Benno wonders: should he describe his sexual past? Benno is ravenous for himself and time it presses on. Benno must cease this night or face yet one other two-day cycle.

[*Out of the shadows comes the* OLD MAN. *He is dressed in a long butcher's apron. It is abnormally white and quite long. The* OLD MAN's *hair has been whitened and so has his face. There is a golden aura about him so that even though he is recognizably a butcher, there is something angelic in his appearance as well. He carries a golden meat cleaver and a black crayon. During the following, as* BENNO *speaks, the* OLD MAN *pulls over his head an enormous white robe. When the robe is fully on* BENNO, *the* OLD MAN *prepares to draw on it with his crayon. He will draw on* BENNO *a butcher's chart identifying the various slices of meat.* BENNO *submits to all this without paying any attention.* BENNO *speaks laconically and with a certain irony. The lights on him becomes brighter and brighter as he speaks.*]

BENNO: Benno and sex: a story. Benno went out one night. He was fourteen. His Pop-pop had been dead—

how many years? They blur too much for Benno to
know for sure. Had Benno been an intellectual he
would have concerned himself with the nature of time.
Benno felt that the secret of time was perhaps his secret. Maybe Benno was the product of a time warp.
Benno then would have been the bloated issue of an
inverted time womb which, due to God-joke, or cosmic
spasm, vomited him out long before, or long after, his
true time. But when, he asks you, when would have
been Benno's time? Some of us, it seems, exist outside
of nature and no one knows where we fit. Nature has
her claws in all of you but not in we who exist outside
her. You have your claws in us. I see that you all think
Benno speaks nonsense. My mouth is dry. Perhaps
what he says to you, even to the very words, is unfa-
miliar. Perhaps it is Hungarian he speaks or some curious combination of frothy diphthongs. Benno always
had a problem with his saliva.

[*Out of the dark come the voices of* FATHER *and*
MOTHER.]

MOTHER'S VOICE: Not only a fatty, but he drools, too.
Looka that: it's like a broken water fountain!

FATHER'S VOICE: Is there something wrong with you, my
son?

BENNO: Benno ran out one night. In the best tradition of
arts and letters there beat in him the age-old despera-
tion. Benno felt those horrible waves of longing wash
over him and tumble back on himself and he could do
nothing about it. There was no cure for that longing in
Benno. No church socials sponsored his dreams of sa-
tiety; no youth organization provided him with a con-
course to fulfillment; and double dating was out. There
was no cure out of popular sentiment, nor out of clinical
misassessment. Benno was singular and had to suffer
alone. Sometimes I want to run to my nailed windows
and vomit out them. The force, the force of my vomit,
would explode through the window onto the passersby
and crush them. And crush them.

[*He pauses for a moment. The* OLD MAN *is now ready
to draw on him.*]

BENNO: Benno Blimpie: The sensuous fatso. Prefatory to
his supper of self.

OLD MAN: Breast! [*Draws the lines around* BENNO'S

breasts, as a butcher's chart would show them, and labels them.]

BENNO: The fourteen-year-old Benno ran out one night . . .

OLD MAN: Rib! [*As before, draws the lines and labels them.*]

BENNO: Benno was looking for love.

OLD MAN: Chuck! [*As before, draws and labels lines.*]

BENNO: Benno was looking for love!

MOTHER'S VOICE: [*Off. In the dark*] You think we should put him away?

FATHER'S VOICE: Who?

MOTHER'S VOICE: Who else? Our humpback of Notre Dame son!

BENNO: For love.

OLD MAN: Round. [*As before, draws on* BENNO *and labels him.*]

BENNO: Benno took a walk. He ended up in Edgar Allan Poe schoolyard. A place of concrete, broken glass, and dog shit. Dried dog shit of the peculiarly urban sort. In the schoolyard, Benno saw three boys. They lounged about in the shadows, some distance from him. They were older than Benno, from his neighborhood. He saw the schoolyard to be a place of waste; to be a locus of the city's fecal matter. Yes, he saw that broken glass, that concrete with the brown grass jutting, and that hard dog shit to be part of a gigantic fecal mass; yes, and he saw those boys with their T-shirts and torn dungarees also as so many turds. Nor was Benno himself exempt; he too was waste. All was waste. Waste. Through the haze of this decay, Benno saw these boys, and chose to wait.

OLD MAN: Sirloin . . . [*As before, draws, then labels.*]

BENNO: In due course, the boys noticed Benno. They performed the usual ritual of greeting Benno. They pointed and giggled.

OLD MAN: Rump. [*As before, draws, then labels.*]

BENNO: Hey, kid, one said, hey, kid. They beckoned me closer. I went. What you name, kid, they asked. They knew already. Benno, he replied. Hey, they sang out, Benno Blimpie. Hey, fellas, meet Benno Blimpie.

OLD MAN: Loin. [*Draws and labels, as before.*]

BENNO: The tallest said: Hey, Benno, know what this is?

He grabbed his crotch. My mouth was dry. Yes, Benno
was heard to whisper, I know. They laughed. Hey, fellas, they sang out, Benno Blimpie knows.

OLD MAN: Liver. [*Draws and labels* BENNO.]

BENNO: The oldest lowered his voice and said: Hey,
Benno, you wanna eat me?

OLD MAN: Kidney. [*Draws and labels* BENNO.]

BENNO: I said nothing. Sure he does, one said. Benno
wants to eat us all. The oldest said: Sure, Benno wants
a big meal, he wants to eat us all. They settled the
order, one taking watch, one watching me, the other
being served. They pushed me down, it took all three.
And one after the other I ate them. I ate all three.

OLD MAN: Heart. [*Labels and draws on* BENNO.]

BENNO: I ate all three. One, two, and three. I caught on
after a bit. They were happy during it and pranced
around. They enjoyed it. When Benno had finished all
three, they bloodied his nose and forced one eye shut
by pounding it. Then they picked up pieces of glass
and dried dog shit and stuffed them into Benno's bleeding mouth. Laughing, they ran off. I was left lying like
a blimp in the middle of the public schoolyard. In the
middle of all that concrete, with come and shit and
glass in my mouth. I couldn't cry; Benno couldn't
scream. He lay there; and in that instant, time stopped.
And feeling, it stopped too, and seemed to merge with
time, and with space. My sense of identity seeped out
of me into the cracks in the concrete. And for a few
seconds I was out of myself, totally free of myself. Totally. Free. Free. And this I call: The Transfiguration
of Benno Blimpie.

Scene 12

Lights come up intensely on everyone. The OLD MAN
hands BENNO *the meat cleaver.*

OLD MAN: You ready now!
    [*Slowly,* BENNO *rises from his chair with great effort.*

*He raises the meat cleaver. Everyone turns and watches
him in silence.*]

BENNO: I am Benno. I am eating myself to death.
[*Slowly he lowers the meat cleaver as though to cut
off some part of himself. The others watch intently. As
he reaches that part, quick blackout.*]

ULYSSES IN TRACTION

TIME

Spring, 1970
Act I: Evening
Act II: Later that night

PLACE

The Rehearsal Hall in the Arts Complex of Chapel University, Detroit.

New Cast List

Bruce Garrick
Emma Konichowski
John Morrisey
Doris Reinlos
Dr. Steven Klipstader
Dr. Stuart Humphreys
Leonard Kaufman
Delores

ACT I

The rehearsal hall at Chapel University. EMMA KONI-
CHOWSKI *is setting up an impending rehearsal. She
mends the tape on the floor, sets props, and starts to
sweep. There are distant noises as of a crowd gathering,*
EMMA *stops to listen, then continues sweeping, working
her way toward a table, which looks onto the rehearsal
area. It has a cloth, actually a large, heavy shawl, thrown
over it, which reaches the floor.* EMMA *sweeps under the
cloth, freezes, and anxiously lifts the shawl. Crouched
under the table is* DELORES; *she looks up at* EMMA, *guilty
and embarrassed.*

DELORES: I'm trapped.

EMMA: Well . . .

DELORES: This is rehearsal hall "A"?

EMMA: Yes.

DELORES: And there's a rehearsal scheduled in here for
the new main stage?

EMMA: Yes.

DELORES: I was going to surprise someone . . .

EMMA: Oh. Well, don't let me stop you. . . .

DELORES: Thanks. [EMMA *drops the shawl,* DELORES *is
hidden again.*]

EMMA: [*Sweeps for a moment, is suddenly struck.*] You
draped that shawl over the table?

DELORES: [*Hidden under the table*] Yes.

EMMA: When I looked over there I knew there was something different, I just couldn't place it.

DELORES: [*Hidden*] Do you think anyone else will notice?

EMMA: Well, I don't know. They are supposed to be actors, observation, memory—

DELORES: But they aren't good actors. . . .

EMMA: That's true—

DELORES: But they're working at it, nonetheless. . . .

EMMA: Yes.

DELORES: I'd hate like hell for someone to lift that cloth before I was ready, not only kill the surprise but make me look like a fool.

EMMA: Probably.

DELORES: Let me think about it.

EMMA: Okay. [*Sweeps some more, more crowd noise.*]

DELORES: [*Hidden*] What's that noise?

EMMA: There's a student/community rally, tonight, against the university, sounds like it's starting early.

DELORES: All those black families?

EMMA: The ones they moved out to build this very building, among many others—

DELORES: I'm getting a cramp. Is there a bar?

EMMA: The safest is the faculty club.

DELORES: I can't go there.

EMMA: There are some neighborhood bars, but I don't know how safe they'd be tonight.

DELORES: I'm an old hand at bars. [*Has pulled the shawl down, but is still under the table, sits back on her heels.*] Have you had children?

EMMA: I beg your pardon.

DELORES: Well, you have big hips and I thought—you're a graduate student, aren't you?

EMMA: Yes.

DELORES: I'd already had my first when I was a graduate student: Tulane in English. It was hard, couldn't afford a baby-sitter, and all that, husband no use, you know: still I read my Blake and did my papers, and rehearsed my orals changing diapers. It added a certain fragrance . . . so you aren't married?

EMMA: [*Annoyed with the questions*] No.

DELORES: When I was in graduate school, everyone was, or looking to be—there weren't all that many women then, there wasn't the romance of higher higher education—and we were all on the lookout, even as undergraduates—I married midway in my senior year,

slightly pregnant and very proud—you're not a virgin,
are you?

EMMA: What?

DELORES: Do you have a cigarette?

EMMA: I don't smoke.

DELORES: I think you're a prude. Or a hippie.

EMMA: I just don't happen to smoke—

DELORES: Well, I didn't for a long time either, but after
a while you have to do something with your mouth, it's
always getting in the way. Mouths are terrible, they
twitch when you get upset, they get wrinkled real easy,
and when you're thirty-six or so you notice them growing little hairs, and they get in the way. I wanted to be
a singer and couldn't drop my jaw, just couldn't no
matter how much I tried, so I read Blake and changed
diapers and a hell of a lot of good that did me. Are you
on something?

EMMA: [*Very annoyed*] No!

DELORES: Well, you act like it, touchy and that compul-
sive sweeping. If you are on something, I understand.
I've tried some pills, but I'd rather get drunk, but I
suppose that makes me a cliché. But you see, I came
home this one day and called out for my youngest son.
I called Billy, Billy. A cliché, wandering through a
clichéd suburban ranch-type house, calling out a clichéd
name, Billy, Billy. No answer. I took off my yellow
sweater, and dropped it on the couch, in the dining
room I kicked off my shoes, they were red and a little
tight, I picked up the *TV Guide*, maybe there was an
Audrey Hepburn movie on, I've given up on Blake, but
on my way to my bedroom I thought: I'll look into
Billy's room. He'd shot his face off. With one of my
husband's guns. Left a four-page note, single-spaced,
with footnotes: he was a brilliant kid, wore thick
glasses. He took them off before he pulled the trigger.
I still carry them with me, in my purse. He hated my
husband, but my husband's analyst pointed out to us,
at one of our joint sessions—sounds like we smoke
something, doesn't it? No, we just squat there, me on
my swelling haunches, him on his giant ass, an otherwise handsome couple in early middle age, dissolving
with hatred, self and other, like stale Alka-Seltzer fizz-

ing slowly in separate glasses ... and listen to Dr.
Chesterton snort and salivate, he has some glandular
problem, and he pointed out that Billy could just as
easily have used my sleeping pills as my husband's
gun. Suicide, he said, is the adolescent's ultimate ploy
for attention, and the gun was simply more dramatic,
and after all Billy was thirteen, and the phallic ...
[*She stops,* DELORES *pulls the shawl down so she is
hidden completely.* EMMA *stares at the table for a moment, is brought back to herself by crowd noises,
shrugs, and continues sweeping. She stops again.
Stares at the table.* JOHN *enters.*]

JOHN: Aha! Derelict in your duty?

[EMMA *is startled.*]

EMMA: What?

JOHN: As ranking stage manageress you are supposed to
be working, and as I sneak in, what do I espy but you
leaning on a broom, moping. A daydream?

EMMA: [*Lying*] No ... I was listening to them.

JOHN: Is it starting already? I thought the notices said six
o'clock?

EMMA: Well, I hear a group assembling. . . .

JOHN: Maybe the muses?

EMMA: They deserted this place a long time ago. [*Stops,
looks at table.*] Do you think I have big hips?

JOHN: [*Pretending not to have heard*] Is there much time
before the rehearsal?

EMMA: Everybody's late.

JOHN: Do you want some coffee—I think I'll go over to
the union and get some, I hate that crap downstairs—

EMMA: Okay—regular, two sugars—no, black.

[JOHN *leaves.* EMMA *sets about working again, but after a moment walks to the table, and not knowing what
else to do, knocks.*]

EMMA: I'm sorry, are you okay?

DELORES: [*Lifts cloth.*] About your hips, I didn't mean
anything by it, I have big hips too and you know, it just
went through my mind: big hips, motherhood ...

EMMA: Maybe you should go home, I'll call a cab if you
like.

[BRUCE *enters, self-preoccupied.*]

BRUCE: Oh, Emma, can you cue me? [*Sits down without
having noticed* DELORES *or paying any attention to*

EMMA.] I'd love to be at that rally, that's where the drama is, like real life, you know? [*Looks up when there is silence, sees* EMMA *and* DELORES.] Hey—

EMMA: We're doing an "improv," Bruce.

BRUCE: Really? Part of a woman's trip?

EMMA: Yes.

BRUCE: [*Getting up and starting to leave*] And I should . . .

EMMA: Thanks. John went to the union for coffee, maybe he'd cue you.

BRUCE: Sure man, dig. [*Off.*]

EMMA: Let me call you a cab, this is no place to be tonight.

DELORES: No, I can survive, I assure you. [*Comes out from under the table.*]

EMMA: What's your name?

DELORES: His name's Crime, mine is Punishment. It's a line from *Rigoletto*, I used to listen to the broadcasts all the time when I was a girl, I got away from it, I think we have one opera record, opera without voice, played by Mantovani, or Kostelanetz. . . . What's your name?

EMMA: Emma Konichowski.

DELORES: Sounds like a wrestler. Okay, Emma, it's all right. I'm going to have a few drinks, then maybe I'll go home, I have my car in lot double "c," is there a good bar near there?

EMMA: As I said, I wouldn't . . .

DELORES: I'm a black belt. . . .

EMMA: There's Giblet's, diagonally across from the north end of lot double "c"—

DELORES: Oops, forgetting my shawl— [*Goes to table, drapes shawl around herself, with mock coquetry goes to outside exit.*] Farewell then, Emma—may we meet again in a better world.

[*Exits.* EMMA *shakes her head.* DORIS *enters.*]

EMMA: Hello, Doris—

[*Crowd noises.*]

DORIS: They're at it! I hear half the Congo has flown over for this rally. What do you think, are we safe in here?

EMMA: I think so, this place is like a fortress, a fortress of art.

DORIS: Oh, please—a fortress of bathrooms is more like it. I was wandering around downstairs last night with—

nevermind, and I went into the ladies' room. I got lost. I opened a door and was in the shower room, I opened that door and was in a makeup room, I opened that door and there were thousands of props, I opened that door and there stood a row of urinals—

EMMA: They do have a lot of urinals in this place, reminds me of the shrines in the Catholic school I went to—

DORIS: Oh that's right, you're Polish. I never saw a urinal until I was in college—my first heavy boyfriend hid me in his bathroom when his father and mother just happened to drop in; it was one of those bathrooms between two dorm rooms and his roommate decided to take a shower while I was in there—well—that was the first day in my life I saw two penises within an hour; quite an educational experience. They're never like what you imagine them to be—and those diagrams in sex ed. class are no help, do you have an interest in penises?

EMMA: Doris!

DORIS: Well, you were looking shocked—so—maybe you're asexual—

EMMA: Because I have big hips—

DORIS: No, actually, I thought big hips meant the opposite—

[JOHN ENTERS WITH COFFEE.]

JOHN: Hi, Doris— [To EMMA] One black coffee—

DORIS: Thanks for bringing me one—

JOHN: Well, I'm working on my ESP, Doris—

EMMA: Did you see Bruce?

JOHN: No—

EMMA: Maybe he went over to the rally for a minute—

DORIS: Oh, come on, Emma, really—they're so boring. On the other hand, maybe if I was nineteen or so . . .

JOHN: Since you're fifty—

DORIS: I'm playing fifty in this piece of shit, and at my age you begin to worry—

EMMA: Your age—

DORIS: Twenty-nine, on July the seventh, three days after the Fourth no symbolism please. Awful age, twenty-nine, awful age to be stuck in this place learning how to teach retarded teenagers how to make flats.

EMMA: Is that why you're here?

DORIS: What else am I going to do? Hook? Well, luckily

there are a lot of high schools in Michigan and this place counts for something with school boards, if you can believe that. I think I'll get good recommendations, I've already had some experience. Can you see me? Developing my own tests for the mature ones, trapping them in the shop after rehearsals, brushing up against them as they hinge the set pieces—

JOHN: That isn't your style, Doris—

DORIS: I think it's going to have to be unless I can find a man who isn't a faggot or married or both. I'd go after you, John, but you're not my type, anybody who went to Yale as a playwright must definitely be weird and Steve's no ... oh well, it slipped out—Steve. Does everybody know about us? Do they say I'm his whore? Maybe I should go to Yale as a playwright? I'm making you both uncomfortable, sorry—

JOHN: Why don't we go down and check out the rally?

EMMA: I wouldn't—they'll be angry with me if you disappear—

JOHN: Well, we can look for Bruce—

DORIS: I'll go, I want some coffee too—and I'd just as soon go alone. You see, I'm sort of—tell me, have either of you ever felt—well, I hate to sound like a popular song—but I mean if I'm going to teach in high schools I might as well stoop to that level now—have you ever felt in love? [*Neither answers.*] Okay, okay, I'm going— [*Out.*]

JOHN: Well ...

EMMA: Maybe Steve is humanizing her.

JOHN: Oh?

EMMA: That's the least abrasive I've ever seen her. Do you think she has any talent?

JOHN: Who knows?

EMMA: You must have an opinion.

JOHN: I take the fifth. [*Sudden upsurge of crowd noise.*] There they are—must be really getting started—

EMMA: I hope she can find Bruce. . . .

JOHN: She's playing his mother, after all—maybe they've developed a bond.

EMMA: Maybe Dr. Humphreys will take a long break and we can go check it out.

JOHN: I doubt it. We open in a week and a half, and we're in bad shape.

EMMA: How can he take this seriously?

JOHN: It's his job.

EMMA: His job?

JOHN: Steve wanted this play, and Stu's was the only slot left by the time they got it organized, so Steve commanded Stu to direct it, or else. He also told him that our professional staff had to have parts, especially our resident professional, Lenny; our glamorous department head, Steve himself; and our most recent Yale graduate: me—being a Yale graduate is a minus in the department and a plus with the press. Since Stu Humphreys is permanently on the outs he had no choice, tenure or no.

EMMA: How do you know all this?

JOHN: I go to faculty meetings, remember? It's all the junior staff does; we sit and take notes on what Steve says, that way we all get renewed for next year.

EMMA: But this play?

JOHN: Glamorous New York success, praised in the *New York Times*—as close to canonization as we get in America. Only four universities have been allowed to do it, and we are amongst those elect—we'll get into magazines, into bulletins, into newspapers, the local critics will come, the alumni will be thrilled, and what else has a department head to worry about?

EMMA: Oh, God, university theater. Was it different when you were here as an undergraduate?

JOHN: Smaller—we all did everything, acted, directed, built sets, about four graduate students—now there are a hundred, and all these undergraduates, maybe two or three hundred. When I was a freshman, college used to get you out of the draft—but now, with this lottery, I don't understand it—maybe it's because everybody fails nowadays, and you might as well fail at theater— and its so impersonal here, all these people, all this specialization, all this compartmentalization—this emphasis on professionalism even though it's just a school, it seems inhuman to me—the grim machine of university theater—all thanks to Steve—

EMMA: But Steve—

JOHN: I know, don't mention it—

EMMA: Did you a favor.

JOHN: Some favor. Chapel University. I've always said

you had to fail tests to be admitted here, and my students prove it—

EMMA: And even after Yale, you couldn't do better?

JOHN: You graduate this spring—

EMMA: M.F.A. in Theater Arts—

JOHN: I'd advise you to take steno, you might do secre-
tarial work, maybe you can drive a taxi—

EMMA: Oh, come on—

JOHN: Everybody I knew at Yale is doing just those things
or nearly—tech people always work, so do administra-
tors, a few get grants—

[STU HUMPHREYS *and* STEVE *enter.*]

STU: Okay, okay, I'm sorry I'm late—call places, Emma—
now, Steve, when you make your—where is everybody?

EMMA: I think Doris and Bruce are at the rally, just looking in—

STEVE: Doris at that rally—might be dangerous—I'll get
her, Stu— [*Off.*]

STU: Shit, and we've already lost so much time— [*Consults
watch, goes to street door, opens it, looks out.*]

EMMA: [*To* JOHN] It just occurred to me—

JOHN: What?

EMMA: This is the longest conversation we've ever had. . . .

JOHN: Don't get your hopes up—

EMMA: I've been interested in you—

JOHN: They told me you were a dyke. . . .

[EMMA *stops, frozen, stares at him.*]

STU: What are they going to do, neck? Why aren't they
back—Emma, go get them—Oh, Christ, I'll go—I
wouldn't mind seeing how many people are there—
[*Leaves.*]

EMMA: Why? Why do they say that? Because I'm a little
heavy? Because I do this fucking tech work, because
it's the only kind of work I can do here? Because I have
a funny last name? It's all costume, isn't it? All ap-
pearances—if you don't look like a heroine in a soap
commercial you're perverted or weird—well, fuck you
and fuck them—

JOHN: Hey, look, I'm sorry—

EMMA: These fucking pea brains and you're one of
them—

JOHN: No, no, I'm sorry, I mean it as a joke, it came out

wrong really—and anyway for God's sake, they must whisper about me too—I catch Steve staring at me, giving me sidelong glances, he hates homosexuals and he doesn't want more than one—Lenny is it. But I don't feel like playing stud just because of Steve, and I hate to be judged because of what my sex life may or may not be—so look, I'm sorry—

[BRUCE *enters.*]

BRUCE: Boy, there are a lot of people at that rally, man, might get heavy. Shit, I wish we didn't have this tonight—it's bad enough to have to do this part, but to have to rehearse it with that . . . you know, I worked on it all weekend, I did all kind of exercises, the kind Lenny teaches—

JOHN: [*Ironic*] To make your part bigger?

BRUCE: [*Serious*] To make the part real, internally, I did all these object exercises, like I was looking down on him from above, seeing his hair, his forehead, his eyebrows, his eyes. I've decided one's blue, one's brown, sort of kinky you know, aquiline nose, like shapely, man, full lips, I think he's a sensualist, strong chin, no beard—that way, I don't have to justify not shaving in the play—

JOHN: Bruce, I appreciate your work, but I'm weak on lines, so if you don't mind—

BRUCE: You mean you memorize? Like really rote? I just let them come to me—well, sometimes.

[JOHN *concentrates.* BRUCE *turns to* EMMA.]

BRUCE: Do you need any help, Emma?

EMMA: A lot of help, Bruce.

BRUCE: Like in rescue—I dig.

EMMA: Do you?

BRUCE: I need it too. I'm afraid, really afraid—you see, Lenny and me—

[STU *enters, followed by* STEVE *and* DORIS, *who are stiff with one another.*]

STU: Okay, we're all here—I hope the rest of you have put this time to good use. Remember we open in little more than a week and we are, to put it mildly and kindly, ragged. God knows with this play we better be good or we'll look like fools. Call places, Emma.

[BRUCE *starts to get into character, the others get ready.*]

STU: Lenny should be here in a little while. I want to run
through as much as we can . . . okay? Now, try to concentrate, Emma will prompt if necessary but I want
everyone off book.

EMMA: Act one—places.

[*Everyone gets into place around the taped area.*]

EMMA: Curtain!

[*Rehearsal of the play.* STU *watches, sitting at the desk.*
EMMA *consults a large prompt script.* STU *mops his
face frequently, takes a swig from a bottle in a bag. In
the taped area representing the stage are* BRUCE *and*
JOHN. BRUCE *is playing the lead—a sensitive poetic
young soldier, trapped in Vietnam,* JOHN, *in a sup-
porting part, playing his tougher, older buddy.* STEVE
and DORIS *are lounging above the taped area, awaiting
their entrances.*]

BRUCE: [*In character*] Look, man, I'll tell you what: life
is like a big tree, a leafy, leafy thing.

[EMMA *makes machine-gun-like noises.*]

JOHN: [*In character*] Was that gunfire?

BRUCE: [*In character*] I hope you can run when the gooks
come, man, for that's all a man has, his legs!

JOHN: [*In character*] Listen!

[EMMA *makes machine-gun noises.*]

JOHN: [*In character, frightened*] We're trapped.

BRUCE: [*In character, dreamy*] It hangs over us, molts in
the fall, greens in the spring. . . .

JOHN: [*In character, nervous*] What?

BRUCE: [*Climbing the "tree"*] Life man, like this tree!

[EMMA *shouts "Bang."* BRUCE, *in character, for this is
that kind of play, falls, then leaps suddenly into a different area, grabs his side, screams, and falls.*]

BRUCE: Mama!

[DORIS *steps forward into the taped area representing
USA, holding an imaginary bowl, and stirring something. She is playing* BRUCE'S *mother.*]

DORIS [*In character*] It's only a scratch, it'll go away.

BRUCE: [*On floor, in character.*] I'm wounded, mom,
wounded! I'm bleeding!

DORIS: [*In character*] Boys have these things happen to
them, they fall and they get scratched.

BRUCE: [*In character*] Hurts, Mom, hurts!

DORIS: [*In character*] Bite your lip, then. Men don't cry.

BRUCE: [*In character, running in slow motion*] I don't know how it happened. I was running, running, but I didn't feel free, running, like I did at track.

[STEVE *steps forward into the taped area, he is playing* BRUCE's *father.*]

STEVE: [*In character*] My son, the track star!

DORIS: [*In character*] We're so proud!

BRUCE: [*In character, playing wounded*] No, not so free, I wasn't flying.

STEVE: [*In character*] Almost a record.

BRUCE: [*In character, wounded*] Then I felt it, in my balls.

[*Falls to his knees.* DORIS *runs to* BRUCE *and slaps his face. This, as are all the others, are very obvious stage slaps.*]

DORIS: [*In character*] Don't use those words!

[BRUCE, *from the impact of the "slap," rolls into the Vietnam area.*]

BRUCE: [*In character*] In my balls, in my belly, everywhere.

JOHN: [*In character.* JOHN *plays as though he has suddenly come upon the wounded* BRUCE.] Don't make it worse.

[*He lifts* BRUCE. *A moment. Another transition within the play.* JOHN *remains frozen, as* STEVE *pulls* BRUCE *up.*]

STEVE: [*In character*] You win that race, and I'll give you five hundred dollars!

BRUCE: [*In character*] You mean it?

STEVE: [*In character*] I'll give you a thousand if you give up the guitar.

BRUCE: [*In character*] It's all I've got, except for Cindy. . . .

DORIS: [*Steps forward, in character, as the mother.*] She's common, her father's just a worker!

BRUCE: [*In character*] She's all I've got!

STEVE: [*In character*] You've got legs, you've got brains, you've got us!

BRUCE: [*In character*] But, Dad, I just want a room of my own, a space to think, to feel music!

STEVE: [*In character*] And screw that girl! She's fast, son, fast! Take what you can get from her, don't get serious.

BRUCE: [*In character. The broomstick in his hands, which up till now represented a gun, now becomes a guitar.*] When I play, the music is in my system like blood, swelling my veins!

STEVE: [*In character*] We used to call that being horny! [*Another transition.* BRUCE *cries out, clutches his side and falls in another area.* JOHN *catches him from behind, very much like in a "trust" exercise, and lowers him gently to the floor.*]

JOHN: [*In character*] I'd offer you some water, buddy, but I'm out, gooks hit my canteen.

BRUCE: [*Forgets next line.*] Line!

EMMA: [*Prompts, mumbles.*] Have you ever seen a tree trunk?

BRUCE: [*Not having heard*] Louder!

EMMA: [*Yells.*] Have you ever seen a tree trunk!

BRUCE: [*In character, soulful*] Have you ever seen a tree trunk?

JOHN: [*In character*] What, buddy?

[*Another transition, as* BRUCE *has a spasm of pain in* JOHN's *arms,* DORIS *and* STEVE *move to another area and play as though they have discovered their son has been killed in action.*]

DORIS: [*In character, to* STEVE] It's your fault, you should have done something, sent him away, to Canada, got him deferred, you boast of connections but no, he had to go, you wanted him dead!

STEVE: [*In character to* DORIS] Get hold of yourself, this won't help! [*He "slaps" her.*]

DORIS: [*In character, to* STEVE] I want him back! My baby! You didn't hold him, inside here, for nine months, you didn't hold him, like this—there was no cord for you!

[BRUCE *is kneeling, as* JOHN, DORIS, *and* STEVE *form a symbolic tree over him.*]

BRUCE: [*In character*] The big tree is folding itself over me!

[*It does. After a moment,* STU *speaks*]

STU: All right. We got that far.

[*The actors break, stretch, yawn, leave the taped area, light cigarettes.* EMMA *strikes the ladder, puts away props, empties ashtrays.*]

BRUCE: [*Himself, earnest. To* STU] Listen, like, I mean, was I real?

STU: Well . . .

BRUCE: I tried to feel it, all weekend, I tried to feel his pain, like I stayed alone. On Sunday I sat in my dark room and thought about trees. . . .

STEVE: Jesus!

BRUCE: [*To* STU] But, like tell me. . . .

STU: [*To* BRUCE.] You might try some speech exercises. You tend to get mud mouth when you get excited.

BRUCE: Speech exercises?

STU: Yes, like gu-da-bu-da, and giddy-lily! And toy boat, toy boat, toy boat.

BRUCE: But look, wait a minute! What has this got to do with truth?

STU: It doesn't have anything to do with the truth; it has to do with the theater and with acting, and the first law of the theater is being understood by the good people out there who have paid their money to see you.

STEVE: The only place they'd pay to see him is a zoo.

STU: Doris, you sentimentalize those last lines.

DORIS: Oh, really, you think that's hard?

STU: That's your problem, it's easy, but she has lost her son. And, John, I really want you to try harder to project interest, I know your plays are better than this but you're acting in this one.

STEVE: [*To* DORIS] Look, Doris, I . . . [*She snubs him.*] Doris . . .

STU: And, Steve, your first entrance needs to be crisper, and you need a sense of character that is clearer. . . .

STEVE: Okay, okay, Stu. . . . [*Goes to* DORIS.] Doris, I . . . [*She stiffens and refuses to look at him. Riot noise.*]

BRUCE: Boy, that's loud, do you think it's going to be dangerous?

STU: [*Sarcastic*] I'm used to being under fire—at faculty meetings—

[JOHN *laughs.*]

STU: Some of those'd make good plays, eh, John?

STEVE: [*So as to be alone with* DORIS] Why don't we take a break, Stu?

STU: Oh, Steve, come on, you realize we have less than two . . .

STEVE: [*Hard*] We'll be able to concentrate better if we relax for fifteen or so minutes.

STU: Okay—ten minutes, but don't anybody wander off,

I know the rally is more interesting, but we have a play to put on.

[STEVE *takes* DORIS's *arm; she pulls away.*]

DORIS: I'll run lines here.

STEVE: Doris, I want to talk to you.

[*Takes her arm again, giving her no choice but to go or make a scene. They leave the room. There is a pause, the others watch.*]

STU: I wonder if Nero talked to his mistress in that tone—

JOHN: Well, I'm glad love continues to flourish—

STU: Love? Between two caricatures in search of a cartoonist?

BRUCE: Dr. Humphreys, can we talk about his inner space—

STU: Oh, Jesus Christ, Bruce—

BRUCE: You're the one who keeps saying we have to work to make this believable!

STU: Okay, okay, you trapped me, but walk me down to the machines, I'm hungry.

[*Takes bottle; they walk off.*]

BRUCE: I think you've got to essentialize the inner particles of his soul to play this character. [*They are off.*]

JOHN: [*Rally noise.*] Speaking of Nero fiddling. while whatever whatevers . . . [EMMA *busies herself.*] I really am sorry about earlier, I didn't mean to be offensive—

EMMA: That's okay, I'm sorry I snapped.

JOHN: God, I feel trapped in here—

EMMA: With the rally?

JOHN: With my life. I feel under siege, I can't escape. When I fled from here to New Haven, I thought it would be a New Haven, good as its name. But it was exactly the same there, more pretension maybe, more promise—ninety miles from New York City, sound the trumpets! But it was essentially the same. In a black ghetto, a back water, a miniature kingdom run at random arbitrarily by a megalomaniac. And now, I'm back here—

EMMA: But this was the best you could do? You didn't have the courage to go to New York and try your luck?

JOHN: Please don't get judgmental. . . .

EMMA: I'm not being judgmental, I'm not in New York either. I'm well acquainted with cowardice.

JOHN: Yes, I was afraid; afraid to go, afraid to come back here. I write plays, why? Who wants to do them, who's interested, who's reached by them, and what are the issues plays can address that everything else doesn't address better? And then, these plays of mine, are they any good? Are they better than what four hundred monkeys could do at random, after an injection of Seconal? I was teetering then, balancing ... and my mind was made up for me. I became very sick, I couldn't get insurance. I was bleeding, there was no one to go to. So I crawled. I alerted Steve to my condition, trying not to beg, and begged him to help me. Well, a new graduate from Yale—looks good in the bulletin. Sick? He needs the job, won't be any trouble. Shrinking opportunities in educational theater? He'll be even less trouble. He hired me. Maybe he was punishing me for being difficult as an undergraduate; putting me on the other side.

EMMA: What do they pay you?

JOHN: Car fare. But there's insurance, a group plan, maybe tenure—

EMMA: I don't know anything about it—but why couldn't you get insurance?

JOHN: Chronic condition, multiple operations, more needed, they won't cover that for any amount of money—

EMMA: Boy you think they'd have a national health plan with all the taxes—

JOHN: Of course not, they don't want people to live. We don't need children, we don't need old people, we don't even need able-bodied people in their prime— they want as many people to die off as possible, less unemployment, less poverty, less overcrowding, less demand on oil, electricity and imports, and only the strong surviving. We're all expendable.

EMMA: Yes, I know—where's the Rifleman when You need him?

JOHN: Or Hopalong Cassidy?

BRUCE: [*Enters.*] Hi. It was no use. I'd like to sneak over to the rally, Emma, I'll come right back—

EMMA: Look, Bruce, you know—

BRUCE: We still have at least ten minutes—

EMMA: Stu called ten and five have passed—

BRUCE: Steve said fifteen and that's what he'll take—I've just got to clear my head for a minute—

EMMA: Okay, okay, but come right back—

[BRUCE *goes out.*]

EMMA: Did you catch it in yourself?

JOHN: What?

EMMA: Death—I'm twenty-five, what would be wrong with reckless confidence, audacity, outrageousness? This need for safety sneaks up like a cancer. Safety first, where can I hide? When does it die?

JOHN: When you come in on the bus from your father's apartment and teach your classes. You talk about Sophocles in one and Beckett in the other and you go home on the bus. Your father comes home from work, heats himself up a TV dinner, drinks himself to sleep in front of the TV, and you sit, in pain, wondering if it will burn as much the next time and how can you face another thirty, forty years of this. . . .

EMMA: Shall we call help?

JOHN: [*Calling*] Help!

EMMA: [*Calling*] Help!

JOHN: Help!

EMMA: Help! [*They strike poses and call help, and finally laugh.*]

STU: [*Running in*] Jesus Christ, what is it?

JOHN: Oh, I'm sorry Stu, a joke—

STU: A joke? Oh, Christ! [*Takes a swig.*] You scared me shitless, and you think it's easy to run up those stairs?

JOHN: I'm sorry, we were just giving vent to our existential despair.

STU: Why?

JOHN: Stuck here in our twenties, we've given up hoping, it's our resolution for nineteen seventy.

STU: Being stuck here in your twenties and you've given up hoping? Is that all it takes? Wait until you're forty-nine and stuck here, and see how you feel.

JOHN: What do you recommend?

STU: Go out and provoke a black kid. Or a white kid—who knows? You could read one of Emma's plays—

EMMA: Dr. Humphreys?

STU: Such as *Hunting Auroras*. That would put you out of your misery.

JOHN: [*To* EMMA] *Et tu, Brute*—

EMMA: Now, Dr. Humphreys—

STU: I was her adviser on that play—we even gave her a grade for it—an A, I recall, ridiculous grading plays: *Ghosts:* A minus, *The Crucible:* C—you see John, Emma's a playwright too.

JOHN: I'd like to meet somebody who isn't a playwright. For the last six years everyone I've met has written a play. You walk along a subway platform and six drunks will fall over offering you their latest. At Yale everyone wrote plays, conductors on trains write during those endless delays. Why do you think there are endless delays? That second act has to be solved. Will it ever end?

EMMA: Well, that was my last.

STU: The futility of art, gets to us all in the end.

JOHN: I think I've heard about this play. Is that possible?

EMMA: Come on, I think everybody talks about it—it's probably why they think I'm a dyke—

STU: Emma!

EMMA: In their pygmy brains any woman who writes must be queer—

STU: Now, Emma ... [*Thinks.*] Come to think of it ... [*Takes a swig.*]

JOHN: It was sort of *Sleeping Beauty*, wasn't it?

EMMA: Inspired by the ballet.

JOHN: Aha, very chic, an "in" play. No dialogue.

EMMA: A lot of it.

JOHN: Too bad, an "out" play.

EMMA: In my play the prince is led to the magic palace by a lame fairy—

STU: Lenny played that.

JOHN: Oh no!

STU: Type casting, except for the limp, or is that swish a limp?

EMMA: It is the palace of the sleeping princess. The prince fights his way through acres of cobwebs to her bed. One kiss from him and she'll awake to eternal happiness. He gazes at all the musty splendor, the sleeping courtiers and dames, the sleeping queen and king, the sleeping pages, particularly the pages. The prince then gazes curiously at the sleeping princess: Aurora by name, a plump, tall girl; then picks his way to the most beautiful sleeping page and kisses him. The page awakes, embraces the prince, they wed, and live happily ever after, and Aurora is forgotten. The moral of the play is: Let sleeping dogs lie.

JOHN: Autobiographical, of course?

STU: Oh, John, be serious. Does Emma look like a sleeping page? All these theories about autobiographical art. Nonsense. You never read about autobiographical criticism, yet that's all modern criticism is. Since they're all illiterate, all these reviewers have to judge from is their own measly pasts; and their amoebic responses. You ever watch the critics at a performance? They're like a bunch of protozoa wired with electrons, they jerk and jump, toss a coin and call it great or awful; and anyway it's all the same nowadays: great or awful, what use is it, who cares? The best that'll happen is it'll be made into a TV series and make somebody—probably not the playwright—a millionaire. Why, I used to write plays, too—oh yes, you'll give up, John, happens to us all in the end. We all become minimalists as we age, what's the least I can do to get by today? But I did write plays, and sure enough they called them autobiographical—as though that meant something. Yet I swear to you that never did I put myself, or my mother, or my brothers in a play, I could never remember them clearly enough. Maybe I'd have been a better writer if I could, and on that note I think we better go back to work: Emma, round everybody up.

JOHN: Shit, I have to go to the bathroom. . . .

STU: Well . . .

JOHN: I'm sorry to bring it up, it's very painful.

EMMA: John?

JOHN: I'm sorry, it's one of those things everybody takes for granted. They think worrying about peeing is funny; I can't very well ask people to hold my hand in the bathroom. . . .

BRUCE: [*Runs in*] Hey, you guys, like it's Lenny, he's in trouble. He's having this fight with these two black dudes. . . .

LENNY: [*Off*] Even if you are butch, I couldn't care less— hey! [*Screams.*] You're keeping an actor from his work, and the Virgin Mary will punish you for it. . . .

STU: Holy shit!

EMMA: Should we call the police?

BRUCE: Do we have time?

STU: Look, let's go get him in—

JOHN: Let me—I'll join you.

[*He runs off to the bathroom.* STU *and* EMMA *run out.* BRUCE *hangs back frightened.* DORIS *walks in, upset, trailed by* STEVE.]

DORIS: What's going on?

BRUCE: It's Lenny, these black dudes—Dr. Humphreys and Emma ran after him. . . .

STEVE: She'll scare them away if she stands in the light. [*Sounds of a scuffle, off.*] Hmm, maybe they'll kill Stu as well, we've been trying to get rid of him—

BRUCE: Should I call the police, do you think? Shit! [*Runs out.*]

STEVE: I detect a bit of the tomboy in that fellow. [*Scuffle heard as* BRUCE *joins in.*] Maybe we should call the police. I'd hate to lose Lenny; token fags are hard to come by, they never want to leave New York, or L.A.

JOHN: [*Enters in pain.*] What's happening with Lenny?

STEVE: Who knows? You look pale, John. . . .

JOHN: I guess I better see what I can do. . . . [*Goes out.*]

DORIS: [*Continuing a fight*] I thought you were different. I have spent my life looking for Daddy, always on a diet, an easy lay and I thought with you there was a future—

STEVE: I just can't leave her—I just can't.

DORIS: They always use their wives in the long run, the same wives they couldn't stand to begin with—

LENNY: [*Off*] Marvelous, simply marvelous. Look at Emma, a regular amazon!

STEVE: He was her favorite, it's ripped her apart—

DORIS: Uh—uh—

STEVE: He'd shot his face off, took off his glasses first, her favorite. Kids do commit suicide, it was no accident and she blames me—

STU: [*Off*] Now look, kids, cool it—

STEVE: Where did Stu pick up that hep talk? Maybe we'll lose everybody, a clean sweep. Look, I didn't love that kid, he wasn't like me, wasn't like his brothers, and he hated me—but when your youngest son goes and—at thirteen no less—

DORIS: So you're dumping me—

STEVE: I am not! I just need time, Doris, just time—

[LENNY *charges in, roughed up, but no worse for wear. He is exhilarated by the experience. The others trail in, a little more shaken.*]

LENNY: What an experience for an artist on the stage. Wait until my next sense memory!

STEVE: What happened, Lenny?

LENNY: They wanted my leather bag. Well, I thought about it, I mean a leather bag is a man's ticket to eternity, how could I walk down Broadway without one, or down Christopher Street, which yields up more parts to the actor-artist, if you understand me, without my leather bag? And besides, there was the principle of the thing: stealing is wrong! And they were worse than the Fourteenth Street Tea Room on the IRT, at least there they tap first if they're interested.

STU: [*Out of breath*] Jesus, I'm not up to that stuff, at my age.

STEVE: Everybody okay?

LENNY: But you know? They gave me a wonderful idea: Romeo and Juliet in black and white. Just see it, the Montagues Negroid, the Capulets Wasp and what bloodshed, what sex—aii bonzai! [*Sweeps out.*]

BRUCE: Boy, that was spooky. . . .

STU: In more senses than one—

DORIS: I thought this was students as well as the black community?

BRUCE: Well, there are lots of students down at the green, but around the edges it's all blacks—

STEVE: Are you absolutely certain that Lenny didn't come on to one of them?

JOHN: Well, that's possible, I guess—

DORIS: You don't think they'd come in here, after us?

STEVE: Why don't we lock this door to be sure? [*Locks door.*]

EMMA: I'm a little shaky after that. . . .

STU: Well, art is the great remedy, solace always in work, and on that note—Emma, start us up.

EMMA: I guess it's act two scene one?

STEVE: Oh oh, the fag scene. Have to have one in every play nowadays. When I was young the writers all had sense enough to hide it. That's why I hate all these new plays. If it's not mom, it's fags and the plays are

always about how rotten life is. I'd rather stick to Noël
Coward.

JOHN: Oh, shit, I have to go to the bathroom . . . sorry.
[*Off.*]

STEVE: Every time John goes wee-wee it's five acts of
King Lear.

STU: We can work around him—read Lenny and John in.
Act two from the top.

[BRUCE *takes time to get into character.*]

STU: Come on, Bruce, what's the trouble?

BRUCE: I'm taking a moment to get into character.

STEVE: Oh, Jesus Christ, actor on the toilet. [*As* BRUCE
continues to concentrate] Constipated.

BRUCE: Look, cool it, it won't be true if I rush in. How
do you suggest I do it?

DORIS: Oh, come on, Bruce, let's get on with it so we can
go home.

BRUCE: No, I want to know, Dr. Humphreys, how do you
suggest I do it?

STU: I'll tell you how: the lights come up, right? You're
there, right? You look up. Why? Because you're onstage
and you want the good people to be able to see your
handsome face.

STEVE: Pretty face is more like it.

STU: You take a moment, just because it's more effective,
then after a deep breath, you say your first line.

BRUCE: And it's phony and empty and dull. . . .

STU: Then why don't you give up? Make-believe is what
it's called. If you're so concerned with reality, why
aren't you out there in Vietnam yourself?

STEVE: Good point, Stu.

STU: But you're not. You're onstage at Chapel University,
safe and sound in the light with people watching you
in a play. Play, get it?

BRUCE: And that's why you're here, teaching, and not in
New York in the professional theater.

STU: Oh ho, the professional theater—

STEVE: Yes indeed, the young man says, the professional
theater.

[*They laugh.*]

BRUCE: What's so funny?

STU: Well, you see, Bruce, the professional theater's sort
of like God: some people think it exists, some people

don't, most people don't see much evidence. . . .

[LENNY *sweeps in.*]

LENNY: Sorry I didn't take longer. I was all set to sulk in the men's room when John came in and started to moan. There's nothing more depressing than a grown man moaning at a urinal, hey what?

STU: Act two from the top, Lenny.

LENNY: [*Mocking* STEVE] Oh oh, the fag scene. Have to have one in every play nowadays, when I was young all the writers had sense enough to hide it, and that's why I hate these new plays—if it's not mom, it's fags. And the plays are all about how rotten life is—

[JOHN *enters in pain.*]

LENNY: Why life is terrific: people pee and cry. . . .

STU: Call places, Emma.

EMMA: Places. Act two from the top.

[BRUCE *takes a long time getting into character.*]

STEVE: Will you look at that, Lenny? I bet that's your doing!

LENNY: What?

STEVE: Encouraging him to stand there like a lump and hold the rest of us up—

LENNY: Didn't you hire me to teach them to be professionals, sweetheart? I mean, I am the professional in residence?

STEVE: You can't tell me professionals behave like that—

LENNY: Well, you tell me, Stevie, how do professionals behave? From your own experience now—

STU: Come on, now—let's try and act, huh?

LENNY: You mean, act out.

STEVE: All those weird exercises you get them to do, theater games—it's all bullshit, if you ask me—I hate to stand here and watch that fucking—

LENNY: That fucking what, Stevie, that fucking what?

STEVE: Nevermind.

LENNY: Look, leave him alone and stop the personal comments—

STEVE: What personal comments? What personal comments?

LENNY: Nobody talks about your shit, so leave him alone—

STEVE: Because he's yours, is that it?

BRUCE: [*Upset*] Hey, look—

EMMA: Don't let him upset you, Bruce, come on—

LENNY: Steve, come on, act like an adult—

STEVE: And as a faggot you know what adult is—

EMMA: Steve, stop it—

STEVE: Oh ho, that's what women's lib teaches, how to interfere—are you going to write another bent fairy tale about it? I should tell you the things the rest of the Communications School staff said about that piece of shit and what it almost cost me in funding.

EMMA: What did it almost cost you?

STEVE: About what you spend on food—and this idiot, Brucie here, playing actor—

EMMA: But he means it, I know that would never occur to you, Dr. Klipstader, Head of the Chapel University Theater Department, but he means it. You would think it the strangest thing in the world if someone actually loved the theater, actually thought it an art form, wouldn't you? When you hear that word "art" you snigger, don't you, Steve, snigger and giggle and point, like the snide little boy you still are. Why didn't you go into accounting or insurance, were you too stupid? So you chose university theater—

LENNY: Touché, Emma—

STEVE: University theater has kept theater alive in Detroit. If we didn't do plays they wouldn't get done. Without Chapel all Detroit would have is Broadway leavings, the worst of the worst. We've done Beckett, we've done Ionesco, we've done Giraudoux—

EMMA: How many of those writers were Americans?

STEVE: If there were good American plays, we'd do them. All they're about is fags and their mothers. . . . Look at John. He went to Yale as a playwright. I've read his plays, they're minority plays, no offense, John, I think you're talented, but our audience wouldn't sit for them. All this despair, all this nihilism. They all write about how ugly life is—they're all a bunch of eunuchs unhappy because they can't come—

EMMA: So now you'd have us believe that homosexuals can't come.

JOHN: No, he means playwrights.

STU: Do you mind if we . . .

STEVE: Shut up, Stu. I've had enough, just enough of this piece of shit.

STU: It was your idea that we do it.

STEVE: Then let's do it, learn the lines, get the blocking and do it.

STU: Well, we're trying. Come on, everybody, call places, Emma.

EMMA: You know, Steve, I am neither a lesbian, nor really even fat. You might not want me for your mistress, so I know that disqualifies me from the human race. But I want you to know that that is a minority opinion, luckily, that increasing numbers of men, straight men, Steve, not fags, would think you were a perverted fool for having that attitude—

STEVE: Then what are you—chubby? Get out of my department, why don't you? I don't need you here—

EMMA: Okay, I will get out rather than submit to—

JOHN: Steve, stop it, it's gone too far—Emma was doing her job as the stage manager, trying to hold things together, now I suggest—

STEVE: Why don't you marry her, John, if you're ever out of the bathroom long enough?

STU: Look, God damn it, shut up, everybody, and listen to me. Okay? Listen? I talk too much. I drink too much, too. I know it, you know it. And after a while alcohol interferes with the functioning of the brain. So I am foggy-minded some of the time, I don't sleep well and I can't get up in the morning. I'm late for class a lot, I don't like this department anymore, although I have been here nineteen years, longer than anyone else on the faculty, and should have succeeded Doc when he retired. That's when they brought you in, Steve. I wonder about education, because educated people act like savages, as you have all just done. I really don't believe in educational theater anymore because I don't believe we are training anybody for anything and just about nobody cares about the theater as anything, even as entertainment, let alone as an art form. I like women. I am not homosexual, I am not comfortable around homosexuals, but I don't hate homosexuals, and my life as a straight buffoon has been nothing to brag about. I go home now to an empty house because my wife is leaving me, and before that she had a lover, unbeknownst to me, for five years. I had cheated on her exactly seven times in twenty-five years of marriage,

and she cheated on me every hour, every second for
five long years, during most of which I thought we were
as happy as any other suburban couple who drink too
much, and fight twice a week, and I am directing this
play. This play is a piece of shit, for which I don't blame
the author, living as he is, probably, in sin in New York
City. I praise him for it, may his next one be better. I
don't blame our department head either, since I know
he must put up with a lot just to keep this department
together, and maybe he is right that if this play is a
success, it will act like a sewer and channel some of
the shit away. So I suggest humbly, as an all too fallible,
flabby, and balding human being, that we please bury
this bitterness, and go back to work. Thank you.

LENNY: I second that motion.

JOHN: Aye aye.

DORIS: The ayes have it.

STEVE: Okay, but let's get on with it—and look, I'm sorry,
I'm on edge and I don't mean a lot of what I said. .

EMMA: Okay, act two scene one—places.

[*As before everyone gets into place,* EMMA *looks at the
prompt book;* STU *sits at the table to watch;* BRUCE
takes a much shorter time getting into character;
LENNY *takes his place;* JOHN, STEVE, *and* DORIS *wait
for entrances.* DORIS *stays away from* STEVE *and pretends to be thoroughly absorbed in the play.* STEVE
*occasionally tries to catch her eye and fails, he is very
nervous and obviously on edge.*]

BRUCE: [*In character*] You summoned me, sir?

LENNY: [*In character*] So, you're PFC Ricky O'Grady. . . .

JOHN: [*Prompting*] Michael MacGovern.

LENNY: Oh, right, sorry.

STU: Enter again, Bruce.

[BRUCE *backs up, takes a moment to center himself,
enters, and snaps to attention in front of* LENNY.]

LENNY: [*In character*] So, you're PFC . . . [*Forgets.*]

EMMA: [*Prompting*] Michael MacGovern . . .

LENNY: [*In character*] Michael MacGovern . . .

BRUCE: I didn't say my line, sorry. . . .

EMMA: [*Prompting*] You summoned me, sir. . . .

BRUCE: I know, I know, let's go back. [BRUCE *centers
himself, enters, snaps to attention in front of* LENNY.
In character] You summoned me, sir?

LENNY: [*In character*] So, you're PFC . . .

BRUCE: [*In character*] Yes, sir!

STU: [*Jumps up.*] Let him get your name out!

EMMA: [*Prompting*] Michael MacGovern . . .

LENNY: Why don't you change your name?

STU: Come on, Lenny!

LENNY: [*To* BRUCE, *doing Mae West*] Come in on me again.

STU: Start again, Bruce.

[BRUCE *prepares, enters, snaps to attention in front of* LENNY.]

BRUCE: [*In character*] You summoned me, sir?

LENNY: [*In character*] So, you're PFC Michael Mac-Govern?

BRUCE: [*In character*] Yes, sir!

LENNY: [*In character*] *The* Michael MacGovern?

BRUCE: [*In character*] The only one in this outfit, sir.

LENNY: [*In character*] I'll say.

BRUCE: [*In character*] Beg pardon, sir?

LENNY: [*In character*] Nothing, Michael. May I call you that?

BRUCE: [*In character*] Yes, sir!

LENNY: [*In character*] Let's drop the sirs! Call me . . . line.

EMMA: [*Prompting*] Laurie . . .

STU: [*Annoyed*] It's only your name in the play, Lenny!

LENNY: I keep blocking it out.

STU: Go back.

EMMA: [*Prompting*] The only one in this outfit, sir.

BRUCE: [*In character*] The only one in this outfit, sir.

LENNY: [*In character*] I'll say.

BRUCE: [*In character*] Beg pardon, sir?

LENNY: [*In character*] Nothing. Michael—may I call you that?

BRUCE: [*In character*] Yes, sir!

LENNY: [*In character*] Let's drop the sirs. Call me . . . Laurie.

BRUCE: [*In character*] Laurie, sir?

LENNY: [*In character*] Short for: Laurence.

BRUCE: [*In character*] I see. . . .

LENNY: [*In character*] Laurie!

BRUCE: [*In character.* LENNY *takes* BRUCE's *"rifle" and is examining it.*] Laurie!

LENNY: [*In character*] Do you like men, Michael?

BRUCE: [*In character*] I suppose, sir.

LENNY: [*In character*] I mean: *really* like!

BRUCE: [*In character*] I don't think I follow you, Laurie. [LENNY *is kneeling in front of* BRUCE, *aiming the* "*rifle*."]

LENNY: [*In character*] A man in my position can do a lot for a man in your position—

BRUCE: [*In character*] What position is that?

LENNY: [*In character, stands up.*] That of a servant. A servant of your country, but some servants share the master's secrets, some clean the toilet. Do you follow me? [*Picks up a riding crop from the table.*]

BRUCE: [*In character*] But . . .

LENNY: [*In character*] There's no butt but yours, Michael! [*Hits* BRUCE'S *butt with the riding crop.*] Your butt is between you and the war out there and a cushy job, here with me.

BRUCE: [*In character*] With you!

LENNY: [*In character*] I'll explain. Smoke? [*Offers cigarettes.* DORIS *steps into area marked USA or home.*]

DORIS: [*In character*] Never take presents from strange men! [*She sits down on bench.*]

LENNY: [*In character*] They're Gauloises. . . .

BRUCE: [*In character*] No thanks.

LENNY: [*In character*] Here's you, see— [*Holds up a finger.*], and here's me— [*Grabs the finger with his fist and squeezes.*] See?

BRUCE: [*In character*] Aaaah!!! [*Recoils, and spins into another area.*]

STEVE: [*Himself. Simultaneously*] Look, Dori, please talk to me, try to understand, he was her favorite—and we've been married almost twenty years, three kids, and I'm afraid he's— [DORIS *turns away.* JOHN *enters the same area, in character as* BRUCE's *buddy.* BRUCE *has recoiled over to him.*]

JOHN: [*In character. As though continuing a conversation*] I mean it, buddy, I love you. But not the way those dirty queers would, but pure, man to man.

BRUCE: [*In character*] I never thought of love that way. . . . [JOHN *makes the sound of a bomb falling and exploding.*]

JOHN: [*In character*] Down! [*Pulls* BRUCE *down and covers him with his own body. They wait a moment, then* JOHN *rolls off* BRUCE.]

BRUCE: [*In character, recovering*] Hey! You saved my life!

JOHN: [*In character, hugging him in a masculine way*] That's what I mean, the pure way.

BRUCE: [*In character, moved*] Gosh, thanks, buddy. [*Punches* JOHN's *shoulder.*]

JOHN: [*In character*] Don't mention it—buddy. [*Punches* BRUCE's *shoulder.*]

STEVE: [*To himself*] Shit, I'd like a drink.

[JOHN *and* BRUCE *do a very elaborate, "in," sixties-type handshake, and then* BRUCE *wheels away, back to* LENNY.]

LENNY: [*In character*] That isn't so hard to understand, is it?

BRUCE: [*In character*] It's the hardest to understand.

LENNY: [*In character*] How?

BRUCE: [*In character*] Have you ever seen a tree, Laurie?

LENNY: [*In character*] All I know, Michael, is I want to climb yours!

BRUCE: [*In character*] Aaaaah!!!

[*Recoils in horror, and spins into USA area.* STEVE *steps forward into the same area, in character, as* BRUCE's *father.*]

STEVE: [*In character*] What were you and Billy . . .

EMMA: [*Prompting*] Johnny . . .

STEVE: I'm sorry. I'm sorry. This moment is very difficult for me to play, you know. Let's go back.

EMMA: [*Prompting*] What were you and Johnny down the street . . .

STEVE: [*In character*] What were you and Johnny down the street doing up in that tree, son?

BRUCE: [*In character, playing a boy*] Playin', Dad.

STEVE: [*In character*] Well, son, you keep your playing above the waist. There isn't anything worse than a queer.

BRUCE: [*In character as before*] What's a queer, Dad?

STEVE: [*In character*] I think Johnny down the street is one.

BRUCE: [*In character, as before*] The only thing I like better than Johnny is my guitar . . .

[STEVE, *in character, whirls into a different area, so does* BRUCE *in character, now playing older.*]

STEVE: [*In character*] That Goddamned guitar! Only faggots play guitar!

BRUCE: [*In character*] I'm not a faggot! I have Cindy!

STEVE: [*In character*] That whore!

BRUCE: [*In character*] Ah! .

[*Hits* STEVE, *who recoils in horror.* DORIS *steps out, in character, as the mother, playing outrage and shock.*]

DORIS: [*In character*] Savage! You hit him! You hit your father! Are you coming to rape me next? You hit your own father! God ought to strike you dead. What are we coming to when son takes up the plow against his father? Animal!

BRUCE: [*In character*] All right, if I'm an animal, I'm going to enlist before the draft gets me, and kill!

DORIS: [*In character, playing hysterical*] That's right, that's all you kids want nowadays, to kill!

BRUCE: [*In character*] If I had a machine gun, right now, I'd kill you!

DORIS: [*In character*] Ah!

[*In character, slaps* BRUCE. BRUCE, *in character, horrorstruck, whirls away from* DORIS *and starts running toward* LENNY. *The run becomes slow motion, as* DORIS *and* STEVE, *as the parents, wave good-bye in slow motion.*]

LENNY: [*In character*] So, you see, Mickey, you're mine, I want you!

BRUCE: [*In character*] No, sir, please . . .

LENNY: [*In character*] And I intend to have you!

[*Suddenly, in character, kisses* BRUCE.]

BRUCE: [*In character*] Ah! [*In character, hits* LENNY.]

LENNY: [*In character*] So you want to play rough, huh?

BRUCE: [*In character*] Faggot!

[*In character, he and* LENNY *struggle.* JOHN *drops the prompt book, and rushes on, in character.*]

JOHN: [*In character to* LENNY *and* BRUCE] We're under attack!

LENNY: [*In character, suddenly masculine*] Man all stations, plans C, F, G, and Zen Buddhist in operation!

JOHN: [*In character, to* BRUCE] Come on, we've got to fight. . . .

BRUCE: [*In character*] I just want to climb my tree, man. [BRUCE, *in character, starts climbing the "tree," with* JOHN *and* LENNY *behind him. They are forming that very famous photo depicting the raising of the American flag at Iwo Jima.* DORIS, *in character as the mother, bowed down with grief, starts a slow circular cross to the tableau.* STEVE, *in character as the father, mirrors* DORIS's *move.*]

DORIS: [*In character*] He's gone, my baby who I cradled. Why is it the fate of mothers . . . [*They begin to hum "Taps."*] . . . to lose their sons to the barbarity of others? I remember him climbing that tree, that tree he loved so much, and playing his guitar. I'd be cooking in the kitchen—pork and beans, his favorite—and I'd hear him plunking away. I'd smile to myself and stir in the molasses. . . .

[DORIS *and* STEVE, *both in character as the bereaved parents, embrace.*]

STEVE: [*Suddenly crying out*] I can't stand it, Jesus Christ—Doris why are you doing this? Come on—am I so hateful, Jesus Christ, and my son—he— [*There is a hammering on the door.*]

BRUCE: Jesus Christ—

DORIS: It's them come for us, don't answer—

DELORES: [*Screams and sobs outside the door.*]

STEVE: Doris, come on—don't. . . .

BRUCE: What are we going to do?

LENNY: [*Listening*] Are you sure that's the mob? Sounds like one woman to me—

EMMA: She might be hurt, open it—

DORIS: No, it's a trick—

STU: Oh, they aren't dangerous, come on—Steve, give me the key—

[STEVE *hands him the key,* STU *opens the door,* DE-LORES *falls in.*]

STEVE: Delores—

LENNY: [*Campy*] Why, it's the wife—

STEVE: Somebody help me—

BRUCE: We're trapped— [STU *locks the door quickly, the others run to* DELORES.]

BLACKOUT

ACT II

The scene is the same. JOHN *and* LENNY *are sitting, obviously bored.* BRUCE *is doing his Yoga exercises, having
removed shirt and shoes. He is pretending to be relaxed
and oblivious but is actually very self-conscious.* STU *is
lying on the table trying to nap. Rally noise is heard very
loud.*

LENNY: [*To* JOHN] What's the answer?

JOHN: Oblivion and turmoil.

LENNY: No, that's the cliché.

BRUCE: [*Still doing exercises*] I can't believe she wasn't
    really hurt.

LENNY: Drunks never are. Haven't you heard the canard
    about drunks getting run over by gas trucks and re-
    maining unscathed?

BRUCE: [*Still doing exercises*] It's taking them a long
    time—

JOHN: Yes, I wish they'd get back here so we could finish
    and go home.

LENNY: She was so out of it, just to bring her around is
    going to take a while. Then they have to clean her up.
    At least we're having an experience, we'll be better
    artists for it, and isn't that what university theater is
    for? To provide burgeoning artists with experiences?
    [*Suddenly grabs and embraces* BRUCE.]

BRUCE: Hey—

LENNY: You want to get rough, huh?
    [*They mock-wrestle, but* BRUCE *is embarrassed by the
    obvious sexual overtones.*]

BRUCE: Come on, Lenny, wrestling is obvious.

LENNY: That's the question. . . .

STU: [*Suddenly, more or less thinking out loud, a little the worse for gin*] University theater! They all laughed. In the old days we did everything ourselves—Doc had been doing it alone since the thirties, and when I came along—in nineteen fifty, I joined him. We worked a twenty-hour day, built sets and props, hung lights, painted, sewed, struck the shows, put posters up, cleaned the theater. The theater! That was an old gym with a platform at one end. We shared it with the basketball team. Then they built this fortress and called it a theater. Theater, that's not fit for men, they'd say. But when I came here it took balls and sweat, physical strength and a sense of purpose. They denied me tenure twice because I used to direct and act in community theater, thought that was undignified. But I never missed a class or was late for one even those mornings when we had teched the entire night before.

BRUCE: [*To* LENNY, *who has continued physically flirting with him*] Come on, Lenny, it's not funny—

LENNY: But I want you—

BRUCE: I told you, it's over and I meant it—

STU: [*Sits, thinks for a minute.*] I thought: my life has meaning, doing art, doing theater, these are meaningful things. And I fought for it, I fought for the principle that a grown man ought to be able to make art and a decent living too. Oh yes, Lenny, I spent my time in New York.

LENNY: We went to different bars, sweetheart.

STU: I might have made it too—

LENNY: John, what time do you have?
[JOHN *lifts arms to show he has no watch.* LENNY *goes to* BRUCE, *who has resumed his Yoga, and makes great show of lifting his arm, even though* BRUCE *is not wearing a watch, and looking at his wrist.*]

STU: I had talent as an actor, was good-looking then, turned many a head.

LENNY: [*Camping*] My, what a nice wrist— [*Shakes* BRUCE's *arm so the wrist waves*] Getting limp, there—

STU: But everyone was driving taxis, you know?

JOHN: [*Whom Stu has addressed*] I know, believe me, I know. . . .

STU: Or they were selling themselves in all sorts of ways, living in slums, doing anything for a walk-on or a shot

at understudy. But I thought, this isn't right, an artist
is entitled to a decent wage, an artist is like the worker,
worthy of his hire, and deserving dignity. So I came
back here and fought.

LENNY: Jesus Christ, I am bored.

STU: And it was a fight, never ending, for funding, recognition, status on campus, priority, they fought us on
everything and I swore to them, the pigs of my day,
theater is necessary, what I am doing with these raw
kids is as meaningful to them at least as gym. Now
you've built three gyms and funded intramural sports
ad infinitum, give the theater a break.

LENNY: Look, Stu, you've made your point—

STU: Okay. [*Goes back to table with bottle, reclines,
takes a sip.*]

JOHN: I can't understand why they are not back from
cleaning her up.

LENNY: Well, she's the department chairman's wife,
maybe they're laving her with frankincense and myrrh;
or perhaps they're having an orgy, Big Steve taking on
all three women. . . .

STU: [*Still reclining*] But you know, I wonder if they
weren't right all along? Maybe theater is ridiculous and
not fit for men. And on that note I am going to the
bathroom. [*Off table, toward hallway exit*] I am going
to wash my face with cold water, and then I am going
to try and get this rehearsal started again. [*Off.*]

LENNY: Pathos on parade.

JOHN: [*To* LENNY] What do you make of Stu?

LENNY: He's not my type, sweetie. Besides, I've learned
better than to grieve over the has-beens, and never-
were's—

BRUCE: It's hard to imagine Dr. Humphreys with talent,
or even being young. . . .

LENNY: You might be looking at yourself, Bruce.

BRUCE: I doubt it.

LENNY: Don't we all when we're twenty? [*Has moved
to* BRUCE *and touches him.* BRUCE *shrugs his hand
off.*]

BRUCE: Just stop it—I've told you it's done, and stop pressuring me.

LENNY: How am I pressuring you?

BRUCE: Touching me all the time. I don't want you to

touch me. Always insinuating, I'm tired of it. You're forcing me to make a scene—

LENNY: So what are you going to do, tell your mother?

BRUCE: I was about to ask you the same, and you're twenty years older than I am. I wonder what's happening at the rally? Dr. Humphreys should just let us go home, with all that we're not going to get anything accomplished. I'm going to find Emma and the others, see what they're up to. [*Off.*]

LENNY: [*To* JOHN] Ah, the distant object. If only I were a metaphysical poet. My problem is I'm all too physical.

JOHN: Isn't gay culture all about rejection?

LENNY: No more than the theater culture is. I don't know why I said yes to being in this thing. It's so sad here.

JOHN: Sad?

LENNY: All these old farts.

JOHN: What are you doing here?

LENNY: Don't you know? Helene sent me.

JOHN: Helene?

LENNY: Mrs. Brecht. I'm Chapel University's walking alienation effect. What are you?

JOHN: How's Naomi?

LENNY: Marvelous, simply marvelous. I'm directing her in *Medea* next semester.

JOHN: That's right. . . .

LENNY: I'm doing it in the nineteen thirties, in Berlin, sort of an *I Am a Camera Medea.* It still freaks Steve out that I have a wife. These straight people are all so simplistic they think sex is everything. I'm proud to say I haven't touched Naomi in twenty years and we have a beautiful marriage. And more, we are not going to end up in divorce court like Steve and his wife, and Stu and his wife, and Steve and Doris in five years, and Stu and whoever he marries next.

JOHN: And Bruce?

LENNY: Well, Bruce. He's the kind who, when young, one always romanticizes and projects upon, such talent, one thinks, such promise, who then winds up with a truck driver from Queens with a plug-in grotto and statues of naked men wrestling.

JOHN: Gay culture.

LENNY: How can you be a playwright if you aren't a faggot?

JOHN: You just said the trouble with straight people is they think sex is everything and now you're saying sex is everything.

LENNY: Depends on the sex.

BRUCE: [*Reenters.*] Well. They're all in the basement where all those ladies' rooms are. They're fussing around Steve's wife. [*Rally noise loud and threatening. The lights go out.*]

JOHN: Jesus Christ!

LENNY: Did they hit the power plant?

BRUCE: They must have.

JOHN: They're stuck downstairs in the dark. Where are the prop flashlights? [*They feel around and find two.*] Do they work? [*Shines one, then the other.*] Isn't there an emergency generator?

BRUCE: How will we find it?

JOHN: Steve should know. Bruce, you know where they are, go with this flashlight and lead them back. Then Steve can find the generator—

LENNY: Why don't we just leave them in the dark and go home?

JOHN: Oh, Lenny, be serious.

LENNY: I am serious. Do you think I could get Steve to participate in an exercise, an improv?

JOHN: But why would you want to?

LENNY: Well, it might help this play we're doing—if we could get some feeling, some believability under it. What do you think? Maybe the muses have caused this opportune darkness, for in dim light or no light it might be easier—

BRUCE: God, that might do us some good. I'd certainly go along with it—

JOHN: I think we should rescue them first.

BRUCE: Okay, I can find my way with this. . . . [*Exit with flashlight.*]

JOHN: [*With other flashlight*] How can we make the best use of this flashlight?

LENNY: Bend over.

[JOHN *grunts impatiently.*]

LENNY: Well, put it out, then, so we don't waste the battery.

JOHN: I'll put it here. [*Puts the flashlight lit on the floor.*]

LENNY: Tell me about yourself, Johnny, I know next to nothing about you.

JOHN: Is this the time?

LENNY: Well, what else can we do? You seem all papery to me. Is there any sinew under that whitish epiderm? I get no aura from you—I should let Naomi loose on you, she's great at auras....

JOHN: I don't think I have an aura, or a halo—

LENNY: That, sweetheart, means you're dead.

[*Uproar from outside.*]

JOHN: What do you think the story is?

LENNY: I'm not afraid of them.

JOHN: No?

LENNY: You mean you are? If you're dead, honey, what can they do to you? What can they do to me—I'm over forty.

JOHN: Does life end at forty?

LENNY: At least I got to forty. When I look at you, or Doris, or Emma, I think you'll all be lucky to get to thirty.

JOHN: You may have a point.

LENNY: You see, I only came up short recently. Since I came here, in fact. For a long time I was sure "it" was going to happen. And there were lots of "its." In my twenties it was world fame as an actor. I took classes, worked hard, and was good. I even got cast once in a while. But not often enough. I asked this renowned acting teacher, he was German, why? Why, Herr Doktor so und so, if I'm so good, don't I get cast more often? "Vell," he said, "do you put out?" Certainly, I said. "Hmmm, zen you are not a commercial type. *Ja, ja,* zat's it. How many parts do you think there are for a tiny, spidery Jew who is obviously a faggot?" Well, I thought about that, so I became a director. Stock, some Off Broadway, an occasional tour, some good reviews ... so I became a teacher. Falling, but full of color. I commute here from New York or Ann Arbor, cruise on the plane, make a good salary, don't have to do much work. It seems like a reward for all those years. But you? You've already given up. I even thought you were cute when I first saw you. Then I looked twice.

JOHN: Thanks.

LENNY: What's wrong with you?

JOHN: Does something have to be wrong with me?

LENNY: From the way you act. Well, if you won't narratize, what else can we do? I know. Fuck!

JOHN: I can't.

LENNY: Oh, that's right. You're not gay.

JOHN: Not only not gay, but physically I can't.

BRUCE: [*Enters with flashlight.*] Hi. I'm here, so's Dr. Klipstader. . . . [*Shines light on* STEVE, *who blinks and pushes light away.*]

STEVE: How are you gentlemen? Bearing up?

JOHN: How's everybody else?

STEVE: The girls are downstairs. Stu's in the men's room—the big one with the ornamental tiles. I told them all to sit tight and keep safe. This reminds me of Korea. I think I can find the generator.

JOHN: I'll go with you.

STEVE: There's no need, John. Bruce can hold the light while I fiddle, there's no point in three of us fumbling around. Come on, Bruce.

LENNY: [*As they leave*] If you meet Dracula, suck back. [*They're out.* LENNY *and* JOHN *are silent for a moment,* LENNY *embarrassed.*]

LENNY: It all goes to show you what this place is like: you make polite conversation with someone, and before you know it, they've told you something that . . . are you serious? I mean, is that the main attraction of those operations? Along with running to the bathroom constantly?

JOHN: Yes.

LENNY: You sure some carnivorous Yalie didn't bite it off?

JOHN: Some Yale surgeon connected it wrong.

LENNY: Did you have VD?

JOHN: Chronic congenital urethral strictures. They trap urine, cause infection, pain. The area is the size of a pencil point, and the operations were essential. They cut you, you see, turn you inside out, then try to remake it so the stricture is absorbed, and the passage stays opened. One tiny, microscopic slip and . . .

LENNY: Well, that gives you an accurate perspective on the modern drama.

[*A terrified screaming is heard from within the build-*

ing. STU *runs into the room screaming at the top of his lungs, knocks over the table.* JOHN *grabs him.*]

JOHN: Stu—Stu!

[STU, *out of breath, almost sobbing, collapses.*]

LENNY: A heart attack?

STU: [*Gasping*] No ... no ... I'm scared of the dark, sorry. . . .

LENNY: Don't move, Stu, I'll try to find your bottle. [*Takes the flashlight from* JOHN, *searches for the bottle, finds it, gives it to* STU, *who takes a long drink, gulping.*]

STU: I'm sorry, I'm sorry, thanks. . . .

[*A long silence.* STU *breathes heavily, sobs occasionally.* JOHN *flips the flashlight off.*]

JOHN: "In darkness let me dwell" . . . A song by John Dowland, Semper Dowland, semper Dowlens. That was his motto. I used to listen to it a lot when I was a boy, before I became neuter, so to speak.

STU: I know that song, don't like it, depressing.

JOHN: Funny what gonads do for you. You take it all for granted, and suddenly it isn't there. Ridiculous, so tiny, relatively. And you know, the worst is a sense of justice. Maybe it's my Catholic upbringing. It's where I was heading all along. Impotence. Writing plays. Synonyms, dear sir. Note that in your thesaurus. Why did I choose to write plays?

STU: Why do we always choose plays? To write them, to be in them. Is it cortical decline?

JOHN: Obsolescence. We have movies now, we have the TV, and whatever function the theater had way back, when it had a life, is filled by them, on a much vaster scale than they ever imagined at the Globe. At Yale they have this program for critics—

STU: What did I tell you? The critics are the artists nowadays, the creators—

JOHN: I sat in on one of their seminars. They never talked about new plays, mine or anybody's, or the possibility of important or interesting new plays. They talked about movies. About thirties movies, about the *auteur* theory, about movies that quote other movies, about narrative in the motion picture, about the theory of signs and the motion picture, about myth and the motion picture, about irony in the film. They took a poll one day of the greatest artistic achievement of the past thirty years. It was a foreign film about a donkey which is beaten for two hours.

LENNY: Did they tie it up first? Whipping isn't any fun without bondage!

JOHN: I'm an anachronism: I believe there is a point to the live theater, to the spoken word, to the feeling that an actor is living and breathing right there, in space, in time, and can die, or laugh, or give birth, or even, in some mysterious way, live for you—right there. If you were a critic, Lenny, what would you call this? A melo-dramatic mess, some kind of muddle? Maybe you'd think it would make a better movie—

LENNY: Just about anything makes a better movie. Even an operation on what was it: genital structures?

JOHN: I feel ashamed. I haven't told anyone, not my father, not the girls who hang around outside my classes. Nobody. I think this is the longest I've ever talked about it. I want to grab on to somebody in the street and shout at them: please, make me whole.

STU: Wait a minute. What are you talking about, John? From the way you're going on you'd think you were impotent. What is this? Another of Lenny's exercises?

JOHN: Afterward, I said to the doctor: I don't know if I can face this, and he said: Well, look on the good side, at least we didn't cut if off.

STU: Pretty kinky, those exercises.

JOHN: What am I going to do?

LENNY: Become gay! You'd be happier. You could be a receptacle. All you'd have to do is turn over. Nothing wrong with giving pleasure, if you're so concerned about it, you'd give more that way than writing plays. And that doctor, was right, it could be worse, you can still take public showers, go to the baths—or does it atrophy like a paralyzed leg? Goodness, I hadn't thought of that.

JOHN: And they say faggots shouldn't be reduced to clichés—

LENNY: I can't think of anything more clichéd than an impotent heterosexual—I think that's the synonym—

JOHN: You have just had what I would expect to be the typical reaction of a New York queen. In a cosmetic universe the most unbearable fact is to be different; and everything must be camped about. After all, if your fate is to wind up drunk in a gay bar, a wreck at forty, invisible at fifty, you have to learn to laugh at everything, right? I don't suppose there is anything wrong with homosexuality in the abstract, but gay culture? If it breeds that level of inhumanity it's disgusting.

LENNY: So, you turn from disgusting self-pity to a viciousness worthy of Chapel University Theater Department—I'm sorry for you, really I am, but no sorrier than I am for anybody trapped with us in the theater—find some strength inside yourself and go on, even write your plays if you have to. You can complain about those bitch critics, and God knows I've wanted to see most of them dead, mangled in the street at least once, but you can't condemn them for lacking what you lack. Not just a functioning prick—I'm sure most of them long ago resigned themselves to impotence—but some kind of blind faith in what you're doing. That's what it takes, bleed and trust your blood, or get out of this profession, but stop pulling back and begging for sympathy. Jesus—I feel like Annie Sullivan with Helen Keller, and that part always gives me a headache. [*Goes to* STU.] Give me that bottle, Stu, I need a swig. [*The lights flicker, then come on, dimmer than before, but the room is illuminated.*] There, you see, I take a drink, and the lights come on. Enough to turn you into an alcoholic. Oh, sorry, Stu, that's your number. Don't want to upstage you.

STU: There was a girl once who kept upstaging me in *Oh, Kay*. Her name was Maggie and I married her. Now she's leaving me. I knew I should have stayed away from actresses—even though she gave it up for me. . . . [*A sudden procession of* EMMA, DORIS, *carrying cookies, a package of doughnuts, a quart of milk, a package of liverwurst.*]

DORIS: We can have a picnic, we raided the refrigerator down there—

EMMA: Liverwurst, bread, milk, cookies and doughnuts. . . .

JOHN: Where's Steve's wife?

DORIS: She passed out after we got her cleaned up, so we figured it would be better to let her sleep.

EMMA: [*To* JOHN] Is something wrong?

JOHN: No . . .

EMMA: Are you sure?

JOHN: No.

EMMA: You're shaking, what is it?

DORIS: Poor, poor woman, I don't know how drunk she was really, just miserable—

LENNY: What's all this concern with Steve's wife, Doris?

DORIS: She's one of us.

STU: A line from *Lord Jim*, I believe—Marlowe in *Lord Jim* says Lord Jim is "one of us," for some reason I've forgotten, with some significance I've also forgotten. . . . [STEVE *and* BRUCE *enter.*]

STEVE: I think we'll be all right for a while, although the lights aren't as bright as I wish they were—are they still out there? [*Listens at door.*]

DORIS: Have a sandwich, Steve—

STEVE: Sure.

[DORIS *fixes him one.*]

STEVE: What do you think? Should we make a run for it?

LENNY: If they hit the power plant they must be pretty worked up.

STEVE: But stuck in here?

[DORIS *hands him the sandwich.*]

STEVE: Thanks, Doris. [*From this point forward the riot noise becomes increasingly more threatening and present. Gunshots, screams, sounds of fighting and glass breaking are all heard clearly.*]

LENNY: Why don't you let me take over for tonight as director? My part's pretty small, I can watch the rest, give you some pointers. I am the professional in residence, after all.

DORIS: Maybe Lenny has a point. Stu's no use to us now and we only have a week and a half.

BRUCE: And we're stuck in here, we might as well put the time to good use.

EMMA: [*To* JOHN] Tell me! What happened here?

JOHN: Nothing.

EMMA: Oh, come on!

JOHN: Leave me alone. [*Joining the others*] Give me a stale doughnut.

STEVE: [*To* LENNY] Can you think of an exercise, Lenny, that might help us with this play?

EMMA: [*Trying to revive* STU] Stu! Stu! Dr. Humphreys? [*To the others*] I think he's out cold.

LENNY: [*To* STEVE, *in answer*] Well, just possibly.

JOHN: [*Handing* LENNY *a doughnut*] A peace offering.

LENNY: [*Taking it*] Bless you, my boy.

STEVE: Okay, Lenny, take over for tonight.

LENNY: [*Pretending unwillingness*] Well, I don't know ... there is professional ethics....

STEVE: And they include not getting drunk and passing out at rehearsal.

LENNY: Well, you have a point. But Steve, if I take over, even just for tonight, I need your complete trust. That means going along with some exercises and improvs to start. That's how I work and I think this play needs them. [*Rally noise.*]

EMMA: God, listen to that. What should we do?

STEVE: Obviously we're stuck here for the duration. We might as well go along with Lenny.

LENNY: [*To* EMMA] Emma, you stay over here in the corner with a notepad, write down what happens. That way, if we stumble onto something maybe Stu can use it when he comes round. Okay?

EMMA: [*After a hesitation*] Okay....

LENNY: [*To the others*] Now, we need a warm-up. So what I suggest is everybody form a circle. [*They do.* LENNY *pushes and pulls them into a tight circle, everyone facing inward.*] I just want you to breathe. Breathe in, breathe out, very slowly, and listen to me. [*His manner becomes suggestive, hypnotic.*] Breathe in. [*They do.*] Breathe out. [*They do.*] Slowly ... slowly ... just breathe. Do nothing, think nothing, feel nothing, just breathe. Breathe in your life, slowly. Breathe out your life, slowly. What are we doing here? Breathe in. This play is about a family. Breathe out. Slowly, slowly and listen. A family and a war. Father, mother, son, friend. Breathe in, pull in the entire world. What is going to happen? The son will be sacrificed. Why? Breathe in, breathe out, slowly, slowly. [*Rally noise,* EMMA *starts, the others are concentrating too hard to notice.*] And there's the war. It will cause the father to sacrifice his son. Breathe in, father, breathe in, son, breathe in, mother, breathe in, friend. Breathe out, slowly, identify yourselves.

BRUCE: Son.

JOHN: Friend, I guess.

DORIS: Mother, right?

STEVE: I don't know. What am I supposed to be?

LENNY: No thinking, no censoring. Keep breathing, don't resist. A war is going on, the son must fight it, but who is he fighting? The mob outside, or the father inside? Breathe in, slowly, very slowly, breathe out. Everybody remember your own mother, father, friend, and son ... identify yourselves. ...

BRUCE: Son. And friend, and maybe ... mother. Is that right?

JOHN: No man, like Ulysses, that's me. No man.

DORIS: Friend, I think, and maybe son, I don't feel like a true mother.

STEVE: I ...

LENNY: Steve?

STEVE: Who can I be? What?

STU: [*Coming to*] What is this? Emma?

EMMA: Exercises, Dr. Humphreys.

STU: Oh, God, I've got to clear my head. [*Goes to outside door, opens it with his key.*]

EMMA: It sounds dangerous out there, Dr. Humphreys. ...

STU: I need air. ...

LENNY: Go with him, Emma. ...

[*They go outside.*]

LENNY: Everyone, keep concentrated. Steve, answer me, who are you? Breathe first, then tell me ... who are you?

STEVE: I ...

[*Outside,* EMMA *screams, drags* STU *back in. They slam the door,* EMMA *grabs* STU's *key, locks the door. There are gunshots near the door.*]

DORIS: What happened—

STU: Cowboys and Indians!

EMMA: Suddenly, there were black people everywhere— they had guns, they shot at us—

JOHN: Jesus, Lenny—

LENNY: Keep breathing. We can't do anything about it, come back, get in the circle. Breathe in, breathe out—

EMMA: Are you all right, Dr. Humphreys?

STU: I want to play.

LENNY: Get in the circle, Stu.

[STU *does, goes along with exercises in a drunken state.*]

EMMA: They wanted to kill us out there! They were after us! Do you hear me, and we are helpless against them—

LENNY: Steve, identify yourself.

STEVE: Father.

LENNY: Again!

STEVE: Father.

LENNY: Fathers, sons, love, hate, need, fear, Abraham and Isaac. Joined in love and hate. Breathe in, so slowly that every particle in the poisoned air is felt. Breathe in, breathe out, slowly, we're all in it. Together, aren't we? In this circle, this magic circle. Breathe in ... breathe out....

JOHN: Are we?

LENNY: What?

JOHN: In it together? Why are you up there and we down here?

LENNY: We'll change places. [*Lies down in the circle,* JOHN *rises.*] Conduct us through, John. Show us the way.

JOHN: There is no way. By all means breathe. In or out, it doesn't matter.

EMMA: John, do you ...

JOHN: Ah! I hear a voice. Is it the muse? It is someone outside the circle, looking on? Perhaps that is the answer. To look on and not care—

EMMA: No, John, you don't understand....

LENNY: Take us backward, John. Backward to the truth.

JOHN: Do you mean primeval time? All right. Breathe yourselves backward into the start. Before all the mistakes. What was the first action? A spasm outward, perhaps. The primal mistake. Breathe in, slowly, breathe out ... breathe yourselves backward. Through time, into time, ones are passing ... [*Rally noise.*] Escape that by fleeing into the past. Breathe in. Breathe out.

EMMA: This is not the answer. Listen to them. And we are trapped here, alone, alone together. We aren't friends, we aren't allies, what is the answer?

JOHN: What do we remember of primeval time? Silence and freshness, newness and the liberation from cliché. Life was not hackneyed then, men and women lived for the first time, died for the first time. And felt for the first time. They didn't age as we do, because to us age means the loss of feeling and to them it meant that feeling grew. Think of Abraham and Sarah, not old at all but young and fertile at one hundred. Breathe in, slowly, breathe out. . . .

STU: Look, I'm a worm crawling through slime. . . . [*Crawls around the floor.*] With luck I'll turn into the fearful dragon. . . . [*Rally noise.*] Ah—it's me, Fafner! [*Roars at the outside door as though to frighten the crowd.*]

LENNY: John. It is Abraham and Isaac, isn't it?

JOHN: No, Anti-Ulysses, Anti-Penelope, Anti-Telemachus. The perversion of what they were but the same configuration. Ulysses bound, but hearing not the sirens, but screams, a mob outraged. Telemachus bound, waiting and longing for a father who never comes, a birthright that dissolves in agony and emptiness. Penelope bound, crying for a husband who will not come back; who has ventured out to war and lost, out to sea and drowned.

BRUCE: Who is Ulysses?

JOHN: We are all Ulysses, paralyzed, our limbs broken and arrayed neatly around us. We lie, crippled, and survey them, and smile perhaps at our helplessness.

EMMA: John, it's so easy to talk that way. If that's true, then what's the answer? The smirk is easy, the simplest thing, to reach out, is so hard and we judge it, call it "sentimental." I want to grasp somebody's hand to feel the pulse, I think that's the answer. . . .

LENNY: Come back to the circle, John. . . .

JOHN: I have to go to the bathroom. . . . [*Exits into the building.*]

LENNY: Who's next in our breathing?

BRUCE: [*Jumping up.*] I am.

LENNY: All right, Bruce.

BRUCE: Breathe in, slowly, breathe out. . . . I know what I am.

LENNY: What?

BRUCE: The sacrifice.

DORIS: I feel that I am the sacrifice.

LENNY: That means you are mother and son, both sacrifices. Offered to whom, these sacrifices, and why? Sarah could not protect her son from the unreasonable demands made of Abraham. She had to bow her head and let her husband lead her son into death.

DORIS: Lead part of herself away, for no reason, into darkness. . . .

LENNY: Abraham took Isaac and bound him on an altar.

DORIS: I feel that way, helpless, a man over me, wanting him to control me.

BRUCE: I understand you, Doris. I know what that feeling is. Yet I'm a man, aren't I, and I must be in control . . . isn't that true? But I never feel in control.

LENNY: The father bound the son on the altar and killed him. Steve, you must take your son and give him to me.

STEVE: Which son, I have three.

LENNY: The youngest.

STEVE: The different one?

LENNY: Yes. Isaac was bound upon the altar. [*Goes to the ladder that serves as the tree in the play within the play.*] Isaac must be bound hand and foot to the tree-altar. [*Gets a prop rope.*] Here—Abraham, bind your son.

STEVE: [*Refuses the rope.*] No—you do it.

BRUCE: Do I have to be tied?

LENNY: It's good practice for life. [*Ties* BRUCE's *hands behind him.*]

BRUCE: It's too tight.

LENNY: This is your son, Steve.

JOHN: [*Enters from bathroom.*] What's happening?

EMMA: Torture of the innocent.

LENNY: This is your father, Bruce. [*Shoves* BRUCE *toward* STEVE, *who punches him.* BRUCE *falls.*]

EMMA: Bruce!

DORIS: [*To* STEVE] Why did you do that?

EMMA: [*To* BRUCE] Are you all right?

BRUCE: I think so. . . .

STEVE: I hated that kid, Doris. I hated him. He wasn't like me. He wasn't like his brothers. They were men, who knows what he was. He didn't even look like me. And you see, Delores and me, we were kids when we met, in school still, and in those days you had to be married, you felt out if you didn't.

EMMA: Untie him, Lenny.

LENNY: Not yet. Bruce? Are you all right?

BRUCE: Are you punishing me for stopping with you?

LENNY: Punishing myself too.

STEVE: [*To* DORIS] You see, Doris, try to understand me, please, she tied me down, she got pregnant once, then twice, and then when we had trouble, again. It became out of the question to leave her.

DORIS: You should have told her.

STEVE: What? That I couldn't stand her any longer? That I never loved her because, way back then, I didn't know what love was? She would gag me with her hurt look, tie me with the boys, with the house, with the cars.

LENNY: [*To* STEVE *continuing*] And now you have to kill the child she loved. The child is bound to the altar. [*Backs* BRUCE *up to the ladder, and ties his feet so he can't move.*]

BRUCE: You tied me so tight. But you know, Lenny, I think I understand. That's what scared me about you. You always held me too tight, always wanted more than I could give. I don't know if I'm gay or not, Lenny, but it was your need for me that terrified me.... I'm sorry—

LENNY: [*Gets a prop knife.*] Here, Steve. Sacrifice your son.

STEVE: I can't. But with my gun he can do it himself.

DORIS: You're a coward, Steve—

STEVE: No!

DORIS: I didn't think you were a coward.

STEVE: I'm not a coward, I've never been afraid—

DORIS: Afraid to tell your wife, afraid to talk to your son—

STEVE: What was I to say to him? Get out of my house? If she had had a lover it would have been easier. You can understand it when it's another man who takes your wife away, but a little boy? Thirteen years old and girlish—how can you understand that? [*Rally noise.*]

JOHN: My God, they sound dangerous—what should we do?

STEVE: Hold on to me, Doris—

DORIS: No—

LENNY: [*To* BRUCE] You don't seem to mind being tied up. Maybe we should have tried it? [*Touches* BRUCE's *face.*] You were right, you know. I did want too much from you. I was trying to screw youth back into me, I guess.

STEVE: [*Tries to embrace her.*] Please. . . .

DORIS: No! I've been in love with men like you my entire life. Men I thought were bigger and smarter and tougher and wilder than me. Men who could hold me down during sex, my arms above my head as though I were bound on their altar. And I wanted to squirm helpless under them and have love wrung from me as though against my will.

EMMA: [*Sounds of glass being broken.*] They're getting wilder. [*A small explosion.*] Jesus!

STEVE: Doris! Doris—don't leave me—

DORIS: [*Pushing him away*] Stay away from me—
   [STEVE *runs to the door.*]

LENNY: What are you doing, Steve?

STEVE: She called me a coward. I must fight them.

DORIS: Are you crazy, Steve?

STEVE: It's a war, isn't it? Which of you is man enough to come and fight it?

STU: [*Suddenly starting up*] I'm a man, look, I'm a man.

STEVE: Come and fight!

STU: No, I'm not a man, I'm a wreck of a man. Look, everybody, look! Male wreckage.

STEVE: You drunk bastard! I want somebody who's not afraid to fight. [*There is banging on the door from outside.*] I'm coming, I'm coming. . . .

STU: This is manhood for you, this is potency. Two sons and a wife who's leaving me. . . .

LENNY: Come on, John, grab him. . . .
   [JOHN *and* LENNY *grab* STEVE *to pull him away from the door. Suddenly he breaks away and runs to the door, unlocking it.*]

EMMA: Steve, don't, if they get in they'll kill us all—
   [DELORES *enters in an elaborate eighteenth-century costume which she has obviously gotten together hastily from the costume shop.*]

DELORES: Didn't people dress well in the eighteenth century?

EMMA: Help us, your husband . . .

STEVE: Delores! What . . . ?

DELORES: Oh dear, I'm embarrassing him again. You can't win. . . .

LENNY: Lock the door, Steve—

STEVE: Delores, forgive me.

DELORES: How can I, Steve? You did it to him—

LENNY: Stu, give me your key— [*Tries to get* STU's *key so he can lock the outside door.* STEVE *continues to stand in front of the door.*]

STEVE: I know, but you too—

DELORES: Yes, I know we were both guilty, we are all guilty of everything nowadays. I think there's a word for it. You were going out?

STEVE: Yes, to fight them, to prove I wasn't a coward.

DELORES: Of course you're not a coward. Come on, then, I'll go with you. We'll face them down together. [*Joins him at the door.* LENNY *finds* STU's *key, goes to the door,* STEVE *pushes him away.*]

STEVE: Together—

[STEVE *and* DELORES *run out, closing the door behind them.* LENNY *runs to the door and locks it with* STU's *key. There is a pause. They listen, expecting to hear* STEVE *and* DELORES *killed. There is no sound. After a moment* EMMA *goes to* BRUCE.]

EMMA: Are you all right?

BRUCE: [*Untied*] Yes. [*The others are still silent and tense, listening.* BRUCE *goes and puts his shirt and shoes on, listening also. After a moment he speaks.*] I don't hear anything, do you?

JOHN: No, nothing.

BRUCE: You'd think if they got them, there'd be gunfire, shouts . . .

JOHN: I didn't hear anything.

STU: [*Drunken*] Austerity.

EMMA: Maybe they let them get away.

STU: Asperity.

LENNY: I didn't hear anything either.

STU: Astarte.

LENNY: God! I wish I were being mugged in Manhatten.

EMMA: Do you think we should go out and see?

DORIS: I should.

LENNY: We all should. Then we can try and get to our cars.

JOHN: That's a good idea. Will somebody give me a lift?

EMMA: I will.

LENNY: All right, we'll have to drag Stu. [*To* BRUCE *and* JOHN] You two, being young, get him up— [*They lift him.*] Marvelous, simply marvelous.

[*Slowly unlocks the door. The others are very tense and frightened.* DELORES *and* STEVE *are standing in the doorway, embracing. They start apart.*]

LENNY: What is this?

STEVE: Oh, I'm sorry everybody. God, that exercise really got to me, Lenny. I guess I gave everybody a scare. I really came out here expecting to be killed. It was crazy.

DELORES: There were people out there with guns, but they just stared at us and disappeared. I think it was my costume—these people always respect mad-women.

LENNY: You mean, you're both all right?

STEVE: Well, alive at least— [*Suddenly a barrage of shots rings out.* EMMA, JOHN, *and* BRUCE *fall down,* DORIS *screams and falls.* STEVE *and* DELORES *are bloodied, scream, and fall outside.* LENNY, *with great presence of mind, slams the door shut and locks it. Bullets are fired into the door, there are shouts outside, banging on the door.*]

LENNY: Holy shit . . . how is everybody—

[*The others, very shaken, stand up, dust themselves off, survey each other.*]

DORIS: [*Suddenly cries out.*] Steve! [*Rushes crying to the door.*]

LENNY: [*Grabs her, pushes her away.*] Stay away from the door.

DORIS: Steve! Steve! [*Sobs.*]

LENNY: Is there any way out of this building?

BRUCE: There are all those underground passages—

DORIS: And I drove him out there—

LENNY: Emma, do you know those passages?

EMMA: They keep them locked. Stu might have keys.

LENNY: Stu, do you have keys to the underground passages?

STU: Christians can always gain entrance to the catacombs.

JOHN: Oh, Jesus, I have to go to the bathroom. [*Off.*]

LENNY: [*Looks through his keys.*] This one is the office, just like mine, these look like house and car keys, a mailbox key—I don't think so—

STU: Somebody call the police.

LENNY: You see? In a crisis you never think of the obvious. I hope the lines are up, I'll use the hall phone. Who has a dime?

[BRUCE *gives him one.*]

LENNY: Thanks. Am I forgiven?

BRUCE: For what?

LENNY: Being who I am, and having no control over it.

BRUCE: I guess.

LENNY: These younger people, so verbal. Marvelous, simply marvelous.

BRUCE: No. I do.

[*Quick embrace of* LENNY. LENNY *leaves,* JOHN *comes in.*]

JOHN: Where was Lenny going?

BRUCE: To call the police.

JOHN: What are we going to do until they come?

EMMA: Take hands.

JOHN: What?

EMMA: What can we do but take hands and wait?

JOHN: You're crazy.

EMMA: I mean it.

JOHN: What good will it do? . . .

BRUCE: [*To* DORIS, *who is still sobbing*] Come on, Doris, it's okay— [*Embraces her.*]

EMMA: We are trapped in here together, and do we have to stay alone, each in his own corner, sneering at the others? What can we do? We can use the perceptions we have as weapons, but we've done that. We can use what art we have to destroy, we've done that. We've done everything but take hands.

JOHN: This sounds like what Spin would say to Marty, or the Rifleman to the one-armed Sheriff—

EMMA: If we were Christians, we'd stand together and sing hymns waiting to be martyred. We're not Christians, and we can't be martyred. We don't believe in anything. Do we believe in art? Hardly. We aren't even sure what it is. Do we believe in life? Hardly, we hold it cheap. Do we believe in love? We confuse it with sex. But take my hand, be my friend, what else can we do?

DORIS: Yes, Emma, what else can we do. [*Takes* EMMA's *hand.*]

BRUCE: Give me your hands. [*Takes hands of* EMMA *and* DORIS.] John? [*Holds his hand out to* JOHN.]

JOHN: You mean you stand and watch Steve and his wife get killed and this is how you react? You have all gone crazy!

[*Riot noise loud, very dangerous sounding.* LENNY *enters.*]

LENNY: They said they'd send police as soon as they could find some. There are fires and riots all over Detroit, and white students who were at the rally have been beaten, maybe killed. They told me we should stay here. They said they knew this building, it's a fortress they said, a fortress of art. So we're trapped.

JOHN: They're holding hands, that's their answer.

LENNY: Holding hands.

EMMA: Take our hands, Lenny, please.

LENNY: I understand. What about Stu? We should take his hand without his will—I think he would if he were sober. Right, Stu?

STU: Right. [LENNY *takes his hand, offers his own hand to the others.*]

LENNY: What can humans do but this?

JOHN: You, Lenny?

LENNY: I think we're heading into another dark age. Doesn't it seem that way to you? Nothing matters, nothing is going to matter, all we can do is this.

DORIS: John?

JOHN: You've all become crazy hippies. With this stupid sentimentality. And you think all this is going to help? What about them outside, what happens when they get in and kill us? Will this stop them? What about my own pain, will it stop it? You don't understand, I'm impotent.

EMMA: Take my hand, then.

JOHN: The healing touch?

EMMA: Precisely.

JOHN: I'm a failure, I have dried up as a writer, I can't put words on paper, or even ordinary thoughts, or pretend any more that I have talent.

EMMA: Then take my hand.

JOHN: And I hate prig hippies with their emotional smugness, and their easy solutions.

EMMA: Then take my hand.

JOHN: And I am wrestling with the temptation to run out there and let that mob tear me to pieces. . . .

EMMA: Then take my hand.

JOHN: This is no answer, it's just the other side of the viciousness and hate this place stands for. God damn all of you—I won't be touched, it's meaningless. . . . [*Runs to the doors at back, hammers on them.*] Let me out—

EMMA: [*Follows him to the door.*] Take my hand.

JOHN: No!

EMMA: Take it, take it. I have nothing to give you but my hand. I have nothing to offer you but a willingness to look foolish and accept failure. So take my hand. It is connected to me, and to all of us, and we are warm and walk on the earth and breathe and think and that's all I have. So please take my hand. . . .

JOHN: No . . . [*Is crying.*]

EMMA: No, then. What are we but poor, silly, middle-class people caught between emptiness and nothing, nowhere to go, nothing to be but failures. It has ended in us, that wonderful energy that begot so much, it has ended in us. No simple joys anymore, no gestures outward, just a bored waiting for death. Poor people in the middle, that's us. Please, John, I am here, take my hand. [JOHN *unwillingly does.*] Squeeze it. [*He does.*] Harder. [*He does.*]

DORIS: Emma?

EMMA: We must stand together. [*She and* JOHN *slowly walk hand in hand to the others. With great dignity they all join hands.*] We are all Ulysses now, and if we try hard enough we might hear the sirens singing. . . . [*Suddenly the door at the back is pushed in. There is an enormous scream from the mob.*]

BLACKOUT

EARTH WORMS

Cast

BERNARD: A man of seventy; heavy, though not obese. He is large-framed, tall, slightly stooped, but in good health and very robust. He has a grand manner, a booming, deep voice, and is inclined to be rhetorical.

MARY: Seventeen at play's beginning; southern accent is heavy at first, in the course of the play it is modified.

ARNOLD LONGESE: Nineteen at play's beginning, from South Philadelphia.

SCODGE: Of the neighborhood, twenty-three.

BUCKY: Of the neighborhood, twenty-three.

MARGE: Of the neighborhood, twenty-nine.

MICHAEL DE FELICE: Eighteen at play's beginning, flamboyant drag queen, but very tough.

THREE NUNS: In old-fashioned habits, long black gowns, wimples, black gloves, oversized weaponlike rosaries; their faces are never visible.

A BOY: Fourteen, of the neighborhood.

EDITH LONGESE: Arnold's aunt, fifty-five, she only crawls, never walks, is blind.

The time of the play is the mid-1950s. The play opens in Virginia, but most of the scenes occur in the Italian section of South Philadelphia.

The Set

The stage is meant to be bare. If possible, there should be two levels connected by a rough stairway. There should be entrances on both levels. Different locations should be suggested by lighting, and the set should be very flexible, able to embrace a variety of locations, in some cases simultaneously.

A number of the scenes occur in a row house in South Philadelphia. The house is meant to be without furniture except for a large desk down right, and a small, dirty kitchen area far left. There can be a small, old-fashioned stove and sink in the kitchen. The balcony or second level, in those scenes, represents the house's second floor.

Certain other scenes occur in a small bar, which can occupy the kitchen section with a small table or bar dragged on. There should never be more than a small attempt to suggest any location.

ACT I

Scene 1

In a spot, BERNARD *appears. He acts as though looking in a mirror. He adjusts on his head a ladies' bonnet and wears an elaborate shawl. Both look as though they were made in the 1890s.*

A light comes up down right. The sound of a stream is heard.

MARY *is lying face down, weeping. She is barefoot and in a rough dress. Her light builds as* BERNARD *starts to speak.*

BERNARD: [*Calling in different tones, now sad, now angry, now pleading*] Ellen Mac Jones! Ellen Mac Jones! Here, Ellen, Ellen, Ellen! Ellen Mac Jones Aberdeen! Ellen! Miss Mac Jones! Please, Ellen. Why do you make me call you and call you? Ellen Mac Jones Aberdeen! Ellen!
[*His light goes out.*
ARNOLD *enters slowly. He wears an army uniform, which is muddy and torn. He is obviously lost and has been wandering, trying to find his way. He sees* MARY, *who is still crying, her head buried in her arms. He approaches shyly and listens to her. Suddenly she speaks without looking up or around. She continues to sob.*]
MARY: [*Heavy southern accent*] Oh, I know you're there. Don't want to hear nothin' from you. You're evil, evil! I bet you think I'm lyin' here just awaitin' for you. Well, you're wrong!
[ARNOLD *startled, looks around.*]

MARY: Oh, I know you're lookin' around just to see if anyone can hear me. A girl callin' her own daddy evil and him a Baptist deacon. It'ud be a scandal. Well, I don't care. You are a prime example of the devourin' parent. I read all about you in that book you ripped away from me.

ARNOLD: [*Urban accent*] Look, I'm sorry, but I think you're makin' a mistake . . .

MARY: [*Whips around*] Who are you?

[ARNOLD *shifts.*]

MARY: Who are you?

ARNOLD: [*Hesitating*] Arnold Longese.

MARY: Why'd you hesitate?

ARNOLD: Well, people around here, well, they ain't used to names like that. You know, they look at me, well, funny.

MARY: Ain't that an Italian name?

ARNOLD: Why, yeah, Longese, that's Italian. [*Embarrassed*] Them wop names, you know.

MARY: Don't you like bein' Italian?

ARNOLD: Who's Italian?

MARY: Why, you just said . . .

ARNOLD: Nah! I'm American. Red-blooded. Got this Italian handle because my pop came over with his sisters, you know, from Italy, when they was kids. But, nah, I'm raised over here, in South Philly.

MARY: South Philly . . . you mean, Philadelphia?

ARNOLD: City of Brotherly Love! Where I come from, everybody's gotta name like mine.

MARY: That true?

ARNOLD: Sure! I mean, Longese, that's my name, that's common. Then there's, let me see, well, Gambone, Mastroangelo, De Felice. . . .

MARY: De Felice . . .

ARNOLD; Yeah. Means "Of Happiness." Boy, was he weird. Then there's Squatarelli. . . .

MARY: Beautiful names.

ARNOLD: [*Looking at her*] Well, lotta beautiful things in this world. [*A pause.*]

MARY: [*Staring back at him*] You at the base?

ARNOLD: Medical orderly.

MARY: Longese, that right?

ARNOLD: You can call me Arn.

MARY: Arn? Don't you read the funny papers?

ARNOLD: Me? Nah!

MARY: Why, Prince Arn, he's Prince Valiant's son. Oh, he's a handsome old boy. Don't know how old. You can't never tell in them funny papers. Some days he looks fourteen, some days he looks twenty. Some of us girls, well, we used to spend time aseein' if we could find us a bulge. Well, you know where. He wears tights, you see. . . .

ARNOLD: You mean them tight things? [*Pulls pants up.*] Up here? In the funny papers?

MARY: Why, yes. But they's never a bulge. Never a bulge on anybody. I looked at Superman, Tarzan, and Lothar, too. Prince Arn . . . he's brave, got curly hair, looks like you. . . .

ARNOLD: Aw, I don' look like nothin'!

MARY: [*Flirtatious*] You do too look like him. Or, I guess, he looks like you, bein' he's in the funny papers and you—you're real. He has brown eyes too and this nice nose, just like yours. [*Touches his nose; he is startled.*] Oh, I'm sorry, I didn't mean to touch it. But I ain't never been this close to a nose like that.

ARNOLD: [*Pause. He shifts.*] Boy, it's hot. That water sounds nice.

MARY: [*Solemn*] Water is a symbol. That's what Jung [*mispronounced*] says. If that's how you say his name. I think that's what he says, somethin' about anima. . . .

ARNOLD: Yeah, animea, that's where you ain't got no blood. . . .

MARY: No, this is somethin' different.

ARNOLD: No it ain't, my mother died from it. . . .

MARY: No, this is about sex. [*Stops, shocked at what she has said.*] I didn't mean that, I mean with the idea of sex. Oh, I better shut up. I worked in the University Library after school. . . .

ARNOLD: You go to college. . . .

MARY: Why, no. My daddy'd never let me. No, I just this summer graduated high school. This teacher, he taught history, Mr. Shingles? Well, he got me this job end of sophomore year in exchange for me lettin' him rub up against me in his Chevvy. I think the pursuit of knowledge justifies anything, don't you? So I'd work there in the afternoons and steal the books—just until I had them read. That's what happened today. Daddy came in early and found me in my room with Jung and got his switch out after me. We're Baptist, you know. Well, he caught me today, let me tell you. He gave me this. [*Shows him her lip, which is cut.*]

ARNOLD: Yeah, I seen that. Looks bad. Have you cleaned it?

MARY: Why, no. Well, he hit on me with that switch. A prime example of hysteria, to judge from Dr. Freud [*mispronounced*]. Of course, I ran off aweepin'. That's what little girls is supposed to do, and to him I'm still a little girl even though I'm a full growed seventeen and don't crowd me so much.

ARNOLD: You ought to wash that cut. Let's go swimmin'.

MARY: Swimmin'? [*A pause; she muses.*] I ain't supposed to go swimmin' with boys. I mean, I go with my brother, but he ain't a boy in the sense I mean.

ARNOLD: I think you should go swimmin' for medical reasons, that cut, after all—

MARY: How old are you?

ARNOLD: Nineteen. Wanted a be sent to Korea. Wound up here. My luck. Let's go swimmin'.

MARY: You start undressin'. [*He takes his shirt off.*] Why, you don't have much hair up here at all. Can I take a hair? Just for me. [*Takes a hair. He giggles. She puts the hair in a pocket.*]

ARNOLD: You take somethin' off.

MARY: Near the river. They's a bush there. [*They get up.*] You won't do nothin' to me?

ARNOLD: Me? Nah! I got lost and have been stumblin' around, tryin' to get back, I'm lost.

MARY: Well, I'm puttin' myself at your mercy, Prince Arn.

ARNOLD: What's your name?

MARY: Why, Mary.

[*A pause. Shyly, he takes her hand, they start off. As they exit, the lights brighten and become very harsh. The entire stage is lit. A street in the Italian section of South Philadelphia is represented.*

SCODGE *and* BUCKY *run on wildly, playing basketball. They are in their early twenties, husky going to fat.* MARGE *appears, twenty-nine, heavy, tough.*]

MARGE: [*Hearty, mocking*] Gee, guys, can I play wit you?

SCODGE: Hi ya, Marge! [*Throws the ball at her; she screams but gets it.*]

MARGE: Bastids!

BUCKY: What's the number, Marge?

MARGE: Nine oh three.

SCODGE: Shit! And I bet nine oh four.

MARGE: You guys and the numbers!

[MARGE *dribbles. The men get the ball away from* MARGE *and play.*

MICHAEL DE FELICE *makes a flashy entrance in full drag. He is wildly effeminate but with more than a hint of toughness underneath. The men greet him with whistles. He flounces all the more.*]

MICHAEL: Keep them balls bouncin', boys!

BUCKY: Hiya, Michael, what's the name today?

MICHAEL: Madame Bovary.

MARGE: Madame Ovary? What the hell kinda name is that?

MICHAEL: Don't judge it, bitch!

SCODGE: Hey, you, show some respect!

[THREE NUNS *enter. They are in old-fashioned habits as would befit the fifties. Their faces are covered. One plays a funeral rhythm on a tambourine, the others carry a large crucifix between them. It is a garish crucifix with Christ's wounds alarmingly clear. They march slowly across the stage. Everyone looks away except* MICHAEL, *who stares at them.*

After the NUNS *exit, the game starts up again. The fourteen-year-old* BOY *runs on;* MICHAEL *grabs him.*]

MICHAEL: Hello, Liù.

BOY: Cut it out. Who?

MICHAEL: That's the victim from the opera *Turandot.*

BOY: Christ, you're weird.

MICHAEL: You think about my offer?

BOY: Up yours.

[*The* BOY *starts off.* BERNARD *enters wearing the shawl and stares at the boy with obvious interest.* MICHAEL *notices this. The* BOY, *confused, starts off.* MICHAEL *calls out to him as he exits.*]

MICHAEL: [*to* BOY] Remember, that's something I know how to do.

[BOY *runs out.* BERNARD, *acting oblivious, passes* MICHAEL.]

MICHAEL: Hi ya, Turandot.
BERNARD: [*Neither stopping nor looking up*] I despise
  Puccini.

BLACKOUT

Scene 2

ONE of the NUNS enters with a chair, she places it in a
dim spot. The TWO OTHERS lead ARNOLD into the spot.
He is wearing undershorts but nothing else; his hands
are bound behind him. The NUNS seat him and tie him
to the chair. ARNOLD is terrified.

FIRST NUN: [*Showing him a picture*] Look at this picture.
ARNOLD: I didn't mean to do it. I'm sorry. I'm ignorant
  even if I did go to high school. [*Tries to look away.*]
SECOND NUN: Hold his head, force his eyes, make him
  look!
FIRST NUN: [*Showing another picture*] Look at this one!
  [NUNS *cluck*, ARNOLD *groans*.]
THIRD NUN: That is not merely a sin of commission but,
  in the end, of emission too.
ARNOLD: Please don' show me no more. I'm sorry. Oh,
  my God, I am heartily sorry for having offended thee
  and . . .
SECOND NUN: [*Clamps her hand over his mouth.*] No!
  Can't repent. You haven't atoned enough.
FIRST NUN: The pursuit of happiness is the filthiest pur-
  suit!
SECOND AND THIRD NUNS: The pursuit of happiness is
  the filthiest pursuit!
  [*The* NUNS *make a jingle of this line and dance in a
  circle around* ARNOLD. *They build until they are
  shrieking, then they freeze. After a pause, they unbind*
  ARNOLD *mechanically and kneel. They cross them-
  selves and pray, whining very softly.*
  ARNOLD *stands up, very shaken. He walks right.*
  A light comes up far right. MARY *is asleep on a cot.*
  ARNOLD's *clothes are piled near the cot. He dresses,*

still very upset. When he is dressed he stares at MARY.
The NUN's *whining increases for a moment.*
MICHAEL *and the* BOY *come on, far left. They settle in
a spot and start to play cards.*
ARNOLD *kisses* MARY, *who awakens.*]

MARY: You goin'?

ARNOLD: Had this awful dream.

MARY: Tell me, I read Dr. Freud [*mispronounced*] on
dreams.

ARNOLD: No.

[MICHAEL *has dealt cards. The* BOY *looks at the back
of his cards curiously.*]

BOY: Hey, Michael, what's this onna back of these
cards?

MICHAEL: They're pictures, hon, play.

BOY: I know they're pictures. Whataya think, I'm ignorant? I go a high school. Who they pictures of?

MICHAEL: You think about my offer? You bring it up wit
you brother? Stop starin' for Christ' sake! It's Arnold
Longese.

[ARNOLD *has tried to leave* MARY, *who has hung on to
him.*]

ARNOLD: See you.

[*He starts to leave. Impulsively,* MARY *hugs him.*]

BOY: [*Laughs, looks more closely at the pictures.*] No
kiddin', that Arnold? He's got his face covered in this
one—yeah, yeah, I guess it's him. Look at what he's
doin' wit you on this one! Can't be him, he was a he-
man.

MICHAEL: That's for sure. And nobody knows it better
than me!

[*They play cards.*

MARY *kisses* ARNOLD. *He is uncomfortable.*]

MARY: Arnold, baby, when you goin'—well, you know,
with me?

ARNOLD: [*Disengaging himself.*] This ain't the time.

MARY: It's been three weeks, I mean, I enjoy the kissin'
and the spendin' the nights, but that's all we done. . . .

ARNOLD: Not now. . . .

MARY: When you comin' back?

ARNOLD: Look, Mary, I been thinkin', I . . . [*Looks at her,
she smiles, he can't bring himself to say it.*] Thursday,
I'll be covered.

MARY: We'll go to a special place I know. A Magic Place.
We'll go at a magic time, I have your hair. . . .

ARNOLD: I'll come. Look, Mary, remember what I asked
you, before? About shavin' . . . down there?

MARY: I'll shave, Prince Arn.

[*They kiss.* ARNOLD *gently gets away from* MARY *and
goes.*
The BOY *and* MICHAEL *play a new hand.*
During their dialogue MARY *rips the sheet from the
bed and begins a dance with it. It is a ritual dance.
She presses it to her breasts, embraces it, treats it as
though it had a human shape.*]

BOY: But how'd you get him to pose? I wouldn't.

MICHAEL: I begged and wept as only I know how. I sang:
"*Ah, non credea mirarti!*" from *Sonnambula,* into his
ear. No luck. So's I knocked over a nigger liquor store
and paid him three hundred dollars. I had the cards
made up. I love him!

[MARY *has finished her dance. She wakes herself as
though she were in a trance and exits. The* NUNS *rise
and take the chair offstage.*]

BOY: Aw, guys don' love other guys!

MICHAEL: You think about my offer?

BOY: [*Triumphant*] Gin!

BLACKOUT

Scene 3

BERNARD *enters wearing an expensive-looking mantilla
from the 1890s. A bus goes by, car horns are heard, a
thumping is heard, as though a ball were being bounced
against the wall of the house.*

*The scene is the row house in South Philadelphia. The
house is meant to be empty except for a desk and desk
chair down right and a small kitchen area stage left. In
the kitchen there can be a small old-fashioned stove and
sink. The desk is old and very battered but large.*

BERNARD *waves his mantilla about, carresses it, treats it as though it had a human shape. He clears his throat. A thump is heard.* BERNARD *goes off, clearing his throat, and returns with a large yellow envelope. He clears his throat. He removes a manuscript from the envelope, along with a letter. He reads the letter in a fury, then crumples it.*

BERNARD: Only editors have names like that!
  [*He puts the manuscript on the desk, clears his throat, rips the letter up, and pads into the kitchen. He passes what appears to be a bundle of old rags near the stove on the floor. He spits in the sink.*
  The bundle of rags starts up violently. This is EDITH. *She is in a rage. She is blind.*]
EDITH: That's right! Spit inna sink! You fat lousy creep! Go 'head, spit inna sink like a pig, and while you're at it, why don' you stick them hairy fingers down your throat and throw up, hanh? And then, why don' you drape that fat ass over the sink and shit in it? Fuckin' fruity Wasp nurd! Why the hell you gotta spit inna sink all the time? Ain't hygienic! All that education and never learned where to spit. Inna toilet! That's where, like a human being. That's the way we do it in civilization. [*Tries to find* BERNARD *by waving her arms about.*] Where are you, creep, where are you? [*Finds his leg and bites it.*] That'll teach you, you bum!
  [BERNARD *yanks his leg away, with a cry;* EDITH *collapses; he kicks her repeatedly.*]
BERNARD: And another thing, you blind odiferous legacy of a fetid past, there wasn't even a postcard from Arnold. He's forgotten his old Aunt Edith. [*Runs out calling*] Ellen Mac Jones, Here, Ellen, Ellen! Ellen Mac Jones Aberdeen!

BLACKOUT

Scene 4

A graveyard. The THREE NUNS *stand like a monument. One of them is holding the heavy crucifix upright.*

A small light goes on. MARY *has lit a small lantern. She has the sheet from the cot laid out on the ground near the nuns. She and* ARNOLD *are sitting on it.*

MARY: [*To* ARNOLD, *whispering*] Watch 'em now, watch 'em, they'll inch out. . . .

ARNOLD: Forget the worms, for Christ' sake!

MARY: Lookit, there's one. . . .

ARNOLD: We shouldn't have drunk so much of that stuff . . . you said it was magic. . . . [MARY *picks up a worm.*] Put that worm down!

MARY: You afraid of a worm?

ARNOLD: Look, Mary, I been thinkin' . . . will you put that down? Jesus Christ, this ain't the place. A graveyard, it gives me the willies. An' these worms . . .

MARY: Do you love me, Arnold? I ain't never felt loved. . . .

ARNOLD: I'm cold. I think I'm gettin' a chill. Hold me? [*She puts her arms around him.*]

ARNOLD: Hey, what is that all over your hands? Jesus Christ, it's worm blood!
[*She puts her hand on his crotch; he leaps up with a cry.*]

ARNOLD: Jesus Christ in heaven, you got my pants dirty. How's that gonna look when I get back to base? [*Takes a handkerchief out, spits in it, starts to work at his pants.*]

MARY: It's time for us to do it, Arnold. To make it hold. The moon is full. I buried your chest hair here, and my hair that I shaved. I buried them here the very instant the cock crowed. I marked the spot. And I'm ripe for love. So we have to do it here, tonight. . . .

ARNOLD: [*Still working at his pants*] It ain't comin' off. Shit, I run outa spit. Here, spit in this, would you? [*She spits in the handkerchief, he works.*
BERNARD *becomes visible in a dim spot, moving his lips but inaudible.*]

MARY: Forget that!

ARNOLD: Let's go!

MARY: Why?

ARNOLD: How'm I gonna screw you wit worm blood all over you, hanh?

MARY: But that's why I brought us here. We must do it

on the earth, crushin' worms as we roll. We must do it on the ground with the dead all around.

ARNOLD: [*Frightened*] Mary! What did I get into with you?

[BERNARD *becomes audible.* MARY *puts up her hand.*]

MARY: Listen!

BERNARD: [*Sadly*] Ellen! Ellen Mac Jones! Ellen Mac Jones! Ellen!

MARY: I hear somethin'.

ARNOLD: Mary!

MARY: It's sayin' this place is right for us. Won't be right anywhere's else. Won't be good. What has to come of it won't come right anywhere else.

ARNOLD: Please, Mary, for me, I'm cold. I'm scared. . . .

MARY: The earth is our mother. She will warm you. Lie back, feel our mother. [*She pushes him back gently.*] You are here, Arnold, your hair is here. Take your shirt off. [*Unbuttons his shirt.*] I'll turn this light off. [*Lantern off.*] Now, take off the rest, Arnold.

[*It is very dark save for the dim spot on* BERNARD *and another even dimmer on the* NUNS.]

MARY: Oh, Arnold, the worms, the worms. . . .

BERNARD: [*Making a crescendo*] Ellen Mac Jones! Ellen Mac Jones! Ellen Mac Jones! Ellen! Ellen!

BLACKOUT

Scene 5

The row house. BERNARD *sits at his desk, writing.* EDITH *is killing roaches in the kitchen.*

EDITH: Hey, fat Wasp creep? I thought I heard weepin' last night. Was it you? [*Kills a roach.*] Gotcha!

BERNARD: [*Reading what he has written*] "Is Reality a Dream of God's? Then we are fragments in the Divine Nightmare. Thus thought Mark as he drove alone in his yellow Volkswagen through the swamp."

EDITH: I asked you a question, fuck-face.

BERNARD: Please, Edith, I'm working.

EDITH: [*Imitating*] Please, Edith, I'm working. [*Kills roach.*] Gotcha!

BERNARD: Must you kill roaches while I work?

EDITH: Only thing I'm good for anymore. Even though I can't see 'em, I can hear 'em. I locate 'em through sensin' them. Lissin, I hear another one comin'. This one's a giant, *madonna me,* a giant. He's thinkin', aw, that Edith, she's blind, she ain't gonna notice me. But I hear his roach feet patterin' onna floor. Why, this *bevone!* He's made a bet he can get by old Edith, The Blindie—that's what them roaches call me, so like the braggart jerk-off he is, he's comin' closer a me. I hear you, roach bastid, and I'm gonna get you. Gotta pray first, this is the big match. [*Crosses herself.*] Oh, *Virgine,* you who was the biggest Mother of them all, help me for once, hanh? I got him located exact. Now: *uno, due, e tre* ... [*Lurches, misses.*]

BERNARD: You missed, Edith.

EDITH: I'll get him this time. [*Lurches, misses.*]

BERNARD: Missed again.

EDITH: Defeated! I massacre a hundred tomorrow. Then when he come back, I can brag a Arnold.

BERNARD: Really, Edith, you haven't heard from that moron in close on three years. He was gone when I arrived and in my time here you have had exactly three postcards from him, all in execrable taste and none of which you could even see.

EDITH: He don' know I'm blind. Happened after Benny left. Three years, hanh? Yeah, yeah, I guess Benny's been gone that long. Tell me, Bernard, did he say where he was goin'? Benny, I mean. Did he say anything about me? [*A silence.*] Yeah, how many times I asked you, hanh? But that wasn't like Benny. Sure he was a bum, he played around, wit my own sister if you believe them stories, but he always come back. And he loved Arnold. Hell, they was gonna put Arnold inna home and it was Benny's idea ... [*Kills roach.*] Gotcha! I think I got him that time, Bernard. Wasn't like Benny. But Arnold, he'll come back, he's gonna rescue me. And he's gonna beat you up, fat Bernard, he's gonna get you. I won't be alone and helpless forever. He's gonna save me! [*Crawls into the kitchen, curls up in her old rags near the stove.*] He'll be back. Then we'll see who's boss. Time to go sleep.

BERNARD: [*Reading his work*] "Is Reality a Dream of God's? . . ." I wonder, should Mark drive a Porsche? "Thus thought Mark as he drove his Porsche through the swamp. . . ." [*Considers, puts down pen.*] Arnold, indeed!

[*A knock at the door.* BERNARD *goes off to answer it. A pause.* BERNARD *comes in again, trailed unwillingly by the fourteen-year-old* BOY.]

BERNARD: Come in, my brave young man, come in. [*He peeks into the kitchen to see if* EDITH *is asleep.*] Tell me about those magazines.

BOY: Coulda told you at the door.

BERNARD: It's more comfortable in here.

BOY: [*Looking around.*] It is? Don' see no furniture.

BERNARD: Disappeared.

BOY: Oh. Bookie?

BERNARD: [*Giggles.*] Oh, my, no.

BOY: That crazy old lady, she lives here, don' she? She your daughter?

BERNARD: [*Mock horror.*] Good Heavens!

BOY: [*Fast, mumbled.*] All right, I'm sellin' these magazines to get me through high school, Bishop Neumann. From the commission on the order you sign I can not only put myself through but buy myself a few extras such as a growin' boy needs.

BERNARD: [*Flirtatious*] You certainly are a growing boy.

BOY: [*Cold*] Yeah. Well, for forty-nine fifty at a saving of twenty-five seventy-nine, you can have the following: *Vogue, Good Housekeeping, House and Garden*, and *Ladies' Home Journal*. Sign here.

BERNARD: Why don't you sit down?

BOY: Where?

BERNARD: On the floor. [*Sits.*]

BOY: Why would I wanna sit down wit you onna floor?

BERNARD: [*All charm and warmth. Pats floor. Boy sits, unwilling.*] We've met, you know. Oh, we haven't exchanged words. Perhaps we were close in a past life. Teacher and pupil, perhaps, father and son. It was recognition I felt when first I saw you, and since then I've been a witness to your spectacular ball playing at Johnson Field. I've sat there in the autumn sun and memorized you, you modern Achilles. And I know you've noticed me watching you like an ancient sage. And you see, my handsome young man, I know good ball playing. My days go back to Cy Cobb and the Great Ruth.

BOY: [*Hard, offhand*] You wanna suck my cock?
[*Street noises. A ball is thrown against the side of the house, making a thumping noise.* EDITH *stirs and wakes.*]

EDITH: [*Drowsy*] Damn kids, always thumpin', get the hell away. . . .

BOY: Well, what gives, you was leadin' up to that?

EDITH: Damn kids . . . ! [*Stretches.*]

BOY: I'll tell you what, you buy the magazines and I'll lay here for a bit. Don' guarantee nothin', though. . . .

BERNARD: [*Shocked, dignified*] You whore, you filthy whore, get out!

EDITH: [*Crawling into living room*] Tell them kids to go thump against their own walls. You hear me, Bernard, I says . . . Wait, there's somebody here, ain't there? Who is it? Arnold? You come back? Benny?

BOY: [*Sniggering*] Jesus Christ!

EDITH: Whoever you are, get the hell outa my house.

BOY: Aw, shut your mouth, you friggin' old lady.

EDITH: You fuckin' jerk-off, where's your respect?!

BOY: It's right here, you witch!
[*Kicks* EDITH. *She grabs his leg. They struggle.* EDITH *fights like a tigress.*]

EDITH: Hey, Bernard! Help me for Christ' sake! This bastid's trying' to kill me!

BERNARD: [*Runs into the kitchen, gets a knife, returns, brandishing it at the* BOY.] Get out!

BOY: Hey! You gonna come at me wit a knife? You fat fuckin' corpse? You gonna come at me? Well, come on, old man, come on, faggot. [*Starts dodging and teasing* BERNARD.] It's like runnin' them bases, like who—Cy Cobb?

EDITH: Bernard! You slit that mother's throat.

BOY: [*Making a game of dodging* BERNARD] Hey, hey, hey! I'm the Great Ruth! Come on, faggot, come on, old man!
[BERNARD *rushes the* BOY, *knocks into him, and knocks him off balance. The* BOY *grabs him for support;* EDITH

*finds them and trips the boy. He falls. She starts to
beat him ferociously.* BERNARD, *out of breath, drops
the knife. The* BOY, *frightened and hurt, gets away
from* EDITH *and runs out, yelling.*]

BOY: [*Running out.*] Hey, they're tryin' to kill me!

BERNARD: [*Stares after the* BOY, *gasping for breath. Suddenly he starts to cry.*] Gone . . .

EDITH: Hanh? Bernard? I didn't hear you. You breathin'
awful heavy, Bernard. Why do you do it, hanh? You're
an old man, why you gotta run out afta kids for, hanh?
An' if you gotta screw around, pick up somebody of
age, for Christ' sake! [*A pause.*] Hey, you cryin', Bernard? Yeah, what you gonna do. You cry and you cry. . . .
Don' cry, Bernard, don' mean so much. Sex! Who cares!
Them kids, they're mean by nature and we old people,
well, we got nothin' for them, can't expect nothin' back
from them. . . .

BERNARD: Oh, Edith, what am I going to do?

EDITH: You could start by acting your age.

BERNARD: And what is acting my age? Dying? [*Exits.*]

EDITH: *Povero vecchio, non acetta nulla.* [*A sudden loud
pounding at the street door.*] They come to lynch you,
Bernard, better make a act of contrition. [*More pounding.*] God damn that kid. All right, I'm comin'. [*Crawls
to street exit, admits* BUCKY *and* SCODGE *with the* BOY.]
Who is it?

BUCKY: [*Looking around, shocked*] Hi ya, Edith, how you
been?

EDITH: Who's 'at? 'At you, Bucky? I recognize you voice.

BUCKY: Yeah, Edith. Scodge is here, too.

EDITH: Hi ya, Scodge.

SCODGE: [*Also shocked*] Hi ya, Edith.

[*A pause. The* BOY *pulls at* SCODGE, *who hits him.*]

EDITH: Ain't seen you guys in years, not since Benny . . .

BUCKY: Yeah, Edith . . .

EDITH: And Arnold . . .

SCODGE: Yeah, yeah, Edith . . .

EDITH: Youse never came around no more afta they . . .

SCODGE: Well, we had it hard gettin' outa the army . . .

BUCKY: Draft board wouldn't take no for an answer. Now,
Arnold . . .

SCODGE: He wanted a go. . . .

EDITH: Well, sit down and talk.

BUCKY: Well, Edith, to tell you the truth, that is, I don' see nothin' to ... well, you know ...

SCODGE: To sit down on.

BUCKY: Yeah, Edith, like Scodge here says, I don' see nothin' ...

SCODGE: To sit down on.

BUCKY: Yeah.

EDITH: [*Pretending to be hurt deeply*] You guys, you guys! Why 'ja hafta go an' say somethin' like that, hanh? Can't you see I'm blind? I can't tell if you sit or not. So's what youse shoulda said was: Sure, Edith, thanks. And then you stands right where you is. That way you don' hurt a poor old blind lady's feelin's. Oh, you guys!

BUCKY: [*Taken aback*] Jeeze, Edith, I didn't think of it that way....

EDITH: [*Laying it on*] First you guys come here and hurt me by bringin' back the good old days, them days when ... Benny ... [*Fakes a sob.*] Then you hurt me by commentin' on the barrenness of my house.... Shit, guys! [*Pretends to break down sobbing.*]

BUCKY: Jeez, Edith, I'm sorry. Didn't mean nothin' by it. Didn't think of it that way. You, Scodge?

SCODGE: Tell you the truth, Bucky, I didn't think of it that way.

BUCKY: Well, Edith, we'll sit right here onna the floor.

SCODGE: That's a good idea, Bucky, we'll sit right here, onna the floor.

BOY: [*Not taken in by* EDITH.] I thought you guys—

SCODGE: Shut up, kid, and respect you elders.
     [BUCKY *sits;* SCODGE *sits and forces the* BOY *to sit.*]

BUCKY: Hey, what is this shit? Sorry, Edith, but there's somethin' ...

SCODGE: Sticky ...

BUCKY: Yeah, somethin' sticky and well ... smelly, onna floor.

EDITH: Dried dog food.

BUCKY: Oh, that explains it, Scodge. Dried dog food.

SCODGE: Yeah, Bucky, that's what I thought it was. Dried dog food.
     [*An uncomfortable pause. The* BOY *squirms.*]

BUCKY: What's dried dog food doin' onna the floor, if I can ask, Edith?

EDITH: Bernard leaves it out for his dead dog.

SCODGE: Well, Edith, now that you mention this . . . this . . .

BUCKY: Bernard . . .

BOY: Wanted a blow me, then tried to kill me wit a knife!

SCODGE: [*Raises a hand, threatening.*] Shut you mouth, kid, we'll take care of this.

EDITH: What about Bernard?

SCODGE: Well, Edith, you know this is a good, clean neighborhood. Catholic. Good Catholic.

BUCKY: No Irish.

SCODGE: Then, all of a sudden, this old guy is here. Right afta Arnie goes away. Never seen him before, ain't related to youse. Then, before we know it, Benny's gone. This old guy ain't Italian, never seen him in church. . . .

BUCKY: We was onna corner, shootin' the breeze, when this kid come outa you house, yellin'. . . .

EDITH: You believe that kid?

BOY: You bitch—

SCODGE: [*Raises a hand.*] Shut you mouth, you!

EDITH: Bernard is a seventy-year-old man. He ain't got it up for years.

BOY: Don' make no difference, queers do other things.

EDITH: Like what, little boy?

BOY: Well, other things. . . .

EDITH: How do you know, you queer?

BOY: Hey, who you shittin'!

EDITH: You out for money, is that it, hanh? I heard, I heard you little bum. That poor old man, he's lonely, he's got nothin' inna whole world and this little creep comes a the door. Hey, mista, I hear him say, I'll let you blow me for a quarter.

BUCKY: Nah, in the neighborhood?

SCODGE: That's for uptown.

EDITH: I heard him say it!

BOY: She's lyin'! [SCODGE *hits him.*] Owww!

EDITH: Well, naturally, Bernard is shocked. Remember, you guys, he was a college professor, he ain't used to reality. He can't believe his seventy-year-old ears. When he says no, this kid starts to holler. Then he runs inna house, runs over to me and starts to kick me. Bernard goes for the knife, then this kid runs out inna street!

BUCKY: I thought there was somethin' fishy in this story.

SCODGE: Yeah, a seventy-year-old Irishman . . .

BUCKY: They can't get it up when they're forty!

SCODGE: All them potatoes.

BOY: But she's lyin'!

EDITH: And ain't he kinda old, this kid, hanh? Ain't he fourteen or so? He can't take care of himself around a seventy-year-old man and a blind old lady?

SCODGE: Well, Edith, you gotta point.

BUCKY: Come on, Scodge. [*Slaps* BOY.] That's for you, shittin' us.

BOY: Hey, but lissin' . . .

SCODGE: Show some respect! [*Hits* BOY.] Sorry to bother you, Edith.

EDITH: Aw, it was a pleasure seein' you guys again, I mean, it woulda been a pleasure seein' youse if I could see. . . .

BUCKY: Let's go. See ya, Edith.

[SCODGE, BOY, *and* BUCKY *leave.*]

EDITH: Friggin' good-for-nothin' bums! Who the hell are you to come around here—to do what? [*Crawls toward kitchen.*] Jeez, Bernard, you're a bundle. Jeez! [*Kills a roach.*] Gotcha! The things a person's gotta put up wit in their own house. [*Curls up in quilt near the stove.*] Time to go bye-bye. Grow-up, Bernard! Sleepy, hope Arnold comes soon. *Mio piccolo,* my Arnie. I'm ready for him.

[BERNARD *sweeps out onto the stage. He is wearing an elaborate ballgown from the 1890s. It is a full gown with a long train.* BERNARD *acts as though he were making an entrance at a grand ball. He uses a large fan coquettishly and hums a slow waltz. A bus goes by. Car horns are heard.* BERNARD *waltzes about and waves at other guests.*

A *spot on* MARY. *She is in a hospital bed attended by the* THREE NUNS. *They are faceless.* MARY *is in labor with* ARNOLD's *child. She is in great pain.*]

MARY: How much longer, sister? [*Silence.*] Why don't you never talk? How much longer? Why ain't Arnold here? Have you really called him? Surely it is my time. This pain has gone on and on. . . .

FIRST NUN: Remember, this is the wages of sin!

SECOND NUN: Next time the flesh calls, remember this agony.

[MARY *screams.*]

BERNARD: [*As though speaking to someone at the ball*] Why, thank you, kind sir. Yes, it is a lovely gown, isn't it? I had it made specially, at Maude's on Fifth Avenue. Oh, you fresh thing! I'd love to. [*Whirls about as though dancing with an uninhibited partner.*]

MARY: Why do they have to be so long? Why does bein' born mean so much pain? Baby? Baby? Are you feelin' it too? Your father ain't been around. That bastard! [*Gasps.*] I'm sorry, baby, I didn't mean to curse your daddy. I'll be good. Just don't twist in me so much.

BERNARD: [*Using his fan as though slapping someone's wrist*] Fresh! Hands to yourself. I'll thank you, sir, to respect me as you ought. I am a young woman worthy of your deference. My, but you do dance well. [*Whirls about again.*]

MARY: Baby, I promise to try and love you but please, please don't stab me like you have a knife. . . . [*Screams.*] God damn you, you monster child!

THIRD NUN: [*Slaps her.*] Cursing is God's business.

MARY: Why does God use women this way?

BERNARD: [*Spreading his fan*] If you wish, you may kiss me behind my fan. [*Hides his face, giggles.*]

MARY: Why ain't your daddy here, baby?

BERNARD: [*Deep curtsy.*] Why, thank you, kind sir.

MARY: [*Screams in agony.*]

BLACKOUT

Scene 6

The BOY *enters walking. Suddenly* MICHAEL DE FELICE *appears, dressed up like an Indian maiden. He jumps on the* BOY *and wrestles him to the ground.*

BOY: Hey, Michael, what the hell!

MICHAEL: [*Stuffs a gag in his mouth and ties him up.*

Very swishy and camping wildly] Oh, John, John Standish, come to your Pocahontas! She's all wet for you and the stream is so far and cold on my Indian Maiden skin!

[MICHAEL *circles the* BOY, *who is quite frightened. Caresses him, circles him again, and whips out an ax. The* BOY *screams in terror through his gag.* MICHAEL, *without warning, jumps into a vaudeville routine, using the ax as part of his dance. He directs his dance to the* BOY.]

MICHAEL: [*Singing and dancing*]
  I wanna be loved by you
  And nobody else will do
  Boo boo dee oop!

[MICHAEL *sings under the following.*

MARY *enters into a spot on the other side of the stage. Her face is set, her manner hostile.* ARNOLD *follows, despondent.*]

ARNOLD: Mary, come on, don' run away. Don' carry on like that, hanh? Okay, tell me I'm a worthless bum, 'cause I am. I shoulda been there, come on, hit me, right here, on the jaw. Oh, please, I'm sorry, it was all my fault. I was guilty but forgive me. . . .

MARY: It's done now.

ARNOLD: No, it ain't. Nothin's done. It's just startin'. We made that baby together. I got inna bed wit you and we made that baby. . . .

MARY Was the graveyard.

ARNOLD: Look, I got drunk, and them nuns, they told me they don' want the father around. Ain't hygienic or somethin'. . . .

MARY: It's dead. All that pain for nothin' and you nowhere to be found. It's like I'm alivin' under some curse. I did all that I could, found the right spot, did the dance, buried your hair and my hair, and it was all for nothin'. And I thought you big-city boys, after all, them city Jezebels, my daddy talks like he knows. . . .

ARNOLD: Your daddy don' know nothin'. . . .

MARY: I left my daddy for you, he'd never take me back. I bore your child. Had to get married at the last minute like two criminals and it was all for nothin'. Oh, you were so handsome in your uniform and you were lost and I felt like you were some prince, like you might be

the one to magic me away. And where did you magic
me? Into a big, cold, white room where they strapped
me up like some animal and where they dug out from
in me a dead thing. And you did it to me!

ARNOLD: [*Very upset*] I'm sorry, I'm sorry, it's so ugly,
stop it. I'll make it up to you!

MARY: I can't stay here, I have to run away!

ARNOLD: Come with me. I'm gonna be discharged soon.
Come with me.

MARY: Where? Is there a hell beyond hell?

ARNOLD: To South Philly. My Aunt Edith's there. She'll
love you, she's good people and, after all, you are my
wife, you're family now. There you can read. We have
huge libraries, you won't have to steal the books. And
I'll go to work—you can go to school. It was my fault,
let me make it up to you, come back wit me. . . .

MARY: One more trap!

ARNOLD: Trap? What trap? Oh, the city's a beauty.
There's so much to do. People ain't stupid, ain't backward like they is here. People are kind. You see, there
are these men on the corners, you know, sellin' pret-
zels, it's like, I don' know, I can't explain it. . . .

MARY: Do you know what I need, Arnold?

ARNOLD: Some love, like me, we're lonely kids. . . .

MARY: Look at what my life has been. It ain't easy for me,
born like I was. I wanted to know, and to be free.
Sounds real simple, real natural. For a boy, a city boy,
it is. But for me it was impossible. Every part of me
was chained, held fast by steel and iron. When I first
saw that library, why I almost died. There was all these
people, they had dresses and suits, they was readin',
and oh, it was so quiet! And everywhere, books, like
stars in the night sky. Well, you can't reach the real
stars, they just twinkle and twinkle and come mornin'
they're gone. But books, why, they're always there, all
it took was some kind of magic that everybody seemed
to know. I wanted it, I wanted to be free of this big
ditch I'm stuck in. But learnin' that magic takes teachers, real teachers, not them prissy old maids. Then, I
met you and thought you might could rescue me
and . . .

ARNOLD: Come wit me, then. You'll find a teacher, I'm
sure. We'll start all over.

MARY: Well . . .

ARNOLD: I owe it to you, let me make it up to you.

MARY: [*After a hesitation, takes his hand.*] All right, Arnold.

[*They walk off hand in hand.*

MICHAEL *finishes his routine with a flourish. He removes the* BOY's *gag and tries to kiss him. The* BOY *turns his face away.*]

BOY: God damn you, I'm too fuckin' old for cowboys and Indians!

[MICHAEL *laughs. The* THREE NUNS *cross the back of the stage with a large baby doll impaled on their crucifix.*]

BLACKOUT

Scene 7

The row house. BERNARD *enters with a large plate of dog food. He puts it up center on the floor, then exits.*

BERNARD: [*Going off, whispering*] Ellen! Ellen Mac Jones! Ellen Mac Jones Aberdeen! Here, Ellen!

[EDITH *crawls on, stopping occasionally to kill roaches.*]

EDITH: Gotcha! Eighteenth today. Almost a record. Smell somethin' weird. Hey, Bernard! You didn't shit inna middle of the floor, did you? Bernard? Well, maybe the bastid went out. He don' talk a me as much as he useda. *Aspett'*—there's this big roach. I sense him. [*She is near the plate of dog food.*] He's enormous. He's the cock-of-the-walk roach. An' he's just sittin' there waitin'. He's sayin': She won't get me, this old, blind lady. Well, I'm gonna get you, roach bastid. Gotta pray first, this is the big match. Holy Virgin, help me massacre this roach and I'll hold my breath for a count of sixty tomorrow. Sometimes I think that Holy Virgin got shit in her ears. I pray and pray and does somethin' good happen? Nah! Not once in fifty years. Hanh? This roach is makin' fun of me. He's sayin I don' know my ass from a rancid pimple. Well, it so happens, roach

bastid, I do know my ass from a rancid pimple. Don'
think there's much difference sometimes.... Oh, he's
laughin'. That Edith, she's funny. She's gotta sense of
humor. Blind, filthy, lonely, ugly, and horny and what
does she do? She makes jokes! Well, just for sayin' that,
I'm gonna smash you. 'Cause it ain't no joke. I got
nothin' and I know it and jokin' don' drown out no
pain! *Uno ... due ... e tre ... [Thinking it is a roach,
she heaves herself into the dog food. She screams.]* Jesus, Mary, and Joseph! I got shit on me. That no-good
bastid shit inna middle of the floor....

[ARNOLD *comes in in a new suit and big smile. He
stops, shocked at the state of the house.* EDITH *thinks
he is* BERNARD.]

EDITH: That you, Bernard? God damn you! *[Hurls herself
on* ARNOLD. *He leaps away.]*

ARNOLD: Get off me!

EDITH: Who are you and how'd you get in?

ARNOLD: You ruined my suit and it's fuckin' new.

EDITH: Answer me, who the hell are you?

ARNOLD: *[Working at his suit]* It's me, Arnold. Whatsa
matter, you blind?

EDITH: Arnold?

ARNOLD: *[Working at his suit]* Shit! Sixty-four bucks
down the drain. *[Realizes.]* Oh, Christ, you are blind!

EDITH: Arnold? *Bello, bello,* is that really you? *[Starts to
cry.]* I waited and waited so long and thought you
wasn't comin' back. You ain't pretendin' a me? Please
don' pretend a me. I'm blind, you see, an'—you're here
at last! Arnold! Look, look, I'm cryin'. Didn't know I
could do that no more....

ARNOLD: What happened, hanh? Where is everything?
Ain't there no furniture no more? Where's Uncle
Benny ... ?

EDITH: ... Kiss your old aunt....

[BERNARD *enters with a large piece of paper.*]

ARNOLD: Who are you?

BERNARD: *[Holds paper out.]* Your landlord. [ARNOLD
stares, shocked.] I realize that Italian ghetto schools are
ineptly run, usually by sexually frustrated primitives
who style themselves "sisters"; but I thought they
taught two things with minimal efficiency. One: to understand English; and two, to read it accurately, how-

ever slowly. You appear to contradict that impression. Read the lease, boy! I own this house, and everything in it, including your aunt. She is my vassal.

ARNOLD: [*To* EDITH, *not comprehending*] Aunt, what the hell . . . ?

EDITH: Let me feel you face, hanh, Arnold? They say that works when you blind and I ain't seen you in three years. Squat down.

ARNOLD: But what the hell is this? There ain't nothin' here and Uncle Benny . . .

EDITH: Squat down, you bastid. [*He does. She feels his face.*] Big nose. I wonder if it's the biggest thing you got, hanh? Feel them cheeks, smooth. He's got all his sufferin' before him. [*She shoves a finger in his eye. He falls back, howling. She crawls to him and whispers.*] Arnie, you mine, you mine. I'm inna this trap and you gotta get me out. You gotta save me. I did that to show you it ain't gonna be easy. . . .

BUCKY: [*Off*] Hey! Getta load of that package on Edith's stoop.

SCODGE: [*Off*] What you doin', honey?

ARNOLD [*to* EDITH] I ain't alone. I mean, I'm . . . Oh, shit. I guess I better . . . Oh, Christ . . . [*Goes out.*]

EDITH: Hey, Bernard, you meet my nephew?

BUCKY and SCODGE: [*Off, crying out*] Hey! Hey! It's Arnie Lungs! He's back, he's back!

MICHAEL: [*Farther off, shrieks.*] What's that I hear? Arnie's back?

BERNARD: He's popular.

[ARNOLD *enters with* MARY. *She is exhausted. She is shocked by the state of the house.* ARNOLD *is frightened.*]

ARNOLD: Here goes. Aunt . . . [*Cannot continue.*]

EDITH: What is it?

BERNARD: [*After a pause*] There is a young lady on your threshold looking wide-eyed and exhausted. Were I to reduce this to cliché, which is all you are capable of understanding, I would say the young lady had traveled awhile without sleep and was a wife.

ARNOLD: Oh, I gotta headache. You got any aspirin, Aunt Edith? I'll go look and see. Jeez, I oughtta change. Aunt Edith, this is my wife, Mary, and oh, the bags is outside. I'll get 'em. . . .

[ARNOLD *runs out.* MARY *stares about her.* BERNARD *peers at* MARY. EDITH *is working to grasp the situation.*]

BUCKY: [*Off*] Hey, Arnie Lungs, let's get drunk!

ARNOLD: [*Off*] Ain't a bad idea, Buck. Say, you got fat.

BUCKY: [*Off*] I don't got a cute chippy like that to work it off.

MICHAEL: [*Off but closer*] Where is my Arnie?

ARNOLD: [*Enters with the suitcases.*] I'll drop the suitcases here. Where'd you say the aspirin was? [*Goes into kitchen and looks around.*]

EDITH: You married, hanh?

ARNOLD: I met Mary near the base.

EDITH: She was smart, got pregnant, then forced you to marry her.

MARY: That ain't true at all.

EDITH: Holy Jesus in heaven, it's a hilly-billy. A fuckin' farm girl! Jesus Christ, he married a turd of cow dung!

ARNOLD: Now, Aunt, she's family. [*Pointing to his stained suit, to* MARY] Had a accident, Mary, better change. [*Opens a suitcase.*] My clothes in this one? Shit! Why'd you have to put my clothes onna bottom? All these friggin' books! [*Throws some books on the floor.* BERNARD *notices them with interest.*] She's ya niece, Aunt, you'll learn to love her. [*Rifles suitcase, sets about changing.*]

EDITH: She's my niece, I'll learn to love her. You hear that, Bernard? You hear what my nephew and god son says the first thing afta leaving me alone for three years, you hear that? You'll learn to love her. That Edith always was a patsy. Well, come on niece, I'm gonna learn to love you. Come on, little girlie, come on little niecie, here niecie, niecie, niecie. . .

ARNOLD: [*To* MARY] Go on for Christ' sake!

EDITH: Here, niecie, niecie, niecie. . . .

MARY: I hear you and I'm comin'.

EDITH [*Imitating*] I hear you and I'm comin'. Isn't she adorable? Isn't this farm girl hilly-billy from the pig pen and the outhouse all sweet and cuddly?

ARNOLD: [*Changing*] Where the fuck's my checker tie? Oh, I found it.

EDITH: [MARY *is close to her.*] This you leg, little hilly-billy? [*Feels* MARY's *leg.*] Feels nice, this leg. I bet you're real pretty. I was never pretty, never had a nice leg. Mine was fat and thick, you could hold the meat away from the bone. Can't do that wit yours. Bernard, is she pretty?

BERNARD: Beautiful. . . .

ARNOLD: [*Still dressing*] Oh, my God, is Uncle Benny dead?

BERNARD: Ran off with good reason.

EDITH: I bet this hilly-billy's got soft white skin and pretty boobies.

BERNARD: Exactly, Edith.

EDITH: Ahhh! *Maledetta!*

[*Bites* MARY's *leg.* MARY *screams and tries to get away, but* EDITH *hangs on.* ARNOLD, *half-dressed, hovers on the periphery of the fight unsure how to stop it.* BER-NARD *is amused.*]

MARGE: [*Off*] Hey, that was a scream in there!

BUCKY: [*Off*] You all right in there? [*Bangs on door.*]

MARY: [*Kicks* EDITH, *who screams.*] You animal, I'll tear your head off!

ARNOLD: Yo, Mary, show some respect!

[*Gets pushed out of the fight, the banging on the door continues,* ARNOLD *after hesitating a moment runs out and admits* SCODGE, MARGE, *and* BUCKY.]

EDITH: [*Kicking by* MARY] I'm hurt, I'm hurt!

MARY: It's just beginnin' for you, you ugly bitch, I'll kill you.

[*Pummels* EDITH *ferociously.* EDITH *defends herself, screaming.* BUCKY *and* SCODGE *hang back, admiring* MARY. MARGE *plunges in, trying to separate the two.*]

MARGE: Come on, you two.

[EDITH *is howling but still fighting.* MARGE *looks to* BUCKY *and* SCODGE.]

MARGE: Help me get them apart.

BUCKY: You do it, Marge, we're printers, we need our hands for work.

MARGE: Edith, for God's sake!

[*Pulls* EDITH *aside.* MARY *is panting.* MICHAEL *runs in in full but hurriedly assembled drag. The* BOY *is with him.*]

MICHAEL: Where is this Arnie that's back? Where? [*Sees him.*] Arnie Sweets! [*Throws his arms around* ARNOLD *and kisses him long and passionately.*]

EDITH: She hurt me, she hurt me. . . .

MARY: You're lucky I didn't kill you!

MARGE: [*To* MARY] That's enough, show some respect.

BUCKY: [*To* SCODGE, *about* MARY] Look at her, Scodge.

SCODGE: I'm lookin', Buck!

[ARNOLD *struggles in* MICHAEL's *grasp, gets away, and is confronted by* MARY *in a rage.*]

MARY: And you're a man? To bring me to this? Two days on the train and you starin' off? This is the mudhole you dragged me into? There's nothin' here, nothin'! After two days and no sleep there's nothin'! Barren, barren, barren!

MICHAEL: Sing it, baby! [*Mocks her in operatic falsetto.*]

MARY: I'm lost!

MICHAEL: Well, honey, these men'll do it every time!

EDITH: She hurt me, she hurt me.

MARGE: [*Looking her over*] You don't look hurt, nothin's broken. . . .

[BERNARD *has been staring at the* BOY. MICHAEL *approaches.*]

MICHAEL: [*To* BERNARD] Ten fifty.

BERNARD: Seven even.

MICHAEL: In advance. [BERNARD *pays.* MICHAEL *turns to the* BOY.] Go on up wit him and relax. I'll give you half and it's just startin'.

[BOY *exits with* BERNARD. ARNOLD *has finished dressing.* MARY *is crying.*]

EDITH: I useda cook him tripe and spareribs and *baccala, mio piccolo,* and pigs' feet in the gravy, that was his favorite. And I have to live and see him come home wit a cowgirl. . . .

MARGE: All right, Edith, relax.

MARY: [*To* ARNOLD] Stop racin' around.

ARNOLD: Gotta finish gettin' ready. Goin' out.

MARY: No you ain't. You ain't gonna leave me. [*Grabs him.*]

MICHAEL: Ding! The Friday Night Fight is on the air.

MARGE: Jesus, not another one! Somebody better call the cops.

[MARY *and* ARNOLD *tussle.* SCODGE *and* BUCKY, *anxious to get their hands on* MARY, *try to pull them apart.*]

SCODGE: She's strong.

MARY: [*Kicks him.*] Don't you touch me.

MARGE: [*Thrusting herself in*] Here! Get over here and quiet down. They're men, honey, and if you don' wan' that pretty face smashed up, give in. [MARY *tries to get away from her,* MARGE *grabs her.*] Stay over here, I says, and relax. [*Gets her across the room.*] Shit! You think this is the worst that can happen or you're the first it happened to?

ARNOLD: Need a mirror. Got a compact, Marge?

MICHAEL: Take mine.

[*Pulls compact out of his purse.* ARNOLD *takes it, brushes his hair.* MICHAEL *feels his muscles.*]

BUCKY: [*Approaching* MARY] Don' you mind Arnie Lungs, he's a regular guy.

[MARY *is about to hit* BUCKY, MARGE *grabs her hand.*]

MARGE: Hold it!

EDITH: [*Has crawled into the kitchen.*] Gotta sleep, sleep. . . .

SCODGE: Boy, is this place a mess.

ARNOLD: Okay, I'm ready, let's get loaded.

BUCKY: Bring your wife, Arn.

MICHAEL: He can't. [*Takes* ARNOLD'*s arm.*] She's a wife, what he needs is a woman.

MARGE: Maybe Michael's gotta point. [*To* MARY] Look, girlie, you stay here, put things away, clean up, wash your face, get some sleep, you been cryin' a lot, take some aspirin. That way, there won't be no trouble. It's better that way.

ARNOLD: [*Not looking at* MARY] Yeah, Mar', you get some sleep. Pick this stuff up, make up wit Aunt Edith, she's family, you know. . . .

MICHAEL: I got some ups.

BUCKY: Let's pick up a pizza. . . .

[*They go off.* MARY *sinks down near the desk, sobbing.*]

EDITH: [*In the kitchen, near the stove.*] Benny? Benny? Shut up, Edith, ain't no Benny. Didn't make no difference when there was a Benny. Oh, *Virgine*, make me die, make me die, this instant; or send me back to when the pain wasn't so big and I could manage it. Shut up, Edith, they'll think you're a crazy, blind, old lady. Chilly. Sleep. Everything ends. I hoped so much. Arnie . . . And now I lost him, I know, I know I lost him. Got nobody. . . . Arnie, *piccolo mio, bambino mio* . . . [*Cries quietly, tries to sleep.*]

[*The* BOY *comes out, peers at* MARY *curiously, then runs out. The room is a shambles. There are books, papers, clothes all over the floor. The suitcases are open. After a moment,* BERNARD *enters. Slowly he picks up the books. He avoids* MARY's *glance. He looks through some of the books, puts them on the desk.*]

BERNARD: Would you like to hear a joke? A man of seventy meets a young woman of twenty on the subway. She invites him to have sexual congress with her. He does. A week later and the old man is in agony and there is a terrible swelling. After a week there is no end to the pain. His doctor says wait a week and see if it goes down and the pain ends. It gets worse. He sees the doctor again. Have you had sex recently? asks the doctor. Why yes, answers the man, three weeks ago. Well, don't get excited, says the doctor, and it may take a week or two, but you are about to come.

[*He looks at* MARY *and laughs. She is puzzled by the joke but smiles politely.* BERNARD *continues picking up the books.*]

BERNARD: I'm sorry, I couldn't help myself. It's disgusting, isn't it? Not just the joke, everything. That thing in there is named Edith. I am Bernard. I gather your name is Mary. How do you do. I take it these books are yours? Jung, Karen Horney, Freud. Why do you read them?

MARY: I don't mean no harm.

BERNARD: Please! I don't mean *any* harm. Repeat, please.

MARY: I don' mean *any* harm.

BERNARD: Why are you afraid? It's wonderful that you read. A girl from your class; I'd say it was remarkable.

MARY: Maybe you are a teacher.

BERNARD: Why yes, for many years I was.

MARY: [*Stands up, very shy.*] I guess I better . . .

BERNARD: I'll help you. . . .

[*Together they pick up the suitcases and clothes.*]

BERNARD: You know, I could put you out. This house is mine now. Do you keep a diary?

MARY: Why no.

BERNARD: I'll teach you. For I've decided, quite on the spur of the moment, you'll be happy to know, to take you in hand. Why are you still crying—gratitude . . .

MARY: He hasn't wanted to touch me in weeks. . . .

BERNARD: I shouldn't want to be touched by him. These
   Wops are an unclean crew, even if the young ones are,
   well, you know what they are. . . .

MARY: Oh, I bet you don't understand about husbands
   and wives.

BERNARD: Don't I indeed? But see here, you've had a
   bad liaison with one man, whom in your southern aris-
   tocratic naïveté you thought attractive because he was
   greasy and had a lot of hair.

MARY: Arnold don't have a lot of hair.

BERNARD: Then he is a mutant and you're lucky to be rid
   of him. How old are you?

MARY: Why, nineteen.

BERNARD: And beautiful. When I was nineteen I was fat
   and had pimples everywhere—do you hear? Everywhere! I was bepimpled in the land of the bronzed
   complexion, smelly in the land of the deodorant, overweight in the country that invented the crash diet, and
   clumsy in the land of the athletic supporter. And look
   at me now I am seventy! Seventy! I am a failure by
   every standard. Look at how I am living. I write, but
   no one wants what I write. What hope is left me?

MARY: [*Earnestly*] Why there is always . . .

BERNARD: It was rhetorical, my dear.

MARY: Rhe—what?

BERNARD: [*Grandly*] You're right, there is no hope!
   [MARY *starts to interrupt.*]

BERNARD: Pray don't interrupt the flow of my narrative.
   I was dreadfully alone, dreadfully. But I wasn't without
   optimism of a sort. So I thought: In the years to come,
   Bernard . . . and didn't fill in the blank, just let it settle
   around me like a hot bath. What came? More misery!
   I have been cursed with a long life. My funds ran out,
   friends died, and to be frank, I never had many, it was
   the state nursing home or this! And thus it happens I
   am a seventy-year-old wreck and worse, that I have
   spent my life in bondage. I was never loved. I always
   paid for what I got, either through the nose, or more
   subtly. I was robbed countless times, I was violated
   and disappointed, and all for boys! For rotten, stupid,
   worthless automatons with penises. But I am strong. I
   have stopped identifying with Virginia Woolf. I no
   longer look longingly toward fast-flowing streams, and

I am going to educate you. Latin tomorrow and our first trip to the library. The museum next, soon German. The works of Shakespeare—I am an expert on Shakespeare, my book—nevermind!

MARY: Hold off a minute! I just got here, he ran off and I don't—

BERNARD: I have so many secrets to impart. Do you like pretty dresses? Do the Gay Nineties appeal to you? I'll turn this pathetic hovel into a finishing school! Miss Bernard's! You'll learn Romantic poetry, Leopardi for the truth, Rilke for pretty affectation.

MARY: But so much has happened. You don't understand, you don't know the half of it. I'm alone here, a stranger, I don't know if I can do it.

BERNARD: Nonsense! You must say one hundred times a day: I shall survive!

MARY: [*Tentative, with heavy accent*] I shall survive!

BERNARD: No, no no! Not in that accent. Try to say it like me. [*Booms, oratorically.*] I shall survive!

MARY: [*Booms in imitation.*] I shall survive!

BERNARD: Closer, you have a good ear.

MARY: I like singin'.

BERNARD: Now, repeat after me: I . . .

MARY: [*Repeating*] I . . .

BERNARD: Good. Shall . . .

MARY: Shall . . .

BERNARD: Survive!

MARY: Survive!

BERNARD: [*Grandly*] I shall survive!

MARY: [*Grandly*] I shall survive!

[BERNARD *prances about, strikes a pose and booms: I shall survive.* MARY *strikes the same pose and booms: I shall survive. The poses become more grandiose, their voices louder, both are nearly yelling. At one point,* MARY *giggles and falls into* BERNARD's *arms. He embraces her. Both become conscious of this, react embarrassed, and are silent for a moment. Suddenly* MARY *booms: I shall survive.* BERNARD *takes it up and they march around the room yelling it again.*

EDITH *has been awakened by the noise. At first she is frightened, then pulls herself together and crawls into the living room.*]

EDITH: Hey! What the hell is this, hanh? You wanna scare

me to death makin' all that noise? Two grown-up people screamin' like niggers prancin' naked inna desert?

BERNARD: Jungle, you cripple, and I shall survive!

EDITH: Youse is both crazy. Well, go on, make some more
noise!

BERNARD: Mary and I are survivors both!

MARY: We shall survive!

EDITH: All right! [*Screams.*] Ellen Mac Jones! Here, Ellen! Ellen Mac Jones Aberdeen!
[*The thumping against the side of the house is heard,
car horns are heard.*]

MARY: I shall survive!

BERNARD: I shall survive!

EDITH: Ellen Mac Jones! Ellen Mac Jones Aberdeen!
[*This builds to an immense noise.*]

BLACKOUT

ACT II

Scene 1

In a dimly lit area the THREE NUNS *appear. They have a paper cutter and a box of cheap dolls. They decapitate the dolls in the paper cutter as the lights build.*

NUNS: [*In chorus*] Amo, amas, amat! [*A doll is decapitated. One nun sprinkles ketchup over the doll as though it were holy water.*] Amo, amas, amat! [*As above.*]
[*Lights build in the row house. A small area to one side is set apart to serve as a street.*
The house looks cleaner, a chair has been added near the desk. A kitchen table has been added in the kitchen.
BERNARD *is in the kitchen finishing breakfast.* EDITH *is eating out of a plate set on the floor.*
A month has passed since MARY's *arrival.*]

BERNARD: [*Calling*] Mary! Come! Come!

EDITH: He calls her like she was his dog. Well, she is a bitch. Oughtta be put asleep!

BERNARD: Be quiet, Edith! Mary!

EDITH: She likes to sleep, she likes to sleep alone. That's why he ain't come back. This is his home, but he don' wanna share it wit her.
[*The* NUNS *hover on the periphery of the scene, well to the back. Eventually they wait in the street area.*]

EDITH: This bacon's too well done. I like it soggy. And you put too much black pepper in the eggs. When you lie on the floor alla time like me, black pepper sets you to sneezin', and that's no picnic!

BERNARD: Mary!

MARY: [*Off*] I'm comin'.
[BERNARD *goes to his desk and opens a notebook.*]

193

EDITH: [*Still in the kitchen*] Why don' you talk a me no
more, hanh? Always wit her, always gigglin', readin' a
her. Never offered to read a me. Thought I was ignorant even though I went a high school. Benny thought
I was dumb too, didn't think I caught on about where
he picked up them fancy smells. . . . [*Calls.*] Mary! He's
waitin'! [*To* BERNARD, *who she thinks is still in the
kitchen*] Tell her to get a job. She oughtta go a the
convent and get a job, that would suit her, workin' for
them nuns. I wouldn't touch a dollar a nun handled,
you don' know where it's been before. The hand or the
dollar. Them nuns got weird ideas.

BERNARD: [*Calling*] Dress warmly, Mary, there is still a
steely spike in the morning air.

EDITH: I remember my brother tellin' me when we was
kids. He knew this nun, see, who kept her rosaries up
her ass as a penance. Nah, I'm serious. My brother
never lied, too dumb, he was Arnold's father, you know,
like father like . . . [*Thinks for a moment.*] Arnold.
Well, he had this nun in school, see, and this one day
she wanted a award this particular kid for doin' somethin' special, see. Don' know what it was. Maybe he
shit without makin' any noise. That's an art. Least it
was in them days, the way we useda eat. Well, that was
durin' the Great Depression. Well, anyways, you lis-
tenin'? She wan's a award this kid, so she reaches back
inna her ass, pulls out the rosary and reaches it to the
kid, sayin', this is for you, you sweet little boy. And the
kid takes it, see, and says, thank you, Sister, and kisses
it! Yeah, I'm serious. That's what my brother told me,
he saw it wit his one good eye, God rest his soul. So
this cowgirl should go to work for them nuns. . . .

BERNARD: [*Ironic*] Don't you realize, Edith, we are all
working for the nuns? God is a nun. I was about to say,
a nun belonging to the Immaculate Conception Order,
save that, A, there is no order in the universe, and B,
God is hardly an Immaculate Conception. [*Chuckles.*]
I think I'll put that in my novel. [*Calls.*] Mary!

MARY: [*Off*] I'll be there.

BERNARD: [*Having found his manuscript, makes a note.*]
"Is Reality a Dream of God's? Then we are all frag-
ments in the Divine Nightmare being dreamed by a
Nun. Thus thought Mark driving through the . . ."

[MARY *enters. She is wearing an attractive old-fashioned dress with a cloak.*]

BERNARD: Mary!

MARY: [*Speaks more carefully than she did.*] Good morning, Bernard. [*Goes into kitchen, pours herself coffee.*]

EDITH: [*Sarcastic*] Good morning, niece.

MARY: Good morning, Aunt Edith. [*Drinks coffee.*]

EDITH: Isn't she sweet? I guess they didn't teach her much about fuckin' in that pigpen she comes from, that's why he ain't come back.

MARY: If you don't want hot coffee poured over you, shut up.

EDITH: Goddamn bully! Gotcha! Shit, was an ant!

MARY: Why don't you eat at the table? That's why there are so many of them roaches.

BERNARD: It was good of you, Mary, to clean up for us.

EDITH: Bitch! Takin' away my work.

BERNARD: Don't worry, Edith. Where you are, there are sure to be roaches. Come, Mary, we must away, matutinal instruction calls. [MARY *is pensive.*] What's the matter, pray? Does something dissatisfy you?

MARY: How could he have just left me?

[*She and* BERNARD *go into the living room.* BERNARD *sets about getting ready to leave, including the donning of a heavy but expensive-looking and old-fashioned ladies' cloak.*]

MARY: I miss him. I like our trips to the library and all, but I remember the way he used to be, at night, beside me, sleeping. I had power then. It was like magic. Him open to me, tender ... that's gone for good.

BERNARD: [*Disturbed*] Perhaps ... perhaps not for good. Perhaps there will be others, maybe not so young as he, no, nor so beautiful.

MARY: That isn't the point, old man.

BERNARD: Then what is the point, young lady? Do you want to be chained to some cretin's marital bed, squeezing out of you one rancid pimple after another, naming one after you, and one after him, and one after your mother?

MARY: You talking about children?

BERNARD: Is that what you want? I can't think of anyone less fitted for the bearing of children than you. You have a mind. And what is the venting of those rubber

mouths we call babies after all? A simple reflex. One
becomes full of an unmentionable substance, it grows,
tumorlike, in one, then comes a day of agony pressing
it out!

MARY: You only talk that way because you never fathered
a child.

BERNARD: Didn't I indeed? I married, and my wife bore
me two sons.

MARY: Bernard! Didn't you say you was homosexual, like
that, that Italian Painter, and that—what was it, Russian
composer . . . ?

BERNARD: What difference does that make? I slept with
my wife enough to make two children, boys both, and
I thought quite handsome boys.

MARY: But what happened?

BERNARD: It is time to go to the library. And did you
remember your Latin text? Today is the fifth declen-
sion. Soon we start on German. [*She tries to interrupt.*]
I may write a monograph about you. You are a living
refutation of Hume. He felt that one's environment was
everything. That were a child to be locked into a dark
room for twenty years, seeing no one, hearing nothing,
he'd never have a thought. I used to believe that. So
passionate was I you might have called me a Hume-
sexual.

MARY: But your wife!

BERNARD: I must call Ellen Mac Jones Aberdeen. [*Calls.*]
Ellen! Ellen! Ellen Mac Jones!

MARY: Haven't you realized that dog is dead?

BERNARD: Of course. I saw her smashed-up corpse near
the baseball diamond at Johnson Field. But I call her
and put out dog food for her in commemoration.

MARY: Commemoration?

BERNARD: Certainly. If a congregation of idiots can eat
bread and drink wine in commemoration of a crucified
charlatan who has been dead two thousand years, I can
do this in commemoration of the best friend I ever had.

MARY: I want to hear about your wife and sons.

BERNARD: What sort of freak are you? Do you want to
hear a seventy-year-old wreck neutered by adversity
muse on his wife? It should be enough I am a wreck.

MARY: You aren't a wreck.

BERNARD: Then come with me this instant to the library.
  [*Calls.*] Good day, Edith, you have your water. . . .
EDITH: If you see Arnold . . .
BERNARD: Good-bye!
  [*They enter the side street; the* NUNS *surround them.*]
FIRST NUN: Taxi?
BERNARD: We'll bus, thank you.
SECOND NUN: Help our convent!
  [*The* FIRST *and* SECOND NUN *intercept* BERNARD, *the*
  THIRD NUN *takes* MARY *aside and whispers to her.*]
MARY: [*To* THIRD NUN] You know where he is? Where?
  [THIRD NUN *whispers.*]
BERNARD: [*Realizing he has been separated from* MARY]
  Away, you harpies!
MARY: [*To* THIRD NUN] I'll come . . .
  [*Runs off with* THIRD NUN. *Other* NUNS *stop* BERNARD
  from following.]
BERNARD: Mary! Why, Mary . . . What's . . .
  [*The two remaining* NUNS *buffet* BERNARD, *rip off his
  cloak.*]
BERNARD: My cloak! Stop!
  [*The* NUNS *push him, until he runs into the house.*]
BERNARD: Mary!
EDITH: Is she dead?
  [*The* TWO NUNS *laugh, drape the cloak over both of
  them and trot off.* BERNARD *collapses at his desk.*]

BLACKOUT

Scene 2

The THIRD NUN *joins the other two in a spot, in a rock-
and-roll dance from the fifties, done without music.
Their routine includes the typical hand gestures and
body movements associated with certain rock groups.
They are describing eternal torment and damnation.*

As lights build, the THIRD NUN *leaves the other two, who,
far to the back, in shadow, watch the scene.*

*The scene is a bar, the hangout of Michael De Felice.
There is little change in the set, another table, or a small
bar can be added. The atmosphere is shady.* ARNOLD
slumped at a table, MICHAEL *watchful.*

ARNOLD: Something in my head . . . veils . . .

MICHAEL: You need some two hundred proof. Kills hangovers. [*Pours.*]

ARNOLD: [*Drinks, coughs.*] Kills more than hangovers.

MICHAEL: Come to! I wanna go to the shore today. Construction workers' convention. You'll do well wit them.
You're their type. Straight-actin' and stiff. I also gotta
blue movie laid out. . . .

ARNOLD: Stop it, I ain't one of them. . . .

MICHAEL: We been through it before. I'm gettin' bored
wit it. I asked you if you wanted a go back to her. Nah,
nah, a week later, you wanna go back to her? Nah, nah.
It's a month now. Make up your mind: me or her. Also,
you gotta start earnin' your keep.

[*The* BOY *runs on.*]

BOY: What's hot?

MICHAEL: We are. I talked a Father Gambone inna the
confessional. You're to go to him at two this afternoon.
He'll need you until three. So be prepared to be patient. If you plays your cards right, there's a bishops'
conference in town next month. We'll hit the big time.

[*The* THIRD NUN *leads* MARY *into the bar, disappears.*]

BOY: [*Seeing* MARY] Holy shit!

MICHAEL: [*To* MARY] I'm sorry, but we don't cater to fish!

MARY: [*Approaching* ARNOLD] Arnold . . .

ARNOLD: [*Covering embarrassment and shame with anger*] What you doin' here? You come to embarrass me?

MARY: Why, no. . . .

ARNOLD: Where'd you get them funny clothes . . . ?

MARY: Why, Bernard, he's been helpin' me—

ARNOLD: Get out of here.

[MARGE *enters.*]

MARGE: Yo, Michael!

MICHAEL: [*To* MARGE] How much?

MARGE: Three scores. Sixty-five fifty. [*Sees* MARY.] Jesus
Christ!

MICHAEL: Count it out.

MARGE: [*Keeping an eye on* MARY, *counts her money.*] Ten ... fifteen ...

MARY: Come back with me, Arnie baby, I miss you. . . .

ARNOLD: Not here.

MICHAEL: [*To* MARGE] Your share, and a bonus.

MARGE: [*Watching* MARY *and* ARNOLD] Thanks.

MARY: Where else, then? You don't come back to me. You left me alone, a stranger here, in this city. I waited for you, by the window I waited, I looked for you, in the streets, everywhere. That first night there wasn't even a mattress for me, or a sofa to lay on. I had no money, but I waited. I've been patient. Maybe I understand a little better now. But you have to do what's right, you're my husband. . . .

ARNOLD: How did you find this place?

MARY: Come back with me.

MICHAEL: [*Contemptuous*] Go 'head, Arnie, go 'head.
[BUCKY *and* SCODGE *enter.*]

BUCKY: Yo, Michael!

SCODGE: Yo, Mich . . . [*Sees* MARY.] Hey, getta load, Buck.

ARNOLD: [*To* MARY] Not now. Get your hands off me.

MARY: I'm beggin' you, don't pay no mind to these people. . . .

ARNOLD: They don' like outsiders like you.

SCODGE: Yes we do, baby.

MICHAEL: [*To* SCODGE] Shut up!

MARY: I ain't no outsider.

ARNOLD: You're a fuckin' hilly-billy. Go on! Get out!

MARY: I won't have you callin' me names.

ARNOLD: You won't have, you won't have! Who the hell are you to talk, hanh? Just like a fuckin' woman, fuckin', fuckin' woman! Always readin' them stupid books, stupid! Hilly-billy! There's no teacher around here for you to rub up against. Get out. Get out!

MARY: You're a coward, a fool!

ARNOLD: Fuckin' southern idiot! And another thing, you don' even fuck good!

[BOY *giggles and applauds,* MICHAEL *hits him.*]

MARY: I don't fuck good? I don't fuck good! Why, who done it all, Superman? I just about had to rape you in that graveyard. And before that, the hints I dropped, God Almighty! And when I first met, I just about put

your hand up me; Innocent Prince Arn, he didn't know
what was happenin'!

BUCKY: Oh, ho, I'd a known, baby. . . . [MICHAEL *silences
him.*]

MARY: "You won't do nothin' to me," and "I'm puttin'
myself at your mercy, Prince Arn"! Shit!

MARGE: What's this Prince Arn crap?

MARY: A grown man from the city, no less. And when I
finally did get you to do it, I had to put you on top of
me like you was a toy and guide you in.

[SCODGE, BUCKY, *and* BOY *much amused by this.* AR-
NOLD *in an agony of embarrassment.*]

ARNOLD: God damn you for this, God damn you, I'd like
to rip them filthy tits off. . . .

MARY: Go ahead! Then I'll be more like a man and you
can love me!

[MARY *runs out.* BUCKY *and* SCODGE *look after her.*]

MARGE: Well, that was better than TV.

MICHAEL: [*Camping*] Nothing is better than TV. . . .

BOY: He means "transvestite."

MARGE: Lissin a that vocabulary!

[*Embarrassed for* ARNOLD, *but also cruel, they ignore
him.*]

BUCKY: [*To* MARGE, *joking*] Come on, baby, let's make
some hay. . . .

MARGE: You ain't got enough to feed you kids and I don'
go on credit.

BUCKY: Well, maybe we'll make a bundle today.

SCODGE: Goin' a the track.

MARGE: Don' you guys ever go to work?

SCODGE: [*False heartiness*] Ho, Arnie Lungs!

BUCKY: Ho, Arnie!

MARGE: Prince Arn!

[*They laugh.*]

ARNOLD: [*To* MICHAEL, *voice breaks*] Give me a scotch!

MICHAEL: What, sweets?

ARNOLD: Scotch! [MICHAEL *pours*, ARNOLD *gulps it.*] Another! [*Gulps again.*]

MARGE: [*To* ARNOLD] Tryin' to put hair on yer chest?

SCODGE: Maybe he's tryin' to put titties there.

BUCKY: That would make it a dyke affair.

[*They laugh.* ARNOLD *hurls his glass at* BUCKY, *barely
misses.*]

ARNOLD: [*To* MICHAEL] Broke that glass, give me another.... [MICHAEL *pours*.]

BUCKY: [*To* ARNOLD] You throw that glass at me, motherfuck?

MARGE: [*Seeing* ARNOLD *gulp another drink*] Whoa, horsie, gonna get snowed.

ARNOLD: Yep.

MARGE: Why?

ARNOLD: Because I need! [*Suddenly grabs and kisses her violently*.]

MARGE: [*Gets away*.] What's that prove?

BUCKY: [*To* ARNOLD] You buy me a drink and I'll forget about the glass.

ARNOLD: Sure. Hey, Michael, go piss inna glass and give it to my friend here, wit my compliments....

BUCKY: You're really spoilin' for it, ain't you? If I wasn't a printer I'd come afta you, but I need my hands for work.

ARNOLD: Why? You don' go in much!

SCODGE: [*Stopping the angry* BUCKY *from attacking* ARNOLD] Come on, you guys, quiet down. [*Pulls* BUCKY *aside, they go over racing forms*.]

[*Suddenly* ARNOLD *again takes* MARGE *roughly in his arms*.]

MARGE: Arnie! Whatsa matter you?

ARNIE: You a whore, ain't you?

BOY: Give it a her, Arnie.

MARGE: Fuck you!

[*Tries to get away, but* ARNOLD *holds her. They struggle*.]

BOY: Oh, oh, that's the way to go. Oh, oh!

MICHAEL: [*To* BOY] Come over here, you. I wanna tell you exactly how to act wit Father Gambone. Always remember the bishops....

MARGE: [*Fighting with* ARNOLD] Get away from me, Arnie, I'm warnin' you, don' start no trouble. Michael, call him off!

MICHAEL: Look afta youself, bitch!

MARGE: [*Still fighting*] Come on, Arnie, I was always nice to you, never said nothin' nasty. You got somethin' a prove, you go afta somebody else. Come on, Arnie.... [*He hits her. She punches him. The fight becomes furious*.]

BUCKY: [*Watching*] If only I didn't need my hands for work.

SCODGE: Marge can take care of herself. I think we oughtta put a deuce on Turandot in the fourth. That's what Tony Putty says.

BUCKY: Oh yeah?

[*They consult the racing forms.*]

MARGE: You're hurtin' me, Arnie, stop it, please. . . .

MICHAEL: [*To* BOY, *ignoring* MARGE] You take a shower before Father Gambone, too, don' wan' them big feet smellin'.

BUCKY: [*Consulting racing form*] Scooter the Dwarf told me Golden Glue was a sure thing inna third. . . .

SCODGE: Italian-owned, that's for sure. . . .

MARGE: [*Kicks* ARNOLD *in the groin. He cries out and falls.*] You rotten queer, you think you can take me just like that, hanh?

SCODGE: No need to use your hands now, Buck.

BUCKY: That so, Scodge?

SCODGE: That's so.

[*They start kicking* ARNOLD.]

ARNOLD: Hey you guys, hey!

BOY: [*To* MICHAEL *about* ARNOLD] Hey, Michael, look— ain't you gonna stop them?

MICHAEL: I'll give you a free lesson, princess, he's gotta call me. Now, when Father Gambone . . .

ARNOLD: You fuckin' killin' me. . . . Michael! Help!

MICHAEL: [*To* BUCKY *and* SCODGE] Stop it, you guys!

SCODGE: Hey, look who's commandin'.

BUCKY: Hey, look who's commandin'.

MARGE: She's Arnie's man.

MICHAEL: Get off him.

SCODGE: You fuckin' pervert, I've been meanin' to . . .

MICHAEL: [*Removes a gun from his purse.*] One more sound and your wife's a hairy-chested widow. You! [*To* BOY, *who takes out a switchblade*] Now, you lissin a me. Arnie's mine, he's my territory, you mess wit him, you messin' wit me, and I don' take no shit from nobody. Now, you all kneel down and beg Arnie's pardon, just like he was the Virgin. Go on. [*They don't move. To* MARGE] You first, cunt. [*She doesn't move.*] All right, I'm gonna start countin'. When I get to three I'm shoot-

in' a tit off, when I get to six I'm goin' for the other tit.
Got that?

MARGE: [*Kneels.*] I'm sorry, Arnie, I didn't mean to kick
you.

SCODGE: [*Kneels.*] I'm sorry, Arnie, I didn't mean to kick
you.

BUCKY: [*Stands.*] Yeah.

MICHAEL: Kneel and say it all!

BUCKY: [*Kneels.*] I'm sorry, Arnie, I didn't mean to kick
you.

MICHAEL: Now, get the fuck out! [*They run out. To the*
BOY] You! Go steal a car, I wanna get him to the hos-
pital. [BOY *runs out,* MICHAEL *kneels beside* ARNOLD.]
Now, just you remember, Prince Arn, you're mine now,
you're my baby, and I'm gonna take care of you.
[*Embraces him.*]

BLACKOUT

Scene 3

The row house. BERNARD *is at his desk, head in his
hands. It is very dark.* EDITH *is in the kitchen.*

EDITH: Geez, it's a hot night. Hey! Bernard! You didn't
leave any dog food out, did you? You should have, that
hilly-billy bitch'll be hungry when she comes back.
Gotcha! [*Kills a roach.*] Shit, I don' hear him. [*Crawls
about.*] Gotta be careful, don' wanna get into dog food.
Dog food is just like shit; smells the same, sticks to you
the same, feels the same, and don' nobody wonder out
loud how comes I know so much about shit. I lived in
it for years, that's how I know. Fifty-eight years, come
February. Yeah, I was born under the sign of *la Pesce*,
the Cold Fish, like Benny useda say. He called me that
because I couldn't get with child. We tried, *Madon'*,
how we tried. Only thing I hadda show from it was
some bruises, only thing he hadda show was some
bites. How I bit him! Well, he run off. Hey, Bernard?

You know anything about it? Why'd he run off? Shut
up, Edith, Bernard ain't here. And now, Arnie . . . [*Kills
a roach.*] Gotcha! I'm a fuckin' survivor, at least. One
of these days I'll get up and walk again, I'm just savin'
my strength. It ain't easy to be over fifty and blind. But
one of these days I'm gonna get up and go lookin' for
that Arnie. And I'm gonna say get the hell home with
your aunt, where you belong. Why ain't he come home?
Maybe it's because he's queer and thinks I don' know.
Christ, it's obvious. Look at that slit he came home wit.
Only a queer would go afta her, look at the old man.
But Arnie, who gives a shit? What's wrong wit bein'
queer? He could use a pineapple for all I care. Ain't
like havin' a big blotch on you face, ain't like havin' no
arms. Ain't no excuse to leave me. You tell my Arnie
his Aunt Edith says there ain't nothin' wrong wit bein'
queer and for him to come and see her once in a while.
Oh, why has he left me wit nothin'?—you ask him that.
I've ended up wit nothin', that's so hard, no eyes, no
legs, no future. Don' think I'm garbage because I got
nothin', I still got feelin's, I still got needs. Just because
I don' got nothin' to give don' mean I don' wan' nothin'.
Oh, Edith, pull yourself together. You're goin' crazy.
Old and blind and horny and now crazy. Geez, you
can't win! Sleep, gotta sleep. Gotcha! [*Kills a roach.*]
How 'bout that, two of them!

[*Curls up near the stove in her rags.* MARY *enters.*]

BERNARD: Mary. I've waited for you. I've been reading
Hopkins. Remember who he is? I dozed off. We've read
him. "I wake and feel the fell of dark not day, What
hours, oh what black hours you have spent this
night . . ." We've read it often.

MARY: Where can I go, Bernard? I have no home, no
money, no husband.

BERNARD: You saw that moron.

MARY: I walked around and around wanting to lose myself. Where can I go? How?

BERNARD: But, Mary, there is no reason for you to leave
here.

MARY: I'll have to get a job. That's the first thing.

BERNARD: Listen to me. . . . [*Touches her.*]

MARY: Please don't touch me.

BERNARD: We must stay together, you and I. I feel it. It

is right. We have known each other in a past life; teacher and pupil, perhaps, father and son. And when you are educated, perhaps there will be a way we can get away, together. . . .

MARY: I wanted so much . . . I can't say it now. I wanted to be free of the mud I was stuck in and here there is more mud and more mud and more—let me hold your hand, I'm sorry I pushed you away.

BERNARD: You mustn't let that fool . . .

MARY: No more about him. Did you go through the same thing with your wife? Is that why you turned against women?

BERNARD: I haven't turned against women.

MARY: How did you meet her?

BERNARD: Well, she wrote, I wrote. I was teaching. I had my book published: *King Lear and the Norns* it was called. Shakespeare criticism from the practical point of view. What practical point of view?! I directed an all-girls' *Macbeth* at a summer camp once. It was peculiar. That was virtually the extent of my acquaintance with the Bard. She came to me with her first novel, a fictionalized treatment of Catherine the Great. I was struck by her elegant prose, her well-turned adverbial phrases, her shapely handling of form. I advised her— Moira, that was her name, it's Gaelic for Fate; actually, its true meaning is Fart, which is what she turned out to be. Drop dead, Moira, if you haven't already! Well, I advised her. The book was published, favorably received, and I became her mentor. She began a book on Dante Gabriel Rossetti. Then, one evening, with nothing better to do, I brushed her upswept breasts. She outlined her second chapter: Dante Gabriel's adolescence, and then, with barely one word spoken, she moved in. We slept together, my first time. I remember kissing her breasts, they were very soft, as yours must be. One night, I said to myself, Bernard, you must be honest with her. You must confess. Confess! She was researching Dante Gabriel's drug addiction. Moira, my fate, I said, drunk, weeping, on my knees, in fact; forehead wrinkled, fourth scotch balanced too carefully on the threadbare rug; Moira, my Fate, I'm queer. Well, since we had slept together not altogether unsuccessfully, and because I was spending more time with her than anyone, she naturally thought this a drunken eccentricity, or better, a sort of personal metaphor. She even used it in her fifth novel. Can you imagine how painful that scene was for me and then, to see it on page seventy-two of a ninety-five-cent paperback twenty-two years later? But then, what excuse did I have? I was hardly truly young at the time. And when had I ever been young? I was born skulking about hiding my premature potbelly, hiding precocious bald spots, covering festering pimples with fluttering hands. There was no excuse for me. Well, Moira was not bothered by my confession. I fascinated her. It's all so dreary! She was overly attached to her father, and whom do you think I reminded her of? We wed. [*Musing*] Moira, I'm queer.

MARY: Well, that's hard for a woman to hear. I never knew anybody like that down home, leastwise, anybody who was open about it. I've got to leave here, leave this city. I have to be free of this, Bernard, I'm going to pack. . . .

BERNARD: Our lessons . . .

MARY: I can't let you support me. I can't stay here with him two blocks away in the arms of that . . .

BERNARD: Don't throw this chance away, Mary, I can give you so much; don't let a silly pride . . .

MARY: Pride? When did I have pride? I was born a beggar. Beggars have no pride. Oh, how I begged, from the time I was two months: love me, teach me, hold me, I begged, if I'd been just a mite crazier I'd have begged the trees and bushes. If you had seen me throw myself on that boy when he found me aweepin' . . . Pride? I did everything. I went to the old women and worked out a spell step by step. I trapped him, I trapped myself, and for what?

BERNARD: I've been so alone. Don't you want to hear about my children? The rest of my life?

MARY: Won't make any difference. . . .

BERNARD: Listen, please, where was I? Moira, I'm queer. Oh yes, I have it here in my diary, volume sixty-eight. [*Rummages through drawers in the desk, comes up with a volume.*] I'll run my eye over it, don't be impatient, Mary, it's very interesting. Someday it will make a novel, like all the best things in anyone's life. [*Continues his narrative.*] Our marriage after eight uneasy months had sustained more cracks than the Parthenon in age. A child was considered the solution. A boy was born; then, for the same reasons, a year later, another boy.

MARY: You as a father . . . ? [*Laughs.*]

BERNARD: I have reserves of tenderness. And pay attention. They loved their mother, she adored them. By this time she was working on the Brontës. She loved the children in the room with her where she worked. The three of them communed, surrounded by copies of her book on Dante Gabriel Rossetti, an enormous success. They'd giggle and make faces at one another, it was a foreign language. *The Atlantic Monthly* accepted three stories from her. How I grew to hate them, those boys, those boys and their noise, their silly babble, their incessant messing. And I hated to hear her cooing over them, whether they'd mouthed their first inanity or had diarrhea. Oh, I tried to conjure up feeling from within me somewhere, how to love these little monsters, these sucking, filthy, little monsters, their goddamned souls are rotting somewhere I hope! And yet, what a hideous monster I was, caught in this quicksand of misery and confusion. I didn't know what I truly felt or where I stood with these three strangers: two messy midgets and their full-grown female trainer. By the time the eldest was eleven they were both emphatically mama's boys. Emphatically. Moira was working on her second novel, an updated version of St. Teresa, the Little Flower. No, I thought, for one summer they'd be truly away from both of us, in a summer camp. I sent them off, over her violent protestations. There was even an excruciating operatic scene between us at the train station. I think she had a bit of the Wop in her. But I held firm, I sent them off, they had to go. One night, in mid-July, they decided, against the rules, to go swimming. The younger had cramps, began to sink, his brother dove in to save him, they both drowned. I thought: Obviously, I've killed them. I was addicted at that time, to the greatest fiction writer of the century, Sigmund Freud, and thought that, unconsciously, I had willed the whole thing. Their mother was prostrate, needless to say. A divorce. She has had considerable success with her books and how have I ended? Look about you.

MARY: [*Touched*] You haven't ended yet.

BERNARD: My boys drowned in lake water and I've drowned in mediocrity, in illusions, in foolish fantasies about myself, about other people. I have been a victim of optimism, an unwillingness to die, to end my life. . . .

MARY: [*Takes him in her arms.*] I never thought you was one of them, you hear? [*Kisses him.*]

BERNARD: [*Starts to cry, stifles it.*] Self-pity. I'm so old. . . .

MARY: Hush. [*They kiss. He allows his hand to brush against her breasts.*]

BERNARD: [*After a pause*] Come, let's dress up. [*She looks surprised.*] I have an extensive wardrobe. [*Runs upstairs and drags a large wardrobe onstage.*]

MARY: You want me to help you?

BERNARD: [*Rushes off and returns with elaborate dresses.*] No, I don't need any. [*Shows her the dresses, opens the trunk.*] Voilà, madame. [MARY *is stunned by the beauty and obvious expense of the dresses.*] Yes, I know, they're miracles of design.

MARY: Where did you get them?

BERNARD: Oh, the museum of art, various collections. I've stolen them all. Remember when I told you that dress you're wearing was one of Edith's old ones? I was lying! This piece of trash was a practice theft. Yes, I've stoken them all. It's very easy once you conquer the inevitable stage fright. I was caught only once and succeeded in passing myself off as a harmless old eccentric. They took the dress in question—it was this one— back politely and said: Mustn't do that. I stole the same dress two weeks later, wearing a false mustache and wig.

MARY: I have never seen the like . . .

BERNARD: [*Displaying another dress*] This one is a ball gown first worn circa 1895. I stole it from the La Modeste Collection. [*Displaying another with particular pride*] This! This one is 1898, first worn by Josephine DuPont, at her coming-out party. She was a beauty. I've seen pictures. Look how thin she was—you take this one. You shall be Josephine DuPont and I shall be your duenna, Madeleine.

MARY: My what?

BERNARD: Your teacher. I'll get into this one. . . .

MARY: You gonna put that dress on you?

BERNARD: Don't worry, it'll fit, I've had it on before. I've been good since you've been here but, why not?

MARY: A big old man like you in a dress like that?

BERNARD: Come, for me, put it on. I want to see you dressed up.

MARY: Well, how?

BERNARD: Here are the bloomers, and the petticoats. First you put on the bloomers, then over them the petticoats, then the gown. Here are stockings, and a corset, just in case. Then these earrings should do nicely, and try these rings, also this necklace. . . .

MARY: Are they real?

BERNARD: Of course not, my dear. But I'm an old hand at high-class paste. I wrote some, remember?

MARY: Oh, Bernard, I don't even think I can play at what you're askin'.

BERNARD: Do it for me.

[*She goes upstairs.* BERNARD *dons his dress and jewelry, all the while behaving like a grande dame who has entered a ballroom and is watching a ball in progress.*]

BERNARD: Oh, my goodness, how full our ballroom is. [*As though to a butler*] Jenkins, Miss Josephine will be down shortly. [*As though watching those present*] Why, there are the Astors, and there, the Carnegies. All here for little Josie. All this grandeur for her, and I can remember when she'd throw up at the drop of a pin. I'm the duenna. [*Primps himself, waltzes.*] Oh, and the intoxication of music. And the beaux, oh, the beaux. So handsome and virile, and, yes, young. Not yet mowed down by the First World War. Oh, were it only 1917 instead of 1897. I'd like to see all this male beauty mangled, blown to bits, all dead, these handsome young boys, all dead! [*Curtsies as though greeting someone who has spoken to him.*] Why, thank you, sir, but I don't dance with hypocrites. [*Fans himself, watches this imaginary interlocutor leave.*] Really! Coming and asking me to dance, just so he'd have Josie's ear through me. I'd never put in a syllable for him. I'm suspicious of that cologne. Only the most virile for Josie! [*Starts to sway to an imagined waltz.*] Oh, that music, that music. [*Calls.*] Josephine, hurry! [*Waltzing*] I'm dancing, yes, dancing alone. What does it matter?

Those young men were never for me, they ignored me and slunk away at my approach. They wilted these young flowers when I cast my rapacious black eyes on them. Well, so be it! Some are beauties, and some turn men to stone. [*Calls.*] Josephine, hurry! You keep them waiting too long. Necks crane in anticipation, the best-bred necks in New York are twisting themselves to see your sweeping entrance. And these mouths, these mouths sweet from having kissed and sucked the lips of the greatest beauties are all whispering: Where is she? Where is she? Josephine, it's time! Josephine!

[MARY *appears at the top of the stairs, very beautiful, radiant in the dress. She stops, embarrassed and uncomfortable.* BERNARD *stares up at her, stunned by the completeness of the transformation. The* NUNS *flicker and swirl at the back of the stage, always in shadow.*]

BERNARD: No, it can't be you. [*He is himself now, not acting Madeleine.*] You know, I didn't really think it would be so ... total. ...

MARY: [*Whispers.*] Bernard ... [*Starts to walk down.*]

BERNARD: No, still, still as stone. ...

MARY: [*Whispers.*] Don't make me stand here, Bernard, the prisoner of your eyes. Don't make me stand here imprisoned in this dress. You've caged me in. You've worked a spell. Stop staring at me. Every second you stare you are stealing me from me. ...

BERNARD: Wait, I'll bring you down. [*Runs up the stairs, trips on his gown, falls.*] No, don't move. Pretend I'm prostrate, laid low by your beauty. [*He rises, takes her hand, escorts her down.*] Now, curtsy. Imagine the applause, the march played by the band, the overpowering scent of the flowers, the most costly perfumes. Curtsy again, and again curtsy. The waltz! They've struck up. Magic. Sway! [*He forces her to sway to his imagined waltz.*]

MARY: [*Swaying*] Something ... familiar ... dressed like this. Swaying in this hole.

[*The* NUNS *are swaying also, always in shadow.*]

MARY: It's as if I'm a corpse laid in earth, new buried. It's like a graveyard filled with turning worms. That's the music, that's the spinning. No! [*Stops swaying.*] Yet it is in the air, that smell, it is in the earth, and it's the eternal earth trapping us and we must dance to the humming of those worms. I've heard them humming and turning and we must dance. Dance ... we must dance....

[BERNARD *takes her and kisses her passionately. They sway together,* BERNARD *kissing her, running his hands over her body.*

The NUNS *continue their swirling.*]

BERNARD: You are the most beautiful creature I've ever seen. More beautiful than a woman can be, a creature, a writhing, soaring, asexual creature. You are the most beautiful thing I've ever held. Don't slip away from me, Mary, don't slip away....

MARY: Too tight. It's too tight. Don't crush me. Oh, please, don't suck on my skin. [*Breaks away from him.*] Vampire! Vampire! Don't take what little I have. I don't want to die.

BERNARD: To die into freedom! [*Takes her roughly in his arms, rips her bodice, kisses her breasts, she struggles momentarily, then goes limp.*] You are mine, now. I can taste myself on your skin. I can smell myself in your hair. I can feel my saliva running along your body. Come with me. Truly, you are my clay, and my wanting you has brought you a new life. Come on!

[*Drags her off. From the* NUNS *emerges a loud, high keening. They swirl about the stage wildly.* EDITH *wakes, shakes her head.*]

EDITH: What's that noise? Arnold, you back? That you? You makin' that bitch whimper and scream like the animal she is?

[*One* NUN *makes baby noises, for a moment all make loud baby noises, particularly of crying.*]

EDITH: I hear a baby. *Bambino.* Arnold. As a baby ... ? What's that noise? Somebody kill that kid, its mother doesn't want it. Oh, Jesus, Mary, and Joseph, it's so ugly, it's always been so ugly. I see these swirlin' things....

[*She tries to see, and listens intently. The* NUNS *whine, make distorted animal noises, pant, their swirling continues, wild and fast, their noises are loud.*]

EDITH: Benny? Benny? That you? You come home afta all these years? You fuckin' that hilly-billy slut, hanh?

Oh, I know, Benny, I know you played around, you couldn't get enough. But you must be old now, ain't you tired? Why don't you come back to me? I need you, she don' need you, she can have her choice. I ain't so awful. I don' care if you do it to her, but then, when you through, come to me, hanh? You goddamn bastid, why did you desert me. Let's make up like we did in the old days. Maybe, if I work at it, I can make some pigs' feet, or some spareribs in the gravy, and we can eat and laugh and get the sauce all over each other like we useda. I remember you drippin' red sauce on me and sayin' I looked like a Red Indian. An' me sayin' it was blood. Love blood. You tongue won't rot off, if you kiss me. Talk to me at least, talk to me, I been dry for years, these tits is dry, my insides is dry, everything, everything is dry except my eyes, and I can't see outa them. Benny . . .

[*The* NUNS *swirl about her, almost touching her but not quite.*]

EDITH: That you, Benny? [*Crawls out of the kitchen, the* NUNS *seem to be leading her toward the stairs.*] You touchin' me? I'm comin' afta you. Like a game . . . [*Laughs.*] Hide and seek. I can kill a dozen roaches just by sensin' them. Touch me again, Benny. I'm comin'. Benny, I can almost see you. . . . Hello, Benny, hello, how you been, hanh? Almost . . . [*On the stairs*] I tell you what, I'll get up—yes? I'll get up, I know I can. . . . I ain't walked in a long time, age, you know how it is, gets to all of us, what you gonna do, *la vecchiaia*, can't see, can't walk, old Edith, the Blindie, them roaches, I'll get up— [*With great difficulty gets up.*] I'm standin', Benny, I can come to you, I love you, I love you just like the old days, I love . . .

[*Loses her balance, tries to grab on to something, can't. Falls, dies. The* NUNS *laugh and shriek, hurl themselves about the stage.*]

BLACKOUT

Scene 4

The beach at Wildwood. The upper level represents a section of the boardwalk. The ocean is front. There is a broken-down bench on the boardwalk.

The BOY *lounges on the boardwalk in tight shorts and shirt.* MICHAEL *and* ARNOLD *are walking up and down the boardwalk,* MICHAEL *forcing* ARNOLD *to walk arm in arm with him.* MICHAEL *is in cheerful beach drag. Eventually they sit on the bench.* MICHAEL *keeps an eye on the* BOY.

MARGE *walks by in a tight summer dress, waves at* MI-CHAEL. *Occasionally she walks through the scene.* BUCKY *and* SCODGE, *very uncomfortable in tight clothes, also walk through on occasion.*

MARY *and* BERNARD *are on the lower level, which represents a section of the beach. Both are dressed in* BER-NARD's *costumes.* BERNARD *has on an old woman's beach costume from the 1890s.* MARY *is dressed in beautiful flowing white. They are sitting, facing front, on a cheerful beach blanket with a picnic basket near by.*

It is fall and everyone is chilly in the summer attire. A month and a half have passed since the preceding scene.

THREE NUNS *walk across the boardwalk. Their habits are tucked up, they wear large beach hats over their wimples. They are turning into cockroaches. They eye the* BOY *as they pass him and giggle.*

MICHAEL: [*To* ARNOLD] Sit still, Arnie babes, I wanna watch him.
ARNOLD: Look . . .
MICHAEL: Don't say it, super sweets, just don't say it. [*Eyes the* BOY.] Look at him, he's a beauty. [*Blows boy a kiss.*] We'll go to the outdoor opera in Rittenhouse Square next week. *Turandot*, it's one of my favorites.

[*Croons in falsetto.*] "*In questa reggia, or son mille anni e mille . . .*" That's where the frozen fish, Princess Turandotty, sings of her desire to avenge her frozen but be-raped ancestress fish, Principessa Lu-Ling. . . .

MARY: [*To* BERNARD] Do you see them, Bernard?

BERNARD: Certainly. Not altogether fortunate, but it will be a test of your ability to withstand that fool who traduced you.

[MICHAEL *tries to neck with* ARNOLD.]

ARNOLD: Cut that out!

MICHAEL: Why? Don' you love me?

ARNOLD: No, for Christ' sake, no!

MICHAEL: That makes it more fun! [*Kisses him.*]

MARY: [*To* BERNARD] He's with that man dressed up as a woman.

BERNARD: So it seems, though that man is very good at it.

MARY: He's not! I could tell right away.

BERNARD: [*Offers her cheese from the picnic basket.*] Brie?

MARY: Bernard! You've already eaten a whole one.

BERNARD: I no longer worry about my weight, thank goodness.

[ARNOLD *has risen from the bench and paces.*]

MICHAEL: Stop pacin', Arnie Princess, you're callin' attention to us.

ARNOLD: *I'm* calling attention to us, Jesus Christ, *I'm* calling attention . . .

MICHAEL: Whatsa matter, Arnie hon?

ARNOLD: She's here wit that old man.

MICHAEL: I seen them. He's weird. I mean, I like his style, but he's sloppy. He looks like a fat teddy bear in somethin' frilly.

ARNOLD: Let's go, hanh? I know she's seen me. Let's go!

MICHAEL: But why, Arnie hon, you don' love her?

ARNOLD: That ain't the point, God damn it!

MICHAEL: What is the point?

ARNOLD: Don' look right for my wife to see me here wit you!

MICHAEL: So who's lookin'?

ARNOLD: Jesus!

[*A man walks on and past the* BOY. *This "man" is obviously one of the* NUNS. *The* NUN, *however, has tucked her habit up and wears a fedora and a fake beard and smokes a cigar. The* NUN *stops and eyes the* BOY, *then starts a conversation.*]

ARNOLD: [*To* MICHAEL] It's one of them nuns.

MICHAEL: So? They got needs, too. So long as they pay . . . [BOY *and* NUN *go off in the same direction as the other* NUNS.]

BERNARD: [*To a nervous* MARY] Be still.

ARNOLD: Shit! Shit! I got nothin', I got nobody, Aunt Edith. . . .

MICHAEL: I showed her respect. All the flowers I sent, I had every male hustler on Market Street send her a rose. But I've been thinkin', I need a house, a place to ply my trade, so to speak. Your house would do fine, we just gotta get rid of the old queen and the young fish—

ARNOLD: My aunt's house?!

MICHAEL: Sweetheart, your aunt's house is Holy Cross Graveyard now. I need to diversify my activity, wit you and that kid, Marge, and now Bucky and Scodge, I'm gonna need a nerve center.

ARNOLD: I gotta get away, you're killin' me!

MICHAEL: I'm feedin' you, I'm puttin' you up, I'm givin' you pocket change, who else is gonna do that, hanh? I'm your whole world!

ARNOLD: Mary! Mary! [*Runs down to* MARY.] You gotta help me. You're all I got. He don' mean nothin' to me.

MICHAEL: [*On the edge of the boardwalk, sings in ugly falsetto.*] 'In questa reggia or son mille anni e mille, un grido disperato risonno . . . [*Continues singing under the scene.*]

BERNARD: [*To* MARY, *ignoring* ARNOLD] Josephine, I hope you like the cheese . . .

MARY: [*Ignoring* ARNOLD] I do, Madeleine. . . .

ARNOLD: [*To* MARY] Ain't you gonna answer me?

BERNARD: It's cold for early fall, Josephine, and here on the beach the wind has an icy edge.

MARY: The wind is icy, Madeleine, as though it wasn't fall at all.

BERNARD: As though it weren't fall; subjunctive, too. . . .

ARNOLD: [*To* MARY] Aw, come on, Mary, come on. I know you're angry at me and you got every right. I ain't denyin' that. I'm a pig. You can hit me, if you like, right here in the kisser. I know I did wrong. I'll tell you what, you help me now and we'll try again. When I get myself set up somewheres away from here, we'll try again, we'll have kids, you can go to school. . . .

BERNARD: Tangerine, Josephine?

MARY: Better a peach, Madeleine.

BERNARD: It's too late for peaches.

ARNOLD: All right, Mary, all right. I got confused. I shouldn't have married you. I wasn't ready to get married. But you trapped me, you know, you chained me up. Maybe I played along wit you a little, but hell, that's what guys do wit broads and the other broads don' take it so serious. . . . Oh, please, God, I don' know what I'm sayin'. Look, my nose. [*Takes her hand, forces her to feel his nose.*] You remember? You said: I'm sorry, I didn't mean to touch it, I ain't never been this close to a nose like that. That's what you said. And you looked at my chest, you took a hair, remember? You said I had a boy's body. But I was a boy, don' you understand? Why won't you help me, for old times' sake. I did the best I could, wasn't good I know but— you see, he trapped me, I gotta get out. Do you have some . . . well, you know . . . that I could . . . well . . . you know . . . borrow . . . I gotta run, understand me, I need, I need, please, I need . . . [*A silence.*]

MICHAEL: [*Finishes his aria in grand style.*] Brava, Brava! She don' know who you are, sugar wafer. She's in a different century. I'm bored wit this game, we both got work to do.

ARNOLD: Mary? [*Watching her, he backs up slowly to the edge of the boardwalk.* MICHAEL *grabs him, pulls him offstage.*]

BERNARD: [*Kisses* MARY.] Brava, brava! You were wonderful. It brought a tear to my eye. You were the very picture of a beauty scorned. Henry James would have loved you. [*Rumbles in a Jamesian manner.*] And she sat there, beached as it were, bleached by the merciless sun, her face, hard as stone, white as the sand shifting listlessly about her. . . .

MARY: Shut up, Bernard!

BERNARD: Well, naturally, you're upset. What you did isn't easy.

MARY: Do you think it's hard to be cruel?

BERNARD: Melodramatic stuff. How grand you were, how like a queen. . . .

MARY: You're the queen, Bernard, not me. . . .

BERNARD: You dropped the cheese. It's all sandy and that's the last of the Brie. Let's read the Hopkins. [*Finds the right page in a book, reads.*]

I wake and feel the fell of dark not day
What hours, oh, what black hours we have spent
This night. What sights you, heart, saw, ways you
    went
And more must in yet longer light's delay.

What does that mean to you, Josephine?

MARY: It means that everything is one long night and an endless nightmare, maybe God's Nightmare. That waking I am twisted, and dreaming I am twisted more. It means there is no end and every cry for help just echoes back, distorted. You know, Bernard, there was a time when I went to sleep and felt my spirit crawl out of my skin and fly. You'll call me silly. Then I'd wake up and feel trapped. And now I don't even dream freedom.

BERNARD: Well, that's a reasonable paraphrase of those lines. Now for this: [*Reads.*]

I am gall, I am heartburn
God's most deep decree bitter would have me
    taste . . .

MARY: I want to stop now, Bernard, I want to stop. And I want to go back to the city. I want to change these clothes, they aren't mine. No, don't say anything. No man ever pleaded with me like that, you know? Not even to get into me. I was pretty but I didn't have enough to give. And some instinct, some male instinct sensed that and went elsewhere. Only Arnold, a half man, couldn't sense it and stayed to play along with me, then to plead with me. And the worst part of it is I was part of his deception. I played maiden in distress by a stream, and I got him to play rescuing prince; and it ended on this beach, cold in the fall with that heaving, indifferent ocean out there, indifferent like the earth . . . so I knew all along how false it was, I played too. What right do I have to act like a beauty scorned?

BERNARD: Josephine!

MARY: Mary is me. I'm not a rag doll you can dress up!

BERNARD: But what's happened to you? We were happy!

MARY: You were happy. You are not a teacher, just a girl man who plays dress up.

BERNARD: Oh, stop it, please. You are all I want, dear Mary, immortal beloved. You are my Diana, my Artemis. I know today has been a strain on you, the long bus ride, this cold beach, a picnic in the fall, it was an idiot's idea, my fault, and then, that cretin, Arnold ... [*Embraces her.*]

MARY: Get away! [*Pushes him away.*]

BERNARD: Oh, but I loved you, don't you realize? I'm not comely, I know that, I'm somewhat overweight, I'm perhaps, well, slightly, all right, I'll be honest, very much past my best. But it's been more than a month, every night in your arms, I can't imagine ... No, no, a mood; Moira had them too, it will pass. Monsoons pass, tidal waves pass, earthquakes are forgotten, volcanic eruptions become legend, thus will it be with my Mary's moods. Now, kiss me, hold me, my Mary, eternally soft, infinitely sweet, return to me. I won't fail you again. That's it, isn't it. It's because I failed you last night. ...

MARY: It's because of all the nights you didn't fail. What do you think it was like lying under you and having your whale's carcass heaving over me? There's nothing in Jung about that. All that sweat! And your seventy-year-old breath! Where does that occur in Freud?

BERNARD: You are condemning yourself to ignorance, you stupid southern— No, I didn't mean that. You are my pupil. I can teach you ...

MARY: How to fake an orgasm? From my father to Arnold to you; one trap to the next, all sucking on me, like I was some dangerous candy to lick, then lock up for tomorrow!

BERNARD: Don't leave me!

MARY: I want to go back to Philadelphia alone. Give me the money!

BERNARD: [*Fumbles in his purse, crying.*] I will die, don't you understand? [*She takes the money.*] I'm so old. I won't live long. How much longer, a few years? Stay with me until then, you'll still be young. And, Mary, listen, when I die there is money. Edith's husband, when he left, hid money in the house. I found it. He

was killed by the Mafia. It isn't all that much but I've
been keeping it, living poor, hoping to use it if ever I
got sick or when I'm certain I'm about to die. I still
hoped for royalties, a benefactor, I'm a stupid optimist,
but there's money, under the first drawer in the desk,
the wood is loose, in there. You can have it. I'll will it
to you if you stay with me, or we can spend it now. . . .

MARY: I'll never touch you again, never kiss or smell you
again. It's finished. Good-bye! [*Runs off.*]

BERNARD: Mary! [*Calls.*] Ellen Mac Jones, Ellen Mac
Jones! What? What? Alone!?? Not after all those nights
of love. Oh, I knew I'd be punished for using that word.
I'll chase after her. [*Makes to leave the stage, stops.*]
Ugly, she said? Rotten breath? [*Breathes into his
palm.*] That's not rotten, it smells like Brie. My teeth
are in good shape. See? I can grind them. [*Grinds
teeth.*] I inherited that from my father. When he took
me to the dentist, the dentist after examining me com-
plimented my teeth, he said I had successful teeth, I'd
be the factory manager or the construction boss, never
merely a worker. . . . Is all hope gone? Into the sea with
me! [*Rushes downstage as though toward the ocean.*]
No! I am not Virginia Woolf. I shall survive! Ellen Mac
Jones! Ellen Mac Jones! Here, Ellen! Oh, Mary, and
she smelled so good. [*Calling off*] I hope the bus
crashes with you in it! No, I don't mean that. [*Looks
down.*] Oh, a good omen. She didn't ruin it for me. That
wasn't the last of the Brie. [*Takes a bite of the Brie,
starts folding the blanket sadly.*]

[*The* NUNS *cross the boardwalk carrying the* BOY
bound like an animal to a pole.]

BLACKOUT

Scene 5

The row house. MARY, *in regular clothes, comes down
the stairs with a small suitcase. She goes to the desk,
opens the drawer, and removes the money. She runs out.*

The THREE NUNS *enter on the upper level. With them,* ARNOLD, *hands bound behind him. Very slowly, they bind him to a chair as they did in Act I.* ARNOLD *wears a look of utter defeat.*

BERNARD *runs in carrying a picnic basket, bonnet askew.*

BERNARD: [*Calling*] Mary! Mary! [*Races upstairs, returns caressing the dress* MARY *wore on the beach. He comes downstairs, collapses in grief.*] Gone! [*He weeps into the dress.*]

[MICHAEL, SCODGE, BUCKY, MARGE, *and the* BOY *materialize very slowly out of the shadows.* MICHAEL *stares at* BERNARD, *then goes upstairs to assure himself the house is empty.* SCODGE *goes through the desk,* MARGE *goes through the kitchen, the* BOY *stares at* BERNARD, BUCKY *stands by the street exit as though on guard.*]

ARNOLD: [*With the* NUNS, *the others do not see him.*] Yes, I'm guilty, guilty of everything. Always guilty, eternally guilty, uniformly guilty. [*The* NUNS *swarm over him like cockroaches.*]

[MICHAEL *returns.*]

MICHAEL: This should do very well. Yes, we'll overhaul it, deck the girls out in his dresses. Whataya think, Marge?

MARGE: Sounds cool a me, Michael.

ARNOLD: Guilty, I am guilty, Arnold Longese, black hair guilty, brown eyes guilty . . .

MICHAEL: [*To* BERNARD] Hey you! Get out! You hear me?

ARNOLD: [*With the* NUNS] Male, guilty, female, guilty, long nose, guilty, dusky skin, guilty, well built, guilty . . . [*The* NUNS *swarm over him.*]

MICHAEL: [*More threatening, to* BERNARD] Get out or die, it's one and the same to me.

ARNOLD: [*With* NUNS] About five nine, guilty, big feet, guilty, stupid, guilty, big hands, guilty . . .

BERNARD: [*Pulls himself together.*] No, no. Let me change. I'll leave. [*Very sadly, goes upstairs to change.*]

ARNOLD: [*With* NUNS] . . . queer, guilty, formerly strong, guilty, formerly promising, guilty, now wasted, guilty, too much a dreamer, guilty, Wop, guilty, greasy, guilty, not very hairy, guilty, scar on right thigh, guilty, scar

on the left palm, guilty, circular birthmark on right
shoulder, guilty, second toe longer than big toe, guilty,
unmanly, guilty, weak, guilty, a faggot, guilty, nonsex-
ual, guilty, worthless, guilty, unfeeling, guilty, a braggart, guilty, a phony, guilty, stubborn, guilty, and guilt-
less, guilty, guilty, guilty!

[*With a wild cry the* NUNS *swarm over him, covering
him completely with their black habits, wimples, and
black-gloved, clawlike hands.*]

[BERNARD *comes downstairs, having changed. He is in
a very old-fashioned, slightly too small suit. He carries
a worn small suitcase. He goes to the desk, opens drawers;* MICHAEL *stops him, angry.*]

BERNARD: I won't give up. I want my manuscripts. I've
still a novel or two in me, maybe a book of reflections. . . .
[*Takes his manuscripts, puts them in a valise.*] And
Mary . . . out there, if I hurry perhaps, no, certainly, I
can find her.

MICHAEL: [*Throws some money at* BERNARD.] Carfare.

BERNARD: [*Hesitates but takes it.*] Thank you, young
man.

MICHAEL: Don't mention it, Turandot.

BERNARD: That's right, once, long ago, you referred to me
in the street as Turandot. Do you like that opera? I saw
Eva Turner sing it with Martinelli in London many
years ago. It's an exciting opera when well sung but
not one of my favorites. You can keep the dresses. I
have my favorite in here. [*Lifts suitcase.*] They're
worth thousands, perhaps hundreds of thousands. I've
stolen them all from famous collections. The jewels,
you'll find, are paste, that means fake. [*Nears the door,
turns, surveys the house.*] Thus I leave all this behind.
This house, poor dear dead Ellen Mac Jones Aberdeen,
she had a long life, fifteen, I think. I wonder if I shall
like the Salvation Army. I shall go there first, then
Goodwill Missions, then a hospital. I'll fake a com-
plaint, how skeptical can they be? A man off the street
at my age with a dress in his suitcase. The least I'd get
would be a month in the Mental Ward. So long as they
have a library it won't be so bad. Who knows? Perhaps
they'd have *Shakespeare and the Norns* in their library—I wrote that, you know. In any case, farewell,
sweet South Philadelphia.

MARGE: Poor old man, why don' you let him stay, hanh, Michael? He could dress up for the clients, add some class. . . .

BERNARD: No, no, my good woman, that is very kind of you. But I'll be off. An artist, it seems, must steel himself, or herself, as the case may be, to be alone if necessary. I only became an artist a few years ago. Before that I was a failure. You may not think there is a difference, but there is, a small one. . . . [*Leaves the house.*]

MICHAEL: All right, let's get busy. . . .

[MARGE, *the* BOY, BUCKY, SCODGE *set about sweeping, rearranging the house, dragging on furniture, etc.*

The NUNS *leave* ARNOLD. *He is a mass of sores, his eyes gouged out. The* NUNS, *shrieking, leap through the house.*]

BLACKOUT

URLICHT

Characters

Gustav
Nun

GUSTAV is about twenty-five, plump, sloppy-looking, in a tattered suit coat and ugly tie.

The NUN is about fifty. She is husky, beefy. She uses, more often then not, a tough, lower-class accent. She behaves as though she has modeled herself on a truck driver. When it suits her, though, she can drop this in an instant and behave like a teaching nun, or a pathetic old lady.

Scene

The scene is the far end of a subway platform, late at night.

The stage represents a subway platform. The drop to the tracks is upstage. Near center is a broken green bench. The light is shadowy; the place is very dirty.

As the lights come up, the sound of a train leaving the station is heard. A young man runs on just as the sound fades. He runs back to the tracks and desperately looks up and down in the hopes another train is coming. Realizing none is, he walks to the bench and sits down dispondently.

He is about twenty-five, shabby and puffy. He hums to himself. He wiggles his legs, he presses his hands into his lap. His face twitches. His humming becomes intense; bits and pieces of a melody emerge. It sounds like a slightly distorted version of the "Toreador Song" from Carmen. *He wiggles his legs more, his face twitches more, he looks acutely uncomfortable.*

His humming grows louder and louder and suddenly, with a cry, he runs back to the tracks, unzips, sighs deeply. A cry is heard from the tracks.

VOICE: [*Off*] Hey! Wiggle it a little at least!
   [GUSTAV *freezes. He looks around in shock.*]
VOICE: [*Off*] Down here, stupid!
   [GUSTAV *looks down. Realizes he has urinated on the speaker. He backs away from the tracks in terror.*]
GUSTAV: Oh, my God, oh, my God . . .
VOICE: [*Off*] Hold it!
   [GUSTAV *freezes in place. A baseball bat is thrown up*

225

from the tracks. Very slowly a NUN *materializes, emerging like a huge black blob. She is a Sister of Mercy in an old-fashioned habit, veil, and long rosaries. She has some trouble climbing up onto the platform and calls to* GUSTAV, *who is terrified and sure of heavenly wrath.*]

NUN: Hey!

GUSTAV: [*Falling to his knees, crosses himself.*] O my God, I am heartily sorry for having offended thee and I resolve to mend my life. . . .

NUN: [*Impatient*] 'Sall right! Occupational hazard. Come on, give me a hand.

GUSTAV: I'm terribly sorry—oh, my God, I . . . [*Removes a handkerchief from his pocket, rushes to her, and starts wiping her off.*]

NUN: Hey! What the hell you tryin' to do, push me back on the tracks? [*Exasperated*] Now come on, help me get up there!
[*He reaches down to help her and gets her up with a great deal of difficulty.*]

NUN: Jesus Christ, get your foot outa my rosaries! Ya wan' me to spend all night pickin' up beads?
[*She is finally up on the platform. He takes one look at her and collapses to his knees.*]

NUN: 'Sall right. I forgive ya. Ya gotta take the shit wit the liquor. Endurance is the first thing a Sister of Mercy is taught.

GUSTAV: But what were you doing on the tracks?

NUN: I kill rats! [*Holds up the baseball bat proudly. He starts, incredulous.*] Yeah! S'on the level! Transportation people hired me. Say! You wanna share my coffee break? C'mon, get off yer knees and say yes. You only get twenty minutes to wait by my schedule.

GUSTAV: Well, thank you, but . . . you see, I never drink coffee.

NUN: You don' drink coffee?

GUSTAV: It's bad for the voice.

NUN: I heard you singing, you don't need to worry. [*Half lifts him off the ground and drags him to the bench.*] C'mon, put hair on yer chest. [*Shoves him onto the bench.*] Gee, thanks. Gets kinda lonely down here. Now, all I gotta do is reach under my habit. That's where I keep everything I got. [*Giggles. Removes ther-*

mos of coffee. Pours coffee into the thermos cup.] You take cream?

GUSTAV: No.

NUN: Good, 'cause I don't got none. Here, you take the cup, I always take mine from the bottle. Here's guts in your mud! [*Takes a healthy swig. He sips and coughs.*] That's the whiskey.

[*A pause. After a moment* GUSTAV *starts humming to himself again. It is what he hummed at the beginning of the play. The* NUN *listens for a bit.*]

NUN: Hey, what's that you hummin'?

GUSTAV: Oh, just a tune from my new opera.

NUN: Hanh?

GUSTAV: My new opera. That's what I do. I write operas.

NUN: [*Explodes in laughter.*] Op'ras? Op'ras? All that screamin'? What kinda op'ras you write?

GUSTAV: Autobiographical.

NUN: [*Huge explosion of laughter*] You mean they went around your life screamin'?

GUSTAV: It isn't screaming, it's art! [*Angrily pours the coffee out and bangs down the cup.*]

NUN: All right, all right, don't get touchy. Can't take a joke? Jeez!

GUSTAV: [*Spiteful*] What time's the next train?

NUN: I said don't get touchy. Soon. [*A pause. The* NUN *stares at* GUSTAV *pointedly. He ignores her. He wiggles his legs, hums, wiggles some more.*] Jesus Christ, didn't you finish? Here, take my holy water bottle, for Christ' sake!

[*He takes it, goes back to the tracks, and urinates in it.*]

NUN: In my day it was up to the man to make conversation.

GUSTAV: Do you find many people down there dead?

NUN: What the hell kinda question is that?

GUSTAV: [*Coming back with the holy water bottle*] All right, forget it.

NUN: [*Takes bottle.*] Nah! I'm sorry. I'll think about it—oooh! Are you touchy! [*Thinks.*] Nah, can't say that I do. Found a artificial arm once. Wore it back to the convent—you shoulda heard them carry on! [*Laughs.*] No dead people, though. Why?

GUSTAV: Oh, I was just wondering.

NUN: You think about doin' it? Jumpin' in front of a train?

GUSTAV: Do you?

NUN: Me? Hell no! Wouldn't work anyway. You think it's so easy to kill a nun? Nah! But why you interested?

GUSTAV: Well, to be frank—

NUN: That was my father's name—

GUSTAV: Really? It was my grandfather's name, too—I have thought about it. In fact, when I was an adolescent I had a fantasy about being thrown under those grinding wheels . . . by my mother.

NUN: What you get her?

GUSTAV: Beg pardon?

NUN: Your mother! What you get her? It's Mother's Day!

GUSTAV: Why, nothing.

NUN: Cheap son of a bitch. At the convent today they had a special mass said, just for me. Then we had a ritual lunch. Ate a Jewish kid. [*He recoils in horror.*] Kosher butcher! [*She laughs.*] Well, come on, ask me!

GUSTAV: Ask you what?

NUN: What a sweet young thing like me is doin' down here—where your manners, where's your social technique, you can't even make conversation! I hope you got better luck wit the dames, though I ain't too sure. Well, anyways, where's your sense of socialness—was you raised wit the animals? Your mother sure as hell didn't raise you.

GUSTAV: [*Touchy*] No, she didn't.

NUN: Well, ask me.

GUSTAV: Ask you what?

NUN: Look, repeat after me. What's a sweet young thing . . .

GUSTAV: What's a sweet young thing . . .

NUN: Like you . . .

GUSTAV: Like you . . .

NUN: Doin' down here . . .

GUSTAV: Doin' down here . . .

NUN: [*Quickly and loudly*] What's a sweet young thing like you doin' down here?

GUSTAV: [*Repeating, almost hysterical*] What's a sweet young thing like you doin' down here?

NUN: Sure you wanna know?

GUSTAV: Yes!

NUN: Well, glad you asked. 'Cause it's a story for our time. It ain't no news that religion is in decline. I know, 'cause I'm in decline wit it. Hell, I'd even say I went down wit it, but you might mistake my meanin'. [*Roars with laughter. He doesn't respond.*] Well, anyways, our convent fell on bad times. We ran outa money. Dere we was. No school. No kids to take milk money from. Dirt poor. Well. Dis cross fell on me, 'cause I'm the mother superior. What was we gonna do? At the beginnin' we took in laundry an' baby-sat. But that wasn't enough to keep a whole convent goin', so's I had to be the man and go out and get a job. It's hard for a gal to get work, God damn it. Only thing they'd hire me for was killin' rats. Seems my years teachin' in the Catholic schools had something to do wit it, I had good aim and plenty of muscle and I was heartless about poundin' the screamin' little mothers. Why, I could kill one wit one swing of the arm—the rats, I mean. Well, it ain't a bad job but I gotta work nights which means I don't get much chance to nun anymore an' shiiiit!, do I miss it! But I'm still a mother and their leader and proud of it. I ain't Mother Superior Mary and Martha not to mention Lazarus for nothin'. [*Offers him thermos.*] Have some more?

GUSTAV: No.

NUN: Aw, come on! Let's drink to Mother's Day.

GUSTAV: I think I'll just be . . .

NUN: What's a matter? Ain't you gotta mom?

GUSTAV: . . . No.

NUN: She dead?

GUSTAV: [*Sorrowfully*] . . . Lost!

NUN: Oh, she is, hanh? Took you long enough to admit it. You kill her?

GUSTAV: No!

NUN: You a bastard?

GUSTAV: Oh, for God's sake!

NUN: Well, shit then, let's drink to Mother's Day! [*Fills the thermos cup, forces it into his hand, lifts the bottle in toast.*] Here's mud in your gut! [*They drink. He coughs.*] That's the whiskey!

GUSTAV: Well, Sister . . .

NUN: Mother Superior Mary and Martha not to mention Lazarus, but you can call me Mother.

GUSTAV: M . . . M . . . M . . . Mother . . .

NUN: Yes, son . . . ?

GUSTAV: There's a bus I can take. [*Tries to run off. She rushes after him and nearly tackles him.*] Let go, let go!

NUN: It's cold out dere and it's dangerous waitin' on them buses. You only got a few minutes to wait. Don't make no sense you runnin' off. I can see your mother didn't raise you!

GUSTAV: Leave my mother out of this! [*Still tries to elude her, but she holds on to him.*]

NUN: Whatsa matter, you don't like my company?

GUSTAV: No, I don't like your company. Let go of me, let go of me—
[*Gets away from her, but she grabs him again. With a difference. She is on her knees and starting to weep. She holds her free hand out to him, supplicating. She sniffles. With part of her nun's habit she wipes the tears from her eyes and blows her nose. She is too overcome with anguish to speak for a moment. Her lips tremble.*]

NUN: [*Finally she can speak.*] Oh, please, don't abandon an aged woman here in the dirty subway. I know my life has hardened me, but once, once was I soft and delicate. Don't leave me to pine alone, especially not on Mother's Day. Think of your mother, I'm sure she'd be my age. Have a heart. An old woman, helpless and alone without solace . . . [*Sobs.*] On Mother's Day!

GUSTAV: Oh, for God's sake. Look, I don't want to stay— [*Weeping, she pulls at his suit coat.*] Please . . . [*She wails.*] Sister . . .

NUN: [*Sobbing*] Mother Superior Mary and Martha not to mention Lazarus, but you can call me Mother—

GUSTAV: M . . . M . . . M . . . Mother . . . !

NUN: Don't you see me kneeling to you? Look at the filth around you—who knows what I'm kneeling in? I lift my rosaries to you—wait until your train comes! Our Father that art in heaven . . . [*Sobbing and wailing*] Succor an elderly woman who has not long . . . to live!!! [*Breaks down.*]

GUSTAV: All right, all right. I'll stay with you until my train comes.

NUN: [*Sobbing in gratitude*] Oh, thank you, thank you. God bless. Wanna shot?

GUSTAV: What?

NUN: A shot, you know. [*Mimes guzzling.*] Jeez, what a

lemon— [*He stiffens, offended.*] No, no, I didn't mean
it. You're a sweet boy. But I got just what you need. A
bottle of bourbon. I carry a bottle between me and my
girdle. Want some?

GUSTAV: No.

NUN: Mind if I have some?

GUSTAV: Do what you like.

NUN: [*Gets the bottle. Drinks.*] That's good. Now, where
was we. Well, look, now that you decided to stay you
can tell me about your op'ras!

GUSTAV: Well, perhaps I can give you some idea. As I've
said already, they are autobiographical.

NUN: Ain't all art? I mean, ain't all art! Get a load of the
shit they scribble on these walls. [*Points at the wall.*]
"Cunnilingus is next to Godliness"!

GUSTAV: Well, as I was saying, I have confronted anew
this problem—

NUN: Think they made that up? Nah! It's autobiographical. Look at the Gospels. Think they made all that shit
up? Jesus, they was too stupid. They wrote from what
they knew. Think anybody can make stuff up outa the
blue like it really happened? Shiit! That's a talent and
don't I know it. [*Takes a swig.*]

GUSTAV: And I have decided that it is justified. That is,
that opera should be—

NUN: Know how I know it? I tried. Sure, I tried to create.
I sent that publisher my novel: *Hot Sally and Her Cold
Tamale.* Did they want it? Nah! [*Another long swig.*]

GUSTAV: Yes, it is hard not to be wanted, but as I was—

NUN: So I sold it to Father Magillacutty, the local porno
maker, for a ten-year indulgence and that was dirt
cheap.

GUSTAV: Well, it's even worse for the composer. Singers,
conductors, even they have an easy time, but who
wants the composer? No one. In any case, my newest
opera—

NUN: Sure, I tried to create. Caaaaarist! Did I wanna create. [*Long swig. Her speech is becoming blurred.*] To
get somethin' lastin' down on paper. Any kinda paper:
toilet tissue; just so's I'd last after my death. An' ain't
that the purpose of bein' alive? Immortality? To survive
beyond them all? [*Long swig.*] Well, sure as hell none
of us can do it physically; but we can do it as artists.

[*Long swig.*] Well, I wanted to like fire—it burned in me! I spent all my time thinkin' about creatin', about becomin' immortal. Create! Naaaaah! All I could create was some snivelin' little monster come outa my inside, that's all. Pus personified wit a rubber mouth, pluckin' at me! Shiiiit! [*Long, bitter swig.*]

GUSTAV: My new opera is called *Urlicht,* that is, *Primal Light.* It is a little autobiographical. It takes place on Mother's Day many years ago—you mean you had a child?

NUN: [*Wary*] What?

GUSTAV: Did you have a child? You just said—

NUN: A kid? Whatever gave you that idea? Caaarist! A kid???!! That was . . . just another novel I tried to write. [*Harsh laugh.*] And anyways, who ever heard of a nun wit a kid? Tell me about your op'ra.

GUSTAV: I'll tell you about my newest—

NUN: You do that. A nun wit a kid! Hahahahahahaha! I think I had enough. [*Puts bottle away.*]

GUSTAV: [*Starts shyly but soon warms up. She settles back sullenly, prepared to be bored.*] The opera is called *Urlicht,* that is, *Primal Light.* It is a little autobiographical. It takes place on Mother's Day many years ago: twelve, to be exact. In the cast there are the little boy . . . and his mom.

[*The* NUN *looks heavenward.*]

GUSTAV: The opera incepts with the *Urlicht* theme: strings softly caressing and undulating; the horns bringing in the theme proper in E flat major. The beginning is happy for the boy and his mom. The *Urlicht* beams contentedly above them. Then they decide: Decision Motive: D major above consecutive fifths to go for a walk. Decision to go for a walk motive: D minor over diminished sevenths. Oh, fateful hapless decision! Fateful Hapless Decision motive: D major above D minor with diminished fifths and consecutive sevenths. And on those notes of premonition: the aria: I've been feeling lumpy and he's sort of strange—the first act ends. Then, I hope I'm not losing you . . . [*The* NUN *looks utterly bewildered.*]

GUSTAV: . . . there AM the second act. They walk, and the boy loses his mom. That's it! Do you understand? The moment! The crux of the tragedy.

[*The rest of the speech, except where noted, is delivered very quickly.*]

GUSTAV: The *Urlicht* at the beginning of the act becomes even more opaque: *Urlicht* Opacity Theme in C minor with E flat major in the background and oboe solo. Oh, unfortunates! They walk in the park! Baleful Urban Renewal Theme counter *Urlicht* Opacity Motive with reminiscences of Decision and Fateful Hapless Decision Motives with French horn barrage and auto exhaust chorale. The *Urlicht* is darker and darker and [*Slowly, with great intensity*] the boy loses his mom. She slips out of her leash and runs off!

[*Very quickly again*] He chases her with no success. With *Urlicht*'s increasing Darkening his figurative eyesight fails. Baleful Urban Renewal Theme accompanied by Figurative Eyesight Failure with Increasing Darkening *Urlicht* in the background. And besides, he's a fat little boy and no match for his mama. Waddling on the old campground sung by four sopranos in the pit.

[*Slowing to a normal rate of speech*] The third act takes place at home. The boy has relinquished the chase. After twelve minutes of dodecaphonic despair, the curtain rises. He paces and looks at his watch. He goes to the door, opens it, and with ever-decreasing optimism calls: [*Sung to a tune similar to "Frère Jacques," in the minor key*] "Mother, Mother, come home, little Mother." All there is is silence and the sound of her lost, desolate howling in the distance.

[*During the last part of the speech increasing horror has dawned on the* NUN's *face.*]

NUN: Oh no . . . no!

GUSTAV: Yes, he calls her to no avail. In the whole opera she never comes.

NUN: [*Singing as though sick to her stomach*] "Mother, Mother, come home, little Mother . . ."

GUSTAV: Yes, that's the opera's greatest aria and my own favorite moment. I've translated it into Italian: "*A casa, a casa, piccola madre.*" Sometimes it hurts for the audience to know too much; this way they can fish for the meaning in the ever-stocked streams of the collective unconscious. Would you like me to sing it for you?

NUN: What? Oh, I'll tell you what . . . [*Starts gathering*

her stuff.] . . . my coffee break's about over, I think I'll be . . .

GUSTAV: Oh, it'll only take me a moment. I'll sing it for you. Remember I'm not a singer really, just a composer, and in reality it's a duet. She punctuates it by howling offstage. It increases the poignancy of the moment. Well, I'll try to give you an idea. [*Sings to the "Toreador Song":*]

> A *casa, a casa, piccola madre*
> *Vieni a me, tuo piccolo figlio!*

[*The* NUN *howls like a dog in response.*]

GUSTAV: [*Shocked*] What? You know her response? How? [*Realizes.*] Oh no!!!

NUN: [*Weeping*] Yes, it's me, your mother!

GUSTAV: [*Weeping*] My . . . M . . . M . . . M . . . Mother!

NUN: I heard you calling every night. But I'd been found by the Sisters of Mercy and chained in their courtyard. All I could do was howl!

GUSTAV: Oh . . . M . . . M . . . M . . . Mother!

NUN: At length came the winter and your calling ceased. The sisters won me over with food and drink. I grew to love and wish to emulate them. After a year I was inducted into their convent.

GUSTAV: M . . . M . . . M . . . Mother!

NUN: Son!

GUSTAV: We must stay together forever and ever, M . . . M . . . Mother!

NUN: Son????

GUSTAV: I said we must stay together forever and ever.

NUN: Forever and ever?

GUSTAV: I know it sounds like a long time, but in each other's arms you'll be surprised at how fast it'll go. Tomorrow a new light, an *Echt Urlicht*, dawns for us. What an opera this will make! Tonight I spend with you in the subway, tomorrow you join me in everlasting communion!

NUN: Communion! Everlasting, with you? Well, look . . . [*She doesn't remember his name.*] . . . sonny . . .

GUSTAV: Gustav, Mom!

NUN: Oh yeah, that's it! [*Wondering who in hell thought that name up*] Gustav???!! Well, we've lived apart these many years; and well, each of us, you know, has led separate lives . . .

GUSTAV: Unhappy, lonely, lonely, unhappy lives!

NUN: Well, My point is I'm used to bein' a nun. I've advanced, too—I'm a mother superior now. To wake up all of a sudden an ordinary everyday MOTHER is more 'n I can take.

GUSTAV: What? You mean to enact that primal rejection again, here and now?

NUN: What? Shit! All I wanna do is kill rats.

GUSTAV: No, no!

NUN: Well, sorry if it hurts you . . . [*Remembers his name at the last minute.*] . . . Gustav . . . but that's the way it is.

GUSTAV: [*With a cry, collapses in a heap.*]

NUN: Now, Gustav, it's not like love really exists or there's any possible tenderness in bein' alive. It's all loneliness, you should know that by now.

GUSTAV: But I've been so alone.

NUN: But . . . Gustav . . . so have I and I've survived. I know for you it's hard and horrifying, and it's calloused me, but you see, in rat killing I've found my true immortality. Every time I kill a rat I prove I exist—I prove my absence or presence can alter the course of a life. It's the function of a god! I need that feeling, we all do, but in creating I couldn't find it. In destroying I've found my essence. You see, I *am* in the swish of this sleeve as I pound them squealing little mothers. I have a purpose now. And to renounce all this . . . ?

GUSTAV: I have nothing against your being a working mother.

NUN: No, Gustav, it just wouldn't work out.

GUSTAV: But I need a mommy.

NUN: You're a man now, a creator!

GUSTAV: No! I want a childhood. Don't leave me again. I want a warm crib and someone to rock me in it. Oh no, Mommy, be a mommy to me. Let me rest in the glen of your motherhood.

NUN: Oh, Gustav, gushing that way. You should be ashamed of yourself!

GUSTAV: Save me and I'll never gush again.

NUN: Don't be stupid! If you wanted to, you could create happiness around yourself. All it takes is a little imagination and will. Now shut up and stop clinging to me.

GUSTAV: I won't let go of you, I won't.

NUN: Now, Gustav, suppose somebody comes along and
catches you? You wanna be arrested for raping a nun?
There's something horrible about raping a nun even if
it is your own mother!

GUSTAV: It's inconceivable to me, do you hear, inconceivable that any mother could be so heartless.

NUN: [*Becoming furious*] Now, Gustav, you're behaving
badly, very badly. Self-control and obedience are the
earmarks by which we know a Catholic youth. Besides,
only pansies cling to their mothers!

GUSTAV: [*shocked*] Oh! Mama!

NUN: Now, don't tell me any son of mine is queer. That's
too much! The op'ras I can take, but queer!

GUSTAV: What's that got to do with anything? Love for
me has always been a wilting phenomenon. For the
operatic stage alone, not for real life. It was after my
first attempt at hetero sex that I tried to commit suicide.
I threw myself into the Walpurgis Stream. They fished
me out and I wrote my first opera. It was called: *You're
Licked*. It concerned a man who, in exchange for
greater potency, loses an eye to the stream of con-
sciousness. All that screaming . . . but you see? It is I
who am screaming—I scream and scream and no one
ever hears, no one ever hears. But finally, you must.
Stay with me.

NUN: Gustav, you're sick! You need a shrink! Caaaarist!
What do you think it is? Have you grown up or not?
You want too much from people, too much from being
alive. You'll always be alone and unhappy. So what?
You shrug that off. And you're ugly. So nobody's gonna
wanna pretend to love you. So what? Each of us got
rules and regulations for our lives, they're yours, you
gotta play within them. Nobody wants to sleep wit
you—play with yourself. Nobody wants to talk wit you,
put mirrors up. Now I'm sick of all this, my coffee
break's over, good-bye.

GUSTAV: But I do all that. And don't you realize? I'm
dying from it!

NUN: God damn it, you don't die from feelin's. You die
from bein' cornered and hit wit a baseball bat. Feelin's.
Bullshit! You wake up one morning with a feeling that
don't agree wit you—turn it off. Otherwise you got
yourself to blame for bein' unhappy. Now let go of me.

GUSTAV: You don't love me anymore?

NUN: God damn you, let go of me!

GUSTAV: You don't love me anymore!!

NUN: No, I don't love you, you son of a bitch! You think I ever loved you? Caaarist! You cause me nine months of agony, you wrinkle and deform my belly, you make me sick after you come, and I'm supposed to love you, just like that? And then, when you was a kid, all you did was cling and pull, and pull and cling! I'm sick of you, sick of the memory of you. Why do you think I slipped outa that leash? Accident? Bullshit! I planned it, I hadda get away from you, you was eatin' me up! You was stranglin' me! Now let me pass!

GUSTAV: So, you want to run off again, you bitch, you, and leave me in the sewer. Well, I won't let you, I'll hold you here, I'll hold you! [*Grabs her.*]

[*They struggle. She tries to escape but he catches her again. A train is heard very distant. She kicks him in the groin and he lets her go. She runs to the baseball bat and beats him with it. He tries to protect himself but fails, and she smashes his skull.*

The train is closer. She runs to the track, locates it, runs back to GUSTAV *and kicks him onto the track. The train runs over his body as it passes.*

The NUN *pauses and pulls herself together. She looks at the baseball bat. She sits down on the bench, pulls out the bottle of bourbon. She takes a swig. She shrugs.*]

NUN: Well, one more rat today!

[*Singing "Mother Machree" lustily, she gathers her stuff together and starts toward the tracks as the lights fade.*]

END

WISDOM AMOK

NOTES

Wisdom Amok is meant to be presented in a very free, yet quite simple style. The stage is meant to be bare. Set pieces may be brought on so as to suggest different locales but no attempt should be made to design any given, permanent set. The larger the space, the better. The style of the piece may be very freely chosen, depending on the participants and their interests.

There are only a few continuing parts. They are as follows:

FATHER AUGUSTINE WISDOM, a man in his thirties.

MOTHER SUPERIOR ELEANORA FRANKLINUS. The woman who plays this part can be of any description, as is clear from the script. However, she must be a virtuoso at playing different kinds of attitudes and aspects of personalities.

NUNCLE, a beautiful young woman who is REX's attendant.

The other parts can melt back into the general ensemble, which should include enough people to suggest a considerable body of MAD NUNS at the Madhouse for Nuns, NURSES and ATTENDANTS at the wake, and so on. The NUNS obviously need not all be female; males may be used as often as necessary in the various parts in the play. The scrim at back should be operable, and slides and film should be clearly used. Those sequences which call for them may be extended if the possibility exists.

A NARRATOR may be used to announce the locations of the scenes.

Improvisations may be used to fill out those scenes which involve the MAD NUNS.

ACT I

Scene 1

A wake is in progress. Downstage an open coffin. Weeping relatives. As lights build, a MIDDLE-AGED WOMAN *kneels at the coffin, crosses herself, and sobs. She bends over and kisses the corpse. A* YOUNG MAN, *evidently her son, escorts her to the side, where she receives the condolences of some of the others. In the background can be heard quiet, sad organ music. Suddenly* FATHER AUGUSTINE WISDOM *enters at back. He stops and looks about. He seems overcome by grief. Very slowly, weeping, he walks to the coffin, kneels, and crosses himself. The relatives look at him curiously.*

FATHER WISDOM: [*A cry*] Chris!
   [*He flings himself over the edge of the coffin and kisses the corpse passionately.*
   This causes a great stir. A group of MEN *confer, and one runs out. The* MIDDLE-AGED WOMAN *peers at* FATHER WISDOM *with huge eyes and looks stunned. The* YOUNG MAN *holds her back.*]
FATHER WISDOM: [*Whispering*] Oh, Chris, Chris, you've deserted me, you've abandoned yourself on death's pointy stake! Why? I waited and waited for your return, and thus must I see you, gelid, waxen, the shattered remains of masculine beauty. [*This last sentence seems especially shocking to the relatives.*]
   Here! Here! My three volumes of poems, dedicated to you, unpublished. [*Reaches under his cassock and drops in three plastic-bound manuscripts.*] Here! Here—my two books of short stories, dedicated to you, unpublished. [*Reaches under and pulls out two thicker manuscripts and drops them into the coffin.*] Here!

243

Here—my first stream-of-consciousness novel, dedicated to you, unpublished. [*Reaches under and drops an enormous manuscript into the coffin.*] Here, here, my volume of memoirs of our childhood, dedicated to you, unpublished. [*Reaches into a briefcase he has carried in with him, pulls out an enormous manuscript and with great difficulty crams this into the coffin.*] I am emptied now, I have surrendered my creativity to the grave! That bitch which begat us, this is her doing! To ruin me, to undo me. She has taken you to her frigid embrace in the coffin! Oh, Chris!

[*Bends over the coffin, weeping. The* MIDDLE-AGED WOMAN'*s horror during all this has grown greatly. Her* SON *has difficulty in holding her back. The relatives look shocked.*

The MAN *who ran out returns with a funeral parlor* OFFICIAL, *who looks very concerned. He quiets the relatives, presses the* MIDDLE-AGED WOMAN'*s hands, then walks to the coffin, kneels beside* FATHER WISDOM, *and crosses himself. He leans very close to* FATHER WISDOM *and almost apologetically whispers:*]

OFFICIAL: Father Wisdom.

[*Looking dazed,* FATHER WISDOM *lifts a tear-stained face.*]

OFFICIAL: Father Wisdom. I'm dreadfully sorry, but you're at the wrong wake. Your brother's wake is down the hall.

FATHER WISDOM: [*Peers at this man, then cries out.*] Chris! [*Again, kisses the corpse, edging around the manuscripts.*]

[*The* MIDDLE-AGED *woman can contain herself no longer. She breaks free of her* SON.]

MIDDLE-AGED WOMAN: You leave my daughter alone.

FATHER WISDOM: This is not your daughter, my good woman, this is my brother, Chris.

MIDDLE-AGED WOMAN: What? That's my daughter, my Diane. [*Weeping*] My baby.

[*The* WOMAN *hurls herself into the coffin. Many people come running up to the coffin, but the* OFFICIAL, *fearing a riot, waves them back.*]

FATHER WISDOM: [*To the* WOMAN] Kindly get off my brother. You are going to mess him up.

OFFICIAL: [*To* RELATIVES] Friends, I'll take care of this. Meanwhile there are coffee and doughnuts down the hall.

WOMAN: [*Lifting her head up out of the coffin*] You stay away from my lily-of-the-valley, you bum! She was pure, you hear me? Pure! She didn't die to get her first kiss at her own funeral from some kinky priest!

FATHER WISDOM: [*Angry*] How dare you refer to my brother as "she"! He was all man! Why, he died for his country. "She," indeed!

WOMAN: And another thing! Your shitty books are in my way. [*With some difficulty, she tosses the plastic-bound poems out of the coffin.*]

FATHER WISDOM: My poems! My stream-of-consciousness novel!

[FATHER WISDOM *runs after his books and crams them into the coffin again. The* WOMAN *continues throwing out manuscripts.* FATHER WISDOM *chases them and then shoves them into the coffin.*]

FATHER WISDOM: God damn you! And I'm a priest, so remember that!

ANOTHER WOMAN: [*Yelling*] Look! It's her kid's wake. You wanna let her enjoy it, hanh?

WOMAN: [*In the coffin*] Oh, Diane! Why'd you have to die so young, hanh? Why didn't the Virgin take me or your brother—he's sixteen—he's had enough of living. But you, my little dove. [*She cannot continue and lies down in the coffin.*]

FATHER WISDOM: [*With priestly dignity, looking sympathetically at the* WOMAN *lying in the coffin*] I'm sorry, my daughter, but you have made so horrible, so embarrassing a mistake in front of all these good people. I know that tomorrow you will be mortified beyond words, but I think I can speak for all present when I say that I understand what grief does to our perceptions, and while your mistake seems a very strange one indeed, we all realize it proceeds from sorrow and not from malice.

WOMAN: [*Leaping out of the coffin*] Holy God! That's her father talkin'. I recognize that drunkard's way with words. He sent you, didn't he? He sent you to ruin my daughter's wake for me. He knew, he knew that was the one thing he could still do that would wreck my life. Look, buddy, you tell that rotten jerk-off I got a dick on his trail, and if he don't come through with the alimony soon, I'm gonna have him put in Alcatraz for life!

FATHER WISDOM: Mother! It's you! You've come back from the grave, borrowing this hideous, wasted form to fool me.

[*The* WOMAN, *shocked, recoils.*]

FATHER WISDOM: Now I understand why I didn't recognize anybody here. You've packed the wake, haven't you, Mother, packed it with these ghouls, these monsters, intimate with you in the nether world.

[*A roar arises from all present. "You bastard!," "Shut up!," "Kill him!" and worse are heard from the crowd. The* OFFICIAL *backs away, frightened.* WISDOM *strides behind the coffin and faces them grandly.*]

WISDOM: Her hordes of night have come! Legions and legions of demons, but I'll win. I'm armed, you see, armed with bravery, armed with beauty, armed with holiness. [*He sweeps down and picks up the corpse. It is a lovely twelve-year-old girl with black hair, fine bones, and a lot of rouge. He waves the corpse about as though elevating the Host.*] I am armed with Chris! [*The* RELATIVES *scream, fall back, turn their eyes away.*]

WISDOM: Ah, I knew it: Chris is a saint. He discomforts Satan. He routs Satan's army.

[WISDOM *runs around the coffin, down the aisle, and out, waving the corpse all the while. A* MAN *starts to run after him, but* WISDOM *turns and waves the corpse at him. The* MAN *freezes in place.* WISDOM *disappears. A shocked pause. Suddenly the* WOMAN *screams:*]

WOMAN: After that creep!

[*Followed by a troop of men, she rushes out after the* PRIEST.

The OFFICIAL *is sick behind the coffin.*]

BLACKOUT

Scene 2

On a screen at back the following is projected. A neutral voice reads:

VOICE ONE: [*Off*] A letter from Our Lady of Eternal Clarity Hospital, The Cups Estate, Willow Grove, Penna. 19139. Dear——. The lack of a name is purposeful, for that sudden stoppage of something you feel you ought to know yet can't quite remember is one of the first signs of madness. It is a symptom we know well here at Our Lady of Eternal Clarity, for we've all experienced it. Yes, we are mad nuns, and we want your sympathy. Many of us went crazy teaching your children in Catholic schools, year after year after year after year after year after year after year after year. Getting stuck—that's another early sign. One of our sisters formed the first Boy Scout troop ever in the Irish-Italian-Polish ghetto to which she had been assigned. She worked hour upon hour upon hour, never shirking her nunly duty. Think of the service she rendered those Irish-Italian-Polish young men, further ingraining into them those values of faith, hope and—oops, forgot the familiar again. She broke down on a campout, driven crazy by an army of preternaturally insistent cicadas. Her story is typical. Every one of our sisters has a similar story behind her—lives of love and service leading to madness and internment for life. We need your prayers. We need your money. We have every confession you ever made on tape in our IBM computer. Do you believe that? If you do, you had better beware of paranoia. Won't you help? Yours in Jesus, his Mother and Saint Jude, Patron of the Hopeless. Mother Superior, Eleanora Franklinus.
[*The slide changes: The picture of a wrecked motorcycle under a Mighty Mouse is shown. Under it the following is printed. A different voice reads:*]
VOICE TWO: [*Off*] Another motorcycle has been found in the Willow Grove Park under the Mighty Mouse. It is

the fourth to be found there in four months. It has been
traced to Billy Humphrey, also known as Jocko, who
disappeared two weeks ago.

Scene 3

*A hospital room. A hospital bed has been rolled on stage,
behind it a screen.* FATHER WISDOM *is in the hospital
bed. He is totally wrapped in bandages; he is in traction
and in splints. Only his eyes show. He cannot speak. A
little white* NUN *ushers in the* ABBOT *of* FATHER WISDOM,
a handsome older man, dressed in a white cassock.

A pause. The ABBOT, *shy, speaks:*

ABBOT: Hello, Augustine. How's your body? I'm glad
you're not in too much pain, or at least one is given to
hope that.
   [WISDOM *tries to speak. Only a gargle can be heard.*]
ABBOT: Good. I would venture, Father Wisdom, that you
realize this meeting is inevitable. There is little in life
more ineluctable than reproach. I had to choose today
for our conversation for I am personally busy with all
our drives, spring being here, I mean charity drives, of
course. I've gotten rid of the other sort long ago. [*He
snorts and runs his tongue over his dry lips.*] I've forgotten my Chap Stick. But I want you to understand
that I understand. Whatever happened, you must understand that I understand, do you understand? Now
that we understand that, I must say I am sorry you
picked a lower-class wake at which to misbehave. Why
couldn't you have chosen an upper-class family? They
at least admit that aberrations exist. In some rich families they honor them. Who knows? Had you chosen
the right wake, they might have made you a totem, or
given us a contribution for our spring drive. You can
never tell with these wealthy sorts. Now, the problem,
Augustine, is not my reaction, but that of our archbishop, our Little Father. He is quite annoyed, to put

it mildly, that you chose this delicate and unhappy time in the history of Holy Mother to act peculiar in public. It is also a pity that you left your unpublished writings behind, for our Little Father has read them. He was not pleased by them. He disapproves of free verse and thinks stream-of-conciousness out of date, both as a novelistic technique and as a model for living. He feels that it drowned with Virginia Woolf, to whom you may remember is related on the maternal side. Finally, he was very unhappy with the subject matter of your work, and the obviously authorial obsessions which he found kept flitting through the pages. Furthermore, your case is not helped by certain reports received from our diocesan spies about certain abuses of yours in the general area referred to as the Flesh. Now you must understand, these adolescent booboos don't bother me in the least, but they do look bad, especially when recorded on videotape by hidden cameras. Now, Augustine, I want you to remain with us, and I mean that. In an age when every cleric under forty is shedding his vestments and racing after nun flesh, it is a pleasure to know a priest like you who loves scholarship, hates women, and fosters guilt in the confessional. It was on the ladder of prelates like yourself the Holy Mother achieved her pinnacle of power in that great age. I have communicated this opinion to our Little Father and he agrees you should be given another chance. You are slated to speak on Holy Mother's position on the abortion controversy in two months' time. This is vital to our archbishop, and he wanted me, nay, urged me, to assign someone else. But I told him that yours was our best yet least ambitious mind in residence. I convinced him with difficulty. But when I reminded him of your obedience and humility he was pleased. Between now and then you may rest. I am relieving you of your teaching load. I want you to relax and compose your speech in peace and quiet. Remember, the speech will be both televised and broadcast on the radio—"simulcast" is, I believe, the ugly term they employ. So rest, think hard, and prepare yourself. Farewell.

[*The* ABBOT *is about to rise when* WISDOM *mumbles desperately through his bandages.*]

ABBOT: That's right. That is your last chance. If you don't
do well in that speech, you will be sent as a missionary
to Our Lady of Eternal Clarity Convent.

[WISDOM *mumbles again, louder and more strangu-
lated.*]

ABBOT: That's right. The madhouse for nuns.

[*The* ABBOT *rushes to the door.* WISDOM *mumbles
again, most loudly.*]

ABBOT: All right. If you insist.

[*Abruptly the* ABBOT *blesses* WISDOM *and leaves.*]

Scene 4

*The stage is bare. Tambourines are heard in the distance.
Gradually a procession appears onstage and crosses the
stage. Two* NUNS *are playing tambourine. They are followed by a* GROUP OF NUNS *walking two by two carrying
parasols. Then* FOUR NUNS, *heavier than the others, carrying between them a* MAN *in a motorcycle jacket and
tight jeans tied to a pole like a beast. Following this
comes a* NUN *who is hunchbacked, crippled, with one
eye, walking with a cane. A very beautiful* YOUNG
WOMAN *holds a parasol over her head. Another* SMALL
GROUP OF NUNS *brings up the rear, walking again in
pairs. Some of the* NUNS *carry holy emblems instead of
parasols. When the procession reaches center stage, all
the* NUNS *turn, face the audience and curtsy. Then they
proceed. After they have left the stage, there is a*

BLACKOUT

Scene 5

*The stage represents a speaker's platform. The audience
is treated as those who have come to hear the program.
There is a small podium. An* ANNOUNCER *appears.*

ANNOUNCER: Good evening, good Catholic friends and others. This evening is the third in a continuing series: Catholicism—Glittering Anachronism or Way to Salvation? This evening our topic is Sexuality and the Abortion, and our speaker is the distinguished teacher, Father Augustine Wisdom. [*He applauds loudly. No one else does.*] After Father Wisdom's speech this evening there will be entertainment from the St. Monica's Boys' Choir . . . [*Very loud applause piped in*] and refreshments furnished us by the sisters of St. Alban's on the Green. And now, Father Augustine Wisdom.

[*Again the* ANNOUNCER *applauds.*

FATHER WISDOM *enters, very nervous. He peers out at the audience.*]

WISDOM: Yes indeed, yes indeed, I see her, her forces gathered. [*He walks to the podium, pauses, arranges his notes on the podium.*] Good evening, friends in the Holy Ghost and Mother. This evening my topic is Sexuality and the Abortion in Holy Mother Church. This, fellow Catholics, is quite a controversial issue, since it concerns issue. [*He looks up expectantly.*] That's a pun. [*Pause.*] We hear so much about sex nowadays, and naturally our young, being people, are more and more anxious to take the great leap into the crevice of pleasure which sex is made to represent. After the flood comes the punishment, though, for the more sinful, the pleasure-giver, the woman. A little sac on the inside of her stomach, a soon-to-be baby, and no father. The wages of her pleasure and that of her filthy amour; nine months of distension, deformation, and agony. This is a tragedy we see every day, and naturally the young woman is tempted to compound her filthy sin with a worse sin: murder—that is, abortion. But since abortions are easy to come by nowadays, some clarification of Holy Mother's sexual position is necessary. First, the act itself. Now no one, certainly not the Pope, wishes to deny the potency of the sexual drive in humans. Certainly no one, especially not his Holiness, would deny the intense pleasure of sex. But are we here to just wallow in our filthy longings for escape and pointless pleasure? Is this surrender of dignity and control the main focus of our earthly existence? What if it is? Look at the consequences: horrible, deforming, brain-dam-

aging gonorrhea for the male, a painful baby for the
female. No! Life is not like that. We are for other, for
better things. The pleasure, the ecstasy of sex is like so
many other pleasures and ecstasies, the devil's weapon
to trap unwary Catholics into sin and self-destruction.
Now in the back row, there must be one unconvinced
by my arguments who is saying, "After all, pleasure is
important. It also attaches itself to eating." But male or
female in the back row—it hardly matters which nowadays—think of this. Why do we eat? We eat to nourish
our bodies, to keep them alive. Go ahead, smirk,
Mother. That's why. There is a certain pleasure in eating, haha, I see the twinkle of disdain there too,
Mother. But if we eat primarily for pleasure, what happens? Our bodies distend and distort. We deform, not
strengthen, ourselves, and shorten, not lengthen, our
lives. If we eat solely for the pleasure of smashing,
chewing, and swilling the food in our mouths, crushing
the meat with our blunted teeth, blunted because we
no longer use them for tearing and to kill, mashing the
meat into wet slobbery lumps, besieging our gums and
our teeth; if we eat purely for the pleasure of darting
our dulled and dented tongues about the prey caught
in our mouths, touching, tasting, caressing, palpating,
kissing, sucking that meat that we have caught; if we
eat solely to joy in the exercise of our jaws, those heady
drawbridges of infinite subtlety and strength which
with the slightest inkling of will, lift and fall, lift and
fall, with the inexorability of a baby's chest asleep; if
we eat for these reasons, we not only are in darkest sin,
but we are destroying ourselves. Food becomes then
not our meat, but our poison. How many of us sin this
way? Eat for no reason but the animal pleasure it gives
us. Yes, as the whole apparatus, delectably complex yet
so concise, tongue, teeth, gum, and jaw, works, works,
up and down, side to side, slaughtering and changing
the food, working miracles of transformation and death,
transfiguring that food into thousands of thick, wet particles, particles which for each of us change their mean-
ings in kaleidoscopic fashion, there in that theater
which is our mouth— [*He is almost in a fit, raging
about the stage, shaking and slobbering.*] Oh, God, the

glory of our mouths. God be praised for them. God be
praised for that holy water, our slobber. God be praised
for those ultimate weapons, our teeth.

[*The* ANNOUNCER *rushes out onstage and yells over*
WISDOM.]

ANNOUNCER: Thank you, Father Augustine Wisdom.

WISDOM: Oh, if only now I could take a meal into my
mouth's embrace.

ANNOUNCER: [*Even louder*] A wonderful, inspiring speech.

WISDOM: Oh, if only now could I hear the delicious music
of the food squishing in my mouth.

ANNOUNCER: [*Screaming*] Now, what you've been waiting for—the St. Monica's Boys' Choir, led by Anselmo
Insorfatti.

[*The* BOY'S CHOIR *troops on in disarray, obviously having not been totally prepared. Their white cassocks are
in disarray, some have on half a cassock, but bravely
they start yelling over* AUGUSTINE. *They are led by a
wild-looking* MAN *who gyrates to the rhythm.*]

BOY'S CHORUS: [*Singing*] "There is nothing like a dame,
nothing in the world. There ain't anything you can
name that is anything like a dame."

WISDOM: [*Eluding the* ANNOUNCER *and some others who
would drag him off*] Mother, I've seen you in a thousand incarnations tonight, in every conceivable mani-
festation, a feat of Indian grandeur. All of you watching
send us signs back to my mother who controls you.
Augustine knows, knows . . .

CHOIR: [*Louder*] This nearly was mine, this nearly was
Paradise. This nearly was Paradise, this nearly was
mine.

WISDOM: [*Still eluding would-be captors*] I'm not alone,
Mother, I'm not alone. I'll win in the end, I'll slaughter
you.

[CHOIR, *louder, sings,* "*I am a cockeyed optimist.*"]

WISDOM: I'll win, I'll win!

ANNOUNCER: Kill the sound!

WISDOM: I'll win!

CHOIR: I'm a cockeyed optimist (. . . etc.)

[*Suddenly the sound is turned off.* WISDOM *continues
to run around the stage screaming but is inaudible.
The* CHOIR *continues its singing, the* CHOIRMASTER *gy-*

*rating and conducting, but they are moving their lips
inaudibly.*
WISDOM *is chased, caught, and, still screaming, dragged
off, still inaudible.*
The BOYS, *very bewildered, continue singing for a few
beats, moving their lips, but again, there is no sound.*]

BLACKOUT

Scene 6

Bare stage. On the back, pictures are projected of
FATHER WISDOM's *arrival and greeting at Our Lady of
Eternal Clarity Convent. They are blurred and grainy.
But what one mostly sees is* FATHER WISDOM *looking
quite terrified. During the slides, a* VOICE, *expressionless,
reads the following.*

VOICE: A letter: My Most Reverend Monsignor Kelly: I
will be delighted to have Father Wisdom. Your news
was the happiest I have had in many a day. I saw his
performance on television and thought it quite one of
the best plays ever brought off on a Catholic theme.
Surely he intended it as a happening. He will stimulate
our sisters, I am positive. I am glad you were able to
reason with the mother of the late Father Rossi. I am
sure she will not regret the statue, which has more uses,
is far more sightly, and is certainly more permanent
than a corpse, even if the corpse is one's own son. If
any other thing must be communicated me re. Father
Wisdom, please communicate it. I would also appreciate all, and may I emphasize all, relevant documents
regarding his physical and mental condition as of his
last examination. Also, I want all of his writings, and
would appreciate a tape recording of memoirs about
him from former students and associates. As you know,
we feel it wise here to have a complete dossier on
everyone who comes to us prior to the day of their
arrival. I trust you will comply. Yours etcetera, Mother
Superior Eleanora Franklinus.

[*The slides end with a large closeup of* WISDOM's *face looking terrified.*]

BLACKOUT

Scene 7

WISDOM *sits at a table eating breakfast. There is a rap on the door. A* NUN *enters. She appears to be a thirty-year-old man, dressed quite accurately as a nun.* WISDOM *stares at her wide-eyed.*

NUN: Hi, Pops. Just checkin' to see if you was done. [*A pause.*] So, Pops, was you done?

WISDOM: What?

NUN: I says, was you done?

WISDOM: [*Uneasy*] Who, who are you?

NUN: Sister Virgilia went off duty today early, you know, woman's trouble—yeah, we nuns get 'em too. Ain't we human, after all? If you prick us, do we not bleed? I'm her sub. Name's Sister St. Delano Eleanor. [*The* NUN *puts out a very hairy hand as though to shake* WISDOM's *hand.*] And you're Pops Augustine Wisdom, the loony, the weirdie. Oh yeah, I heard all about you. Be careful, Mac, they're watchin' you. So what's doin'? [WISDOM *continues to stare at the* NUN *wide-eyed.*] 'Sat so? [*A pause.*] Don't say? [*A pause. Suddenly the* NUN *explodes.*] Look! It's because I'm a man, ain't it? That's why. Oh, I know all about it. You priests are all alike. What you priests got against men? I come here, livin' in poverty and obedience for the greater glory of da Virgin, and all you priests clam up like I'm a leper. What the hell is it, Mac? [*The* NUN *lights a cigarette, takes a long puff, suddenly starts coughing, hacking and huffing against the door.*] All my life they discriminated against me because I'm a man, and I'm tired of it. You got some coffee left? [*The* NUN *goes to the table, pours himself coffee, belches.*] Ah, dat hits the spot. Sit down!

WISDOM: [*Sits down.*] Well, I didn't mean to . . .

NUN: [*Takes a doughnut, crams it into his mouth.*] You know what 'at's like? Discrimination just because of your sex? Somethin' you can't control? You know what 'at's like? Hearin' all the time men can't do this and men can't do that, and why? 'Cause they're men. And each of them things you always wanted to do. That's the kicker. Like onna the corner, you know how they look at you, when one guy says he wants to be a plumber and the other guy says he wants to be a cop and you says you wanna be a fat lady? You know what dat's like? And then at the family's Christmas dinner, you know how they look at you? Your own family, when one brother says he wants to be a mechanic, and your kid brother says he wants to be a bookie like Pop-pop, and you says you wanna be a fat lady? [*The* NUN *pours another cup of coffee, spills some on the tablecloth.*] Den I got my vocation. I wanted to serve da Lord and da Virgin the right way, like a nun. It came to me in a flash like the light bouncin' all blindin' off a new Korvette ... Be a nun! Well, it was the same story—men can't be nuns, and why? 'Cause they're men. Well, I wasn't gonna take this lyin' down. If I couldn't be a fat lady, I was sure as hell gonna be a nun. [*The* NUN *takes another drag on the cigarette, has another coughing fit, sips more coffee.*] Well there was this big rigama-role about it. They thought I was a queer. Can you imagine that? They thought I was some sort of queer. [*The* NUN *laughs in a huge, belching way.*] Well, I proved I was no queer. I also proved I had the will-power to renounce sex and remain chaste, even while livin' with the other novices. It wasn't easy, I'm here to tell ya. Well, I guess you know, hanh? You know all about keepin' your hands off. Well, it meant a lot of trouble for everybody. They had to go all over to get permission. Even to the Pope, can you imagine? Fi-nally they worked it out and I became the first man who ever was a nun.

WISDOM: I . . .

NUN: You gonna say you ain't so sure. Went to Catholic school too, hanh? Nah. It's on the level.

WISDOM: That's wonderful.

NUN: You're damn tootin' it is. I'm in all the magazines and newspapers. You seen it in *Life*, ain't ya? A big picture of me and my brothers with the caption "Their Brother's a Sister"? They even did a TV special on me called "We're on Our Way to a Unisex Clergy." And I was born in South Philly, just like Eddie Fisher. Well, anyways, thanks for the coffee and stuff. I'm here to take you to Moms St. Sebastian Anselme. She's one of our holiest—missionary work in China, with the Zulus, and at Yale—tough as hell. When I was a novice we used to call her da Red Guard. She's going kinda slow, mostly old age I guess.

[*The* NUN *puts a number of pats of butter into the little patch reserved for medals on his habit.*]

WISDOM: What's her . . . er . . . her . . .

NUN: Para. schitz. with L.I.s.

WISDOM: I beg your pardon?

NUN: Paranoid schizophrenia with lucid intervals.

WISDOM: I hate to be indelicate.

NUN: What's indelicate? It's a fact. She's nuts like all our sisters here. Nuts, crazies, loonies, weirdies, kooks, way-out, spaced-out, far-out, anything you like. I know it, they know it, you know it, what's the use of pretendin'? It don't do no good to pretend, to hide, don't cure 'em. Just the opposite, in fact. For the old South Philly sayin' goes: The long road back to sanity begins at the toll booth marked "I know I'm nuts." So Moms St. Sebastian Anselme's got her problems up here, but that don't make her any the more lovable or in need of a priest. [*The* NUN *picks up the last doughnut on the table, stuffs it in his mouth in one gesture.*] Don't mind me. I'm supposed to be fastin', but I can't keep my mitts off the food.

WISDOM: Help yourself.

NUN: I guess we better go off.

WISDOM: I believe so.

[*The* NUN *leads* WISDOM *out of the room.*]

BLACKOUT

Scene 8

A nun's cell. An old nun sits in a rocking chair, rocking slowly back and forth. This is MOTHER ST. SEBASTIAN ANSELME. *In the course of the scene, all she says is "Christ have mercy on us." Sometimes it is prayerlike, sometimes an imprecation, sometimes a gentle plea, sometimes a shrewd observation, sometimes she sings it, and sometimes it is a scream. She tells her rosary beads over and over. Suddenly, violently,* FATHER WISDOM *bursts into the room. A pause.*

FATHER WISDOM: Good morning. My name is Father Augustine Wisdom and I am here for the confession.

NUN: [*Mumbling*] Christ have mercy on us.

WISDOM: [*Sitting on a small chair*] I live here now. I'm a missionary to all your sisters. I've been appointed. By the archbishop. Our Little Father. I was greeted officially last week by all your sisters in great convocation. I don't suppose you were there. I was surprised by the elaborateness of it all. I haven't heard a brass band in years, and I found the ballet a bit of a shock, and those fireworks! I used to teach. I'll go back to it someday. I'm here for a rest. As a sort of missionary. Or did I say that? Who are you again? [*He reaches into his cassock pocket and pulls out an index card.*] Oh. Mother St. Sebastian Anselme. How do you do? I am Father Augustine Wisdom. I am here for the confession. This is such a lovely place. The grounds are gorgeous. All those lovely slopes and sculptured gardens, and that rippling lake, right in the middle of things. One stumbles onto it and is shocked to have come upon a body without warning, a body of water, that is.

THE NUN: [*Screams.*] Christ have mercy on us!

WISDOM: Well. [*Puts back the index card.*] I suppose we should get on. Death waits round the bend and we don't want to meet Him, our duties undone. What are your sins? [*The* NUN *does not answer but continues to say her rosary without acknowledging him.*] Well, I know it is difficult to own up to Christ's representative. Don't be shy. It is difficult, hurling oneself on one's

sins as if one meant them bodily harm. Can I help you
remember, perhaps? Put your fingers where they didn't
belong lately? [WISDOM *laughs.*] You see, it is difficult
not to be indelicate. No active sins of the flesh? How
about unreciprocated lust? Please allow me to be clear.
Have you felt a longing for another, glimpsed perhaps
without words in the shadowy secret distance, a feeling
you knew never could come to fruition, but a feeling
you nonetheless hugged to your aging nun's breast?
Hugged there until after hours until you ran your
tongue over it in secret? Please be open with me if you
have, for you see, I understand about the absence of
reciprocity in love. I've experienced it.

THE NUN: [*Clicking*] Christ have mercy on us.

WISDOM: You may well sympathize. It is very sad. You
know, there is a kind of poignancy in a lack of reciprocation. And yet also a sort of feverish joy, a comfort
even. At least there isn't all that anxious wondering
about how it will end. You see, there won't be an end.
There won't even be a beginning. And that knowledge
produces an exalted shiver of neverness up and down
the spine which in its way is comforting. I felt that from
my brother Chris.

THE NUN: [*Screams harshly.*] Christ have mercy on us!

WISDOM: Oh dear. I hope that doesn't shock you. I suppose that does amount to an incest of sorts. Well, it
hardly matters now, except *sub specie aeternitatis*, of
course; he died in the war, the one in Asia.

NUN: [*Slobbering*] Christ have mercy on us.

WISDOM: Yes, it was awful for me, awful. You cannot
imagine. I loved him, you see, totally. I felt he was the
only thing I had in an otherwise barren existence, although I didn't even have him in truth.

NUN: Christ have mercy on us.

WISDOM: [*Settles into the chair.*] So most of us fervently
hope. On the other hand, I am a believer in our own
responsibility for salvation and mercy. You see, we cannot be sure there is a Christ, or, being one, that he
cares. What then? Anomie? Despair? The answer is
choice and will: the choice to live our life as though
there were a Christ, and the will to shape our lives, and
lives after death, as we wish. In short, the will and
choice to believe in Christ, not from fear or any hope

of glory—it's been many years since there was any of
that for Catholics—but from a desire to take upon ourselves the responsibility for what we do and for what
befalls us. That is verbatim from a lecture that scan-
dalized my Theology 132 last year—a very bad year for
me, by the way. Well, hardly original thoughts, these.
I am not conscious of imitating anyone, but anymore,
those syllables I would have once identified as my
words have a familiar taste to them and are stale. It is
as though I were taking already chewed meat from
someone else's mouth, and pretending I am the first to
chew. The meat's juices mingle with another's saliva.
Where does it come from. [*Suddenly his voice hard-
ens.*] You know, Mother, don't you? [*He smiles.*] A
cliché. I'm such a cliché. I'll entitle my autobiography
Incident in Cliché, as soon as I invent the incident.
Everything has happened to me before, everything in
my life has such a hackneyed tinge. Oh, I'm not claiming to be an old soul tired after too many lives. This
life! This life! If you can call it a life. I've met you all
before, yes, all before. Well, that too—what I've just
said—has the old taste of cliché in it. You've heard it
all before. Come now, admit it: not original, not original, Augustine. It's not a sin to be unoriginal, but that
doesn't change the truth. Everyone in my life radiates
from that all-powerful One. Who is that, you ask? No
matter, I say. But you all come from her, are her, in
fact, that is why I am going to commit the most dramatic
cliché—Mother-murther.

NUN: Christ have mercy on us.

WISDOM: I am going to creep up to you like this: slowly
in a circle, getting nearer and nearer your chair. When
I'm behind you, I am going to touch your neck as
though to caress it, as though to bathe those gray hairs
there gently with my breath. I am going to inch up your
shoulders with my fingers slowly, then circle your neck
with them and squeeze, squeeze, squeeze, squeeze.
[*At this moment, as he is strangling the* OLD NUN, *a*
NUN *enters. She is humpbacked, walks with a limp,
one eye is missing, and she seems to have a skin problem on face and hands.*]

REX: Ave, pater sapientum!

WISDOM: [*Sees her and shrieks.*] Ah! [*He faints.*]

REX: Thank you, Father Wisdom, I admire correct form in a man. Father Wisdom? He's fainted dead away. And I thought he was prostrating himself. What deceivers men are. Help ho, sistern, the priest's fainted. [FOUR NUNS *enter and set about reviving* AUGUSTINE. REX *approaches the* OLD NUN.] And how are you, dear Mother St. Sebastian Anselme? Have you kept your fingers clean? [*Examines the* OLD NUN's *hand.*] Hmm, there's a wart on your mound of Venus. Glamorous. [*Drops the hand. The* NUNS *are having a hard time reviving* WISDOM.] I'm melancholy today. My humor's turned sour. What ho, my fool, my fool! [*A beautiful young* NOVICE *enters. She wears a white dress and small veil. She carries a lute.*] Well, Nuncle, did you beat yourself today?

YOUNG NUN: No, Reverend Mother.

REX: Kiss me! [*The* YOUNG NUN *does.*] Sweet. Now play. [*The* YOUNG NUN *strums the lute.* REX *sings in a cracked and mostly toneless voice:*]

O mistress mine, where are you roaming?
O come and hear thy true love's coming
That can sing both high and low.

[*The* LUTENIST *continues playing, but* REX *speaks.*]

REX: I was always suspicious of that song. Singing it is like doing a stations of the acrostic.

[*The* YOUNG NUN *laughs.* REX *sings again as the* NUN *plays. As she is singing,* WISDOM *revives slowly, and seems dazed.*]

WISDOM: [*Speaking softly over* REX's *voice*] What is that old, sad tune that revives me with its plaintive sound?

REX: Ah, Father Wisdom, you're quoting from *Tristan.* You are a true intellectual. You cannot resist being allusive even when unconscious. The line, with which you were taking liberties goes, I believe: "*Muss ich dich so versteh'n, du alte ernste Weise, mit deiner klage klang.*" Sung as it is in the third act by the dying, death-devoted Tristan. I am Mother Superior Eleanora Franklinus and no unpleasant remarks about the Roosevelts, please. I am the abbess of this establishment, and regret I could not be here for your arrival last week, which I gather was a moment of some pomp.

WISDOM: But I met the . . .

REX: You are going to say you met the abbess yesterday.

A statuesque woman of mid-forty, six-feet high and
deep of voice. That is my surrogate abbess, you might
call her my mother manqué. I wheel her out of the
closet and wind her up when I cannot be present.
When I can be, I wheel her back into the closet and let
her wind down with a clothes hanger or two. [*To the*
YOUNG NUN] Stop that tinkling. And you, weird sisters,
thank you, the priest seems awake. [*The* FOUR NUNS
leave.] Yes indeed, I am the queen here. I've been a
cripple all my life. My right leg is wooden—see? [*Lifts
her dress and shows him.*] My eye was poked out to
allow me greater wisdom and is now walled up. This
eczema is a special favor of the Virgin, and none of my
teeth are real. And how are you? That's good, I'm fine.
Now repeat after me: *Sehnsucht!*
WISDOM: *Sehnsucht!*
REX: Good. Now, *sehnen.*
WISDOM: [*Repeating*] *Sehnen.*
REX: Good. *Sehnsucht* and *sehnen*, longing and desire.
Now you know the secret of my being. [*She reaches
forward and kisses* WISDOM *full on the mouth. He
screams and wrenches away.*] Not only kissed by a
cripple, but worse, by a woman! Your altar boys, Father
Wisdom, how many of them were cripples, emotional
cripples, their souls as deformed as my body? But a
woman, no woman has ever touched you, that I can see
on your face, that I could feel on your lips. Oh, to suck
those lips into mine. [*She laughs.*] My career has been
varied, to say the least. Someday I shall tell you about
it, taking tea perhaps. I often swim in it; tannic acid
helps my eczema. You might summarize by saying:
here am I, mother superior, artist's model, model artist,
administratrix, translatrix, and sometime actress. My
best role is the angel of death in our theatricals, but my
favorite role in those plays is the friendly yet formi-
dable dog. You may call me Rex. Say good day, Rex.
WISDOM: Good day, Rex.
REX: Good day, Father Wisdom. It's been delightful
meeting you, *Herz an herz, mund an mund* to further
quote *Tristan.* Come, Nuncle! [*She and the* YOUNG
NUN *start to leave.*] Oh, how were you progressing with
Mother St. Sebastian Anselme?
WISDOM: She wasn't quite finished.

REX: Mothers rarely are. We will leave you to finish her.
[*She walks farther toward the exit, then stops.*] Oh yes,
I came not only to greet you but also to invite you.
Tomorrow you must tour my establishment and see a
play. You will also meet the sisters in a more intimate
way. Further, you and I must become friends. I am sure
we shall. Will you?

WISDOM: Yes.

REX: Yes what?

WISDOM: Yes, Rex.

REX: Bravo, Little Father. Adieu, Mother St. Sebastian
Anselme, safe journey. . . .

NUN: Christ have mercy on us!

REX: Why, the same to you. Come, Nuncle.
[*They leave.*]

WISDOM: Mother! No reprieve was granted you, I see.
For I am the instrument of God! You must confess now,
for you are to die soon. [*Rips off her veil.*] Yes, it is
you! If you didn't want to die this way you should have
crushed me between your walls, terminated my life at
its beginning. [*He caresses her hair.*] I've seen you for
years like this: an aged woman, a fortune-teller, a clair-
voyant. I see you in dreams thus, austere and beautiful
in age, dealing destinies, having dealt mine and
triumphed. You made my future, pushing it out of you
like a dead twisted thing. I am going to avenge not only
myself but Chris whom you called to death. Die now,
die! [*He knocks her out of the rocking chair.*]

NUN: Christ have mercy on us!

[WISDOM *throws himself on top of her and starts strangling her.*]

NUN: [*Struggling*] Christ . . . Christ . . .

WISDOM: You killed my faith, sucked it from me with that
toothless, aging mouth! [*He slaps her. She screams. He
hits her again.*] This is my filial caress! [*He finishes
strangling her. He does so slowly, obviously relishing
her terror and pain. She dies.*] No, no, too soon, too
soon! Too quick for what I've suffered! [*He continues
strangling her corpse.*] More and more and more and
more! [*He bangs her head down and hits her repeatedly.*] Too easy, too easy. More and more and more. [*He
weeps with frustration and rage.*] Bitch! [*He screams
and throws himself on her body. The lights begin to*

dim out.] No ... no ... too easy, too easy ... I must find you again—too easy, too easy, I must find you again! [*He runs off.*]

BLACKOUT

· ACT II

Scene 1

*Lights up on a coffin downstage. Then lights build. A
funeral mass is in progress for* MOTHER ST. SEBASTIAN
ANSELME *whom* FATHER WISDOM *murdered in the first
act. At an altar up center,* WISDOM *officiates. He is as-
sisted by an attractive* ALTAR BOY. *A large number of
inmates*—MAD NUNS—*are present. They are guarded by*
HEFTY NURSES *dressed in one of two ways: (1) as Infants
of Prague (with papier-mâché elaborate crown and flowing terrycloth regal robes) or (2) as Virgin Marys. All
nurses are armed with lethal-looking steel rosaries. A
number of nurses patrol the outskirts of the group. These
have crossbows loaded with tranquilizer darts.*

The MAD NUNS *giggle, masturbate, salivate, quarrel,
nudge each other, sometimes at the same time. Others
stare off vacantly; still others manifest strange tics, a
very few seem to be in continual prayer.*

REX *is present with her party, sitting apart from the rest.*
REX *is on a throne. All of these wear black veils and
indications of mourning.*

*Organ music is heard in the distance, sad but strange-
sounding.*

WISDOM [*Saying the funeral mass*] Requiem aeternam
  dona eis, Domine. Et lux perpetua luceat eis.
  [TWO MAD NUNS *break away and run up to* WISDOM.
  *They appear to be trying to bite him. He stops the mass
  in terror and hides behind the* ALTAR BOY, *who seems
  unconcerned and is not menaced by the* MAD NUNS.]

REX: [*From her throne*] You nurses, do your duty! Lash those wayward sisters! This is a disgraceful lapse, I shall inform God and have her punish you!

[TWO NURSES—*an infant and a virgin—rush to the escaped two and beat them mercilessly with rosaries as they scream. Some of the other* NUNS *applaud, others seem oblivious. The beaten two are pushed out by the* NURSES.]

REX: Please to pardon our inattentive nurses, dear Father, but it isn't easy to be dressed up as an Infant of Prague and concentrate at the same time. And the Blessed Mothers are rather a dizzy crew. Please to continue the mass.

WISDOM: [*Shaking and frightened*] Dear God . . . Dear God . . .

REX: Dear Father, be comforted and experience no pain or fright at our dear sisters. They are like children and haven't had a man in a while. Your smell sends them crazy with longing.

WISDOM: Holy Mother of God . . .

REX: How long has it been since they've had a man, Nurse Cohen?

NURSE COHEN: [*Dressed as a Virgin Mary*] Two months, Mother Rex!

REX: Has it indeed been that long?

NURSE: [*Virgin Mary*] That's when we sacrificed old Mr. Otaruanni to them.

REX: Indeed, indeed! You would have liked him, Father Wisdom. He was a dear old man—a former playwright. He cleaned toilets for us and taught drama. A bit stiff he was, but he went far.

WISDOM: [*Shocked*] They ate him?

REX: Well, of course, dear Father. What do you think I meant—they didn't read his plays! [*She and her party laugh.*]

WISDOM: [*Near a faint*] Oh . . .

REX: Go ahead and faint, Father Widsom. Then your altar boy can give you mouth to mouth—er, mouth to mouth . . . reciprocation? [*She and her party laugh.*]

WISDOM: No, I'm all right.

REX: Then continue Mother St. Sebastian Anselme's funeral mass.

WISDOM: [*With a sigh, continues the mass.*] *Libera me, Domine, de morte aeterna* . . .

REX: I think it's time for the eulogy. Deliver it, Father.

WISDOM: I haven't gotten far enough in the . . .

REX: [*With an imperious gesture*] Please!

WISDOM:
  [*Both annoyed and frightened, comes forward.*] Dearly . . . [*The* MAD NUNS *applaud him. Some of them run tongues over lips.*]

REX: They like you, Father!

WISDOM: Dearly beloved. We are here to send the soul of Mother St. Sebastian Anselme into eternity!

A NUN: How'd she die, Augie?

ANOTHER NUN: You kill her?

WISDOM: Oh, I have a cramp! [*Bends over, holding his stomach.*]

REX: I myself registered suspicion of those boysenberry pancakes, though you seemed to eat them with relish. Relish on pancakes, mark you—no wonder he feels cramped. And be ye quiet, dear sisters, he isn't a race-horse and doesn't need cheering on, though perhaps he could do with a jockey! [*She and her party laugh.*]

WISDOM: How dare you, you twisted cripple! I will leave here this instant! You . . . you . . .

REX: Oh, please to pardon, dear Father Wisdom, my oblique little jokes. And pity me, for they are a cripple's only compensation. And please, continue with the eulogy!

WISDOM: Dearly beloved, let me say a bit about Mother St. Sebastian. [*With meaning and glancing toward* REX] She was a saintly, handsome old woman; her limbs were strong and well formed and she could carry the cross of a nun with a strong back. She was an old-fashioned woman with real backbone, and she disported herself with dignity!

REX: Oh ho! [*She and her party titter.*]

WISDOM: Her work amongst the Red Chinese, the rabid Congolese, and at Yale won Holy Mother dozens of souls she would not otherwise have had.

A NUN: [*Yelling*] She was a good fuck too!

REX: Lash that liar!

  [*The* NUN *is lashed and driven out.*]

WISDOM: She ended her life as she lived it: saying her rosary and praying Christ to have mercy on us.

NUN: How do you know, Augie?

WISDOM: I had just finished hearing her confession. She died very shortly after I left. Her last thoughts were of our great need for love, so often unanswered in this life, and the death that replaces it for all of us!

A NUN: here's her teeth! [*Hurls molars at* AUGUSTINE, *who ducks but continues his speech, choosing to ignore this.*]

WISDOM: I am unwell, she is dead, there is no more to say!

REX: [*She and her party applaud.*] An eulogy as good as your name, Father! You may kiss the corpse.

WISDOM: [*Shocked*] What?!

NUNS: [*Variously*]
Go ahead!
Tongue her!
Stick it in!

WISDOM: I won't—

REX: Do so this time—

WISDOM: No, no, I won't! What am I to do, defile her spirit, defile myself, don't forget, you grotesque horror, I am an ordained priest, the minister of God on earth. . . .

REX: [*Kindly*] Nonetheless, this is our madhouse and we have our rules. A corpse—the remains of a mad sister who has spent her life loveless—must be sent into the Beyond with an inkling of the physical pleasure that awaits her there. Kiss her.

WISDOM: No!

REX: [*Still patient*] Do not risk or dare too much, Father Wisdom. It is little enough to ask. A second and it is done. There are other tasks which are harder and last longer. Do this now and the ordeal will be over.

[WISDOM *looks at the* MAD NUNS, *who are glowering at him and looking ferocious, looks back at the determined* REX, *then decides to kiss the corpse. He does so and is immediately sick, bending down and retching behind the coffin. The* NUNS *make loud noises of disapproval. The* NUNS *who haven't seen or understood have it explained to them: "The priest has puked" is heard in a number of different places.*]

REX: Very poor taste, Father, poor taste! Time was when

a priest had a stronger stomach. You'd be quite a loss amongst lepers. Why the gracious St. Teresa drank their pus in order to discipline herself and her eyes! Can we find a more appropriate example? Now, if you've recovered, bless us!

WISDOM: [*Blessing the sisters*] In nomine Patris, et Filius, et Spiritu sancti, Amen.

REX: You may thank him, dear sisters!

[*The* NUNS *crowd forward to thank* AUGUSTINE. *At first they are quiet and humble. Soon one takes a playful swipe at the* PRIEST. *Another follows her example, and a third. The fourth who does this is less playful.* AUGUSTINE *pushes her away. Others crowd around him, pushing him and laughing. He fights back, but the* NUNS *become more vicious. Once again, one takes a bite at him. He cries out and kicks her. A melee starts and is vicious. The* NURSES *watch, waiting for a sign to interfere from* REX. *Finally she gives it.*]

REX: Help ho, nurses.

[*The* NURSES *rush in wielding their rosaries violently. The* NUNS, *however, don't want to stop and continue hitting and clawing at* AUGUSTINE. *He fights back, crying out in anger. Most of the* NUNS *are cleared away and pushed out, but a few remain clustered about the* PRIEST.]

REX: Darts for those recalcitrants in the middle.

A NURSE: [*With a crossbow, takes aim. She is dressed as a Virgin.*] Yes, Mother Rex. . . .

REX: Well, come on . . . get them. . . .

NURSE: [*Takes aim but finds the target difficult.*] I'm trying. . . .

REX: Some Virgin you are!

NURSE: I don't want to hit the priest. . . .

[*Aims and fires. The dart hits a particularly rambunctious* SISTER, *who keels over with a cry. Her fainting helps the* NURSES *by causing confusion among the* NUNS. *They are all driven out and the fainted one carried off.* AUGUSTINE's *vestments are torn and shredded. He has a few minor cuts.*]

REX: Father Augustine, are you all right?

WISDOM: I . . .

REX: I thought you would be. You look like you can take care of yourself.

WISDOM: I . . .

REX: I'm not surprised. I wager you've spent your life
fending off excited females. There is something so tit-
illating about a supposedly celebate priest. Many
women consider it a great challenge, like hunting
muskrat.

WISDOM: That wasn't playful, or erotic. . . .

REX: Oh, they've angered you. Please to accept my apol-
ogies for them. In them is combined love and the need
to devour. A combination common in humankind but
perhaps uncomfortable in multitudes. [*She speaks to
the last few* NUNS *who are exiting.*] That's right, sisters,
back to our lovely cells. We've been bad girls, but Rex
loves us, that's right. And remember, sweet sisters, if
you are good today and God gives a good report on you
. . . [*To* AUGUSTINE] —God is our head nurse, it's convenient short hand—if God gives me a good report on
you, we'll have Sister St. Ignatius' play. That's right.
You must also see that play, Father Wisdom.

[*He is silent, glaring at her.*]

REX: Father, are you ill?

WISDOM: I have never been so insulted and treated with
so much disregard and I am convinced it is your fault.
And what did you mean by those vicious jokes before?
Cripple's compensation indeed! I don't believe cripples should be given such easy sympathy or indulgence.

REX: Please, Father, no bitterness. See how deformed I
am. [*Does a turn so he can see.*] Am I bitter about it?
What is a little nasty humor between friends such as
we, compared to such ugliness and deformity? No, my
hump is my concern and I carry it upright, expecting
sympathy from none—and it's a good thing too. Often
I am glad I have a hump, it has its uses. At night, when
I cannot sleep, which is often the case, I lay on my
side—I have no choice, you see—and count the pimples on my hump. It works better than sheep. But I
must go; come, Nuncle. [REX, *followed by the* YOUNG
NUN, *starts out but turns back.*] Father, come to my
office later this afternoon. We will talk out any trouble,
then, like beaux, go to the play.

[WISDOM *is still looking ill.*]

REX: Are you all right, Father?

WISDOM: I'm feeling a little faint. . . .

REX: Then put your head between your legs. It's always a help to confront the reality principle.

[REX *leaves with the* YOUNG NUN.]

WISDOM: [*Alone with the* ALTAR BOY] Oh, thank God that thing is gone. Her smell, her looks, her language. I wonder where she had her novitiate? They weren't trained to be like that in my day. [*To the* ALTAR BOY] You may go, my son. Thank you. [*The* BOY *smiles at him.*] You want to stay? What is your name? Why are you in this place? [*The* BOY *doesn't answer, but looks down, as though shy.*] Perhaps you are an orphan, I often feel an orphan. An orphan with a bitch mother— dead now. At least, that's what the conventional-minded say. They have no conception of how malevolence lives on. What is your name? [*The* BOY *giggles.*] No matter. I have often felt we should dispense with names like James, Robert, or Jesus, or Chris. Chris! Dispense with them, I say, and call people instead: Object Number One, Object Number Two, Pursuer Number Three, Failure Number Four, Ugly Hopeless on down the line, Number Five, and so on and so on. But then, you argue, that confuses people with their roles and with their successes and failures. But that's precisely it, don't you see—people *are* their successes and failures. That is verbatim from a lecture I gave my Sacred Text class 197. It was off the topic but to the point. [*Reaches under his cassock and retrieves some papers.*] Here are my notes, you may have them. [*The* ALTAR BOY *takes the notes but touches* WISDOM's *hand in so doing.*] It was not a success. It was ahead of its time. But that was a bad year for me all around. I gained weight, lost hair and forgot things. [*The* ALTAR BOY *lies back, seductive.*] Why are you so concerned with being ugly, Father Wisdom, you ask me in your sweet, high voice? Because, my son, it is so important to be linked in some way with beauty. To hold it in one's hand—that is the melody of living. One strives to be within the beatific vision. One cannot be, one is outside, in hell, cast out, if one is ugly, You will never have that problem. [*The* BOY *puts his arms about* AUGUSTINE.] What's the matter? Are you ill? [*Feels the* BOY's *forehead.*] No fever . . . are you crazy? To want me . . . it's not possible.

You've gotten a good look, haven't you, and heard me rattle on. . . . I have nothing to give you. I am so poor and pudgy, and look at my face. [*The* BOY *kisses* AUGUSTINE.] Oh . . . oh my . . . [*The* BOY *kisses him passionately, then rubs up and down along* AUGUSTINE's *body.*] I suppose your need for a parent, for a father image, is strong enough to overcome any repugnance you might feel. [*They kiss.* AUGUSTINE *becomes excited and embraces the* BOY, *holding him to him.*] Oh, my dear one, you are beautiful, beautiful. [*Another kiss.*] I need you, come to me. . . . [*He feels the* BOY's *crotch.*] What? There's nothing there. [*Terrified, he feels the* BOY's *breasts. The* BOY *is a* MAD NUN *dressed up as a boy. She pulls down her cassock and shows her breasts, then runs off laughing.*] Oh, my God . . . [WISDOM *falls down, horrified.*] Chris! [*Faints.* REX *suddenly appears at back and laughs loudly.*]

BLACKOUT

Scene 2

The recreation room in the madhouse. At back a balcony or elevated section with a blank scrim or drop. MAD NUNS *cavort;* NURSES *patrol. Much noise and confusion. At right a large statue of the Sacred Heart. The heart is very large and formed like a target. A group of mad nuns with bows and arrows take aim and fire at the target, supervised by an Infant of Prague nurse.*

NURSE: [*Infant of Prague*] [*As one* NUN *steps up with bow and arrow*] C'mon, sister, let's see you hit that target like it was one of your eighth graders—c'mon, let's see that famous elbow grease and them muscles work! [*The* NUN *raises her bow. She is spastic and has enormous trouble fitting the arrow into the bow. She draws back with great difficulty and lets loose, hitting a* NUN *nearby, who falls over.*] Nope! You scored a great big zero for your team, sister! No wonder they kept you teachin' in the ghetto! Next!

[*The fallen* NUN *is carried off and another* NUN *steps up as the* SPASTIC NUN *retires weeping.*]

[*At stage left a Virgin Mary* NURSE *has been putting a group of very hefty, uncoordinated* NUNS *through calisthenics.*]

NURSE: [*Virgin Mary*] Now, sisters: one, two, three— squat! One, two, three—squat! Up! Now again with grace: one, two three—squat!

[*Trumpets on every side.*]

A NURSE: Sisters, fall prostrate, God is coming!

[*A burning bush is projected onto the scrim, as is lightning.*]

NUNS: [*Prostrate, calling out*] Hosanna, hosanna, Adonai, Adonai!

[*Renewed trumpet blasts, thunder and lightning projected and heard. Cries of greeting from prostrate* NUNS. GOD *enters. This is a very beefy female* NURSE *in white, low-cut uniform and noticeable cleavage. She wears a flowing white beard and golden hair.*]

GOD: [*As a* NURSE *with averted eyes hands her the day's report*] My children, I greet you. I hope you are behaving yourselves this glorious day. Remember Paradise awaits the good, the other place the bad, lamb is for supper, and maybe a play later if you behave!

NUNS: [*Still prostrate*] Hosanna, hosanna, hosanna!

GOD: Don't mention it. Play ball.

[*Much cheering. Suddenly* AUGUSTINE *enters. A silence. He looks very self-conscious.*]

GOD: Oh, you must be Father Augustine Wisdom, known in some quarters as the weirdie. How do you do? I am God.

WISDOM: Oh . . .

GOD: I'm the head nurse. You may address me as God. I dispense with formality.

WISDOM: How do you do, God.

GOD: Very well. And you are just in time for our daily baseball game!

WISDOM: Baseball?

GOD: Yes, as part of physical therapy.

WISDOM: Baseball as physical therapy? Does it work?

GOD: No, but it tires them out, the first rule of dealing
with the spiritually ill. You must watch the game!

WISDOM: Oh no, I . . .

GOD: You must!

[*The* NUNS *cry out that* WISDOM *must watch them.*]

WISDOM: I'd really like to, it's just that . . .

GOD: No excuses. . . .

WISDOM: I hate baseball! And besides, Mother Rex summoned me to see her this afternoon. I made a wrong
turn, else I wouldn't even be here. . . .

GOD: There are no wrong turns in this universe. Every
corridor leads here. You must stay. I command it.

[*A roll of thunder. the* NUNS *cry out that* AUGUSTINE
must stay and the NURSES *look poised to follow any
commands* GOD *might have. With a shrug,* WISDOM
agrees.]

WISDOM: All right.

GOD: We have a guest today, sisters! Be good and play
ball! And in honor of our guest, we'll name the ball
Wisdom!

WISDOM: Thank you.

[*The* NUNS *divide into teams and spectators. Much
crying out and noise. The* PITCHER *steps up to the
mound. A three-foot replica of a blond young boy,
about ten, is used as the ball. The* BATTER *steps up.
The bats are long, sharp, double-edged swords. The*
BATTER *swings a few until satisfied with one. The
bases are attended by* NUNS *with gladitorial costumes
over their habits and weapons out of a gladiator
movie—tri-pronged spears, long swords, nets, etc. A
few nuns play lions. An Infant of Prague* NURSE *acts
as the umpire.*]

FIRST PITCH

[*The boy is hurled. The* BATTER *swings with the sword
and misses completely.*]

UMPIRE: Steeeeeerike!

[*Much argument. A few* NURSES *with rosaries are
needed to restore order.*]

SECOND PITCH

[*The boy is hurled.* BATTER *swings and cuts off one
hand. Blood and sawdust flow out.*]

UMPIRE: Baaaaaallll!

[*Much argument.*]

PITCHER: That was no ball, that was a strike if ever I saw one!

BATTER: You mother, you, that was a ball and no strike!

GOD: [*As the argument grows intense and involves the teams and their supporters,* GOD *speaks through a megaphone.*] Children, children, be calm. The boyball which we in deference to our holy guest have named Wisdom was only maimed. This is clearly by our rules a ball!

PITCHER: Look you! I ain't snowed by no bull dyke dressed up as God.

[*A shocked silence.*]

GOD: Blasphemer!

[*Points a finger imperiously at the* PITCHER. *A thunderclap and lightning projected on the scrim. The* PITCHER *falls flat, apparently dead. After a silence,* GOD *speaks.*]

GOD: Don't nobody fuck with me! Now, God commands a relief pitcher!

[*A new* NUN *trots out, and mounts the mound.*]

GOD: Play fair, sister, and abide my rules, that's how I run my world!

RELIEF PITCHER: Yes, God. Hosanna!

GOD: Play ball!

THIRD PITCH

[*The boy is hurled. The* BATTER *swings her sword and lops his head off. To cries of encouragement or booing, the* BATTER *runs the bases. These are obstacle courses constructed of* MAD NUNS. *The head, with blood dripping out of it, is hurled first by the* CATCHER, *then by a* MAD NUN *at each base. All try to hit the* BATTER *with the head. They fail. She gets to the last base, which is a calvary constructed by* MAD NUNS. *She stands, arms outstretched, and is cheered.*]

UMPIRE: Homer!

[*Much acclaim for the* BATTER.]

GOD: There is joy in the heavens today. I will make a rainbow.

[*A rainbow is projected onto the scrim.*]

WISDOM: [*Uncomfortable*] Well, that is certainly a spectacle to warm a Christian's heart.

GOD: I'm pleased you enjoyed it, Father.

WISDOM: May I go now, God?

GOD: Well, of course, dear Father Wisdom. Pass through them, the seas will part at my command!

WISDOM Thank you.

[*With much fear,* WISDOM *passes through the mass of* MAD NUNS. *At his approach, those on the floor part like a black sea. Very quickly,* WISDOM *makes his exit. The* NUNS *cheer, then return to lauding or booing the* BATTER.]

BLACKOUT

Scene 3

REX'*s cell.* REX *in a chair,* NUNCLE *at her feet playing a sad tune on her lute.* WISDOM *enters, out of breath.*

REX: Father Wisdom, thee I greet.

WISDOM: [*Cold*] You wished to see me?

REX: See you? Ah, could I but. To see you in all your masculine beauty . . . oh, don't be alarmed, be flattered, it's the more appealing thing to be. Nuncle, Nuncle, Nuncle, croon to me.

[NUNCLE *hums the sad tune.* REX *strokes her sensuously.* WISDOM *looks on, revolted.*]

REX: [*Without ceasing to stroke* NUNCLE] And does the physical so disgust you, Father Wisdom?

WISDOM: The unnatural does.

REX: I gather you are expert at that.

WISDOM: You then must be my mirror. Look at you, feeling that innocent child. . . .

REX: Innocent child? Because she's young and pretty. Neither noun nor adjective follows. Very inexact in observation, Father Wisdom. Your writings must have been abysmal.

WISDOM: Be quiet about them. Not only a cripple but a . . .

REX: Lesbian, my lovely? [*She laughs.*] A lesbian indeed. And what is lesbian, and what isn't? Is the human heart a lesbian, is the human soul? Does the heart say to itself—only the approved object, my friend? Nonsense.

WISDOM: The typical rationalization of the deviate.

REX: And what a large vocabulary you have, Father Wisdom. Are you yourself, titillated as you are by the feel of boy flesh and the smell, the smell of boy loins, not a deviate, as you put it, or a pervert?

WISDOM: Precisely, I am those things precisely! A sore, a cancer in the eyes of God, in the dark in our society's reckoning—a disease, a degenerate. Oh, the shame I've felt! But that shame also purifies and cuts deep! In being all malignancy I am none. That purity, that isolated purity—that is part of what makes me an artist.

REX: I hope the other part of what makes you an artist isn't the way you use words.

WISDOM: Naturally you wouldn't understand.

REX: The babbling of a fool? Naturally, being no fool. But you see, I am neither normal nor ab, just me. My longings do not say "men only," or "women only," or "only oxen need apply"; my longings take me where they will. Nature creates sexual differentiation but doesn't acknowledge it. Nature does not move in discreet patterns.

WISDOM: You've been reading that fraud Kinsey.

REX: Reading? Living! For I have done it all—rampaged through the hips and hearts of dozens of both sexes. Further, I've experimented with animals, vegetables, and machinery. Yet I still consider myself and say with absolute confidence I am a whole, normal woman! And I want you! [*Leaps on* WISDOM, *who falls back with her on top of him. He screams.*]

NUNCLE: Ah, ah, ah . . .

[REX *stops ripping at* WISDOM's *clothes and runs to* NUNCLE. NUNCLE *continues sobbing and gasping.*]

REX: She's having her insulin shock! I must run and get my hypodermic. You hear confessions, we'll meet later for the play. [*Running off*] A hypodermic, what ho, a hypodermic!

NUNCLE: Ah, ah, ah! [*She has a fit.*]

[WISDOM *rushes to the exit, then comes back on and speaks to the screaming* NUNCLE.]

WISDOM: Child, your diabetes may be a cross to you, but it is the resurrection and salvation of the body to me! [*Runs off as* NUNCLE *foams at the mouth.*]

BLACKOUT

Scene 4

A room in which WISDOM *hears confessions.* WISDOM *sits in a chair with surplice on. A* MAD NUN *enters and kneels.*

MAD NUN: [*Crossing herself*] Bless me, Father, for I have sinned. . .
WISDOM: Sister, when was the last time you were happy?
MAD NUN: On listening to a Bach fugue in spring.
WISDOM: Wrong!
    [*He stabs her. She dies.*]

BLACKOUT

Scene 5

The same as Scene 4. The FIRST MAD NUN's *body lies left. A* MAD NUN *enters and kneels.*

MAD NUN: [*Crossing herself*] Bless me, Father, for I have sinned . . .
WISDOM: Sister, have you ever thought about the mystery of character? I mean, really thought about it, pondered it naked on your bed, late at night with only a candle, a hopeless, flickering candle fluttering all alone at your bedside? [*A pause.*] No, I can see you have not. Do I exist in any profound sense, sister? I doubt it. Of course I am capable of activity, of what one in a generous mood might even call actions—but am I real in any sense? Characters in plays are capable of activities and in good plays even actions, but are they real? Real in the sense we suppose ourselves to be? No, they aren't. But that's how I feel—like a character in a play. I am only now—at this instant; I feel that I have no life "offstage," as it were. I always seem to be performing,

entertaining, acting as others expect me to act, as though every morning some super-director whispered stage directions in my ear and sometimes, are you listening, sometimes I seem to hear the applause of some super-audience hidden somewhere out there. Oh, ye of little imagination say it is merely the wind rustling through foliage or some such. But I think it is the rustle of gloved hands applauding a scene in life very well played. Once in a while I even hear a "bravo" as though shouted from some hidden gallery. And think of the ironies of life—the coincidences, the outrageous fate of most of us. The fact that we never fall in love with the right people. Or never fall in love at all but only think we do, knowing all the time in some hidden crevice that we are only playing at some painful game, like rugby. Or take the suddenness of murder, the fact that in some way we are all unsuspecting victims of a master killer. Take the tragicomic action of eating. Are these not the ironies, the actions of plays? Oh, it is all so confusing. I should have entered the DFA program at Yale. I am so poor, so poverty-stricken—the comic relief in a bad Russian play in an early draft. My hair is falling out. [*Pulls out a wad of hair and shows it to the* MAD NUN.] Look! I have no ideas anymore, nothing winds through my brain save snippets of basic theology and simple Latin—*sum, es, est, sumus, estis, sunt.* What does all that tell me? O ye stars—ye hair tufts of the angels, I am losing, daily, I am losing! I wake up and am farther back, more ignorant, I open my eyes and a segment of the universe falls out backwards like part of a badly constructed stage set. And there is space where once there was . . . what? Where are you?

MAD NUN: [*Very fast*] Joan of Arc was a transvestite who didn't burn up but lived out her life surrounded by hot faggots feeling there was nothing at stake!

WISDOM: Cynic! [*Stabs her.*]

BLACKOUT

Scene 6

Scene the same. Two bodies are stacked stage left. A MAD NUN *enters and kneels.*

MAD NUN: Bless me, Father, for I have sinned. . . .

WISDOM: You ask me: "Tell me, Father Wisdom, did you have a brother?" Well . . . yes. And then you ask: "And were you close?" No, I say, no. I felt very deeply for him, very deeply. "And whatever happened to him?" you ask. I reply: Dead. On a pongi stick in the mud. The war. Impaled. Stuck right through like a butterfly. Elusive Chris, pinned at last by boyfriend Death. I loved him deeply, totally. I saw him die. I saw it in the back garden, the garden with the stagnant pond, the overgrown garden at the seminary. I was reading my breviary. Something drew my attention to the pond. I walked there. In the water I saw it. He was penetrated quite slowly, quite slowly, all the way through. The more he struggled, the more he sank onto the pointy stick. Red mud and black hair, fair features ripped in pain, and fine hands all aflutter, dying. Then I taught Theology One-o-two, pretending not every face was his split in death. But it was no use. Everywhere there was Chris, in dreams, in a thousand incarnations, I saw him. And every time I saw him I became hard. One day elevating the host, it was his face I saw on the wafer. My body shook, my thighs grew moist, I thought my spine would crumble. *You* did it to me! He alone of the entire world was not your minion; you took him away from me by that horrible death, left me bereft, and then forced me into continual confrontation with his ghost. [WISDOM *slaps the* NUN.]

MAD NUN: [*As if nothing out of the ordinary has occurred*] Mother Rex sent me to summon you. The play is about to begin.

WISDOM: The play?

MAD NUN: Sister St. Ignatius Loyola's play.

WISDOM: Rex?

MAD NUN: Yes.

   [*Absentmindedly* WISDOM *stabs her.*]

MAD NUN: Father! Give me the extreme unction. . . .

WISDOM: [*Absently*] What do you think I am, Uriah Heep?

   [*The* MAD NUN *dies.*]

WISDOM: I wish life were like the opera, *Madama Butterfly*. It would be comforting to marry a sailor, bear his child, then fall on one's sword. A well-characterized life but an uncluttered one. . . .

   [*Sad lute music is heard.* REX *and* NUNCLE *enter, being carried by the* FOUR HEAVY NUNS *usually in* REX's *party.* NUNCLE *plays a sad tune on her lute. A* NURSE *with a crossbow stands on the platform with* REX *and* NUNCLE.]

REX: *O caro padre, gegrüsset.* I love mixing languages. I've come to pick you up. Stand over there as though you were a male hustler.

WISDOM: What?

REX: Oh, come on!

WISDOM: No!

REX: All right, shoot him, nurse!

   [NURSE *raises the crossbow.*]

WISDOM: Wait! I don't know how a male hustler stands.

REX: Oh, come on, papa, what do you take me for? I know what your life was like before you came here. Do you think I believe those poor-box donations went to the leper missions in the Congo? I bet many a hustler with randomly bepimpled buttocks ate the better for you— in a number of senses.

WISDOM: You vile bitch! [*Moves threateningly.*]

REX: Shoot him, nurse!

   [NURSE *raises crossbow.*]

WISDOM: Wait! I'll stand like a male hustler—I've seen them in movies. [*Lounges nearby.*]

REX: Take his picture, Nuncle. [NUNCLE *does so.*] You shouldn't be so frightened of the crossbows, Father. They only contain tranquilizer darts. You swoon for a few minutes, then wake up, mute and happy. [NUNCLE *hands* REX *the picture which has come out of her instant camera.*] *Brava*, Nuncle. That's for my scrapbook. I take one of every priest who is sent here as our missionary. That makes the fourth this month. I usually put them in compromising positions. I like the idea of combining the priestly with the perverted. It's called creating an irony. But here I go rattling on again. So, Father, ask me about the play.

WISDOM: Well, actually, plays are a sore point with me.

REX: Foreplays certainly are—I noticed that earlier.

WISDOM: I mean because I have written plays—six.

REX: Ask me about the play we are to see today. It's called being polite and making conversation. Since you don't seem to want to make anything else.

WISDOM: I find you tedious and unfunny.

REX: Ask me about the play or I'll have the nurse . . .

WISDOM: Who wrote it?

REX: Sister St. Ignatius Loyola. Poor dear, she so wanted to write operas, but she punctured her eardrums in a suicide attempt, and so had to make do with writing plays. Ask something else.

WISDOM: Have I met her?

REX: She cut her throat last night. Dance this story for us, Nuncle! [NUNCLE *dances as* REX *talks.*] Playing Oedipus in a director's project, she got carried away on Sophoclean rhetoric and a roll of ups and really put her eyes out. What was she to do? She couldn't hear to compose, and couldn't see to write, and since most of the sweet sisters in her circle were teaching sisters, and had never learned to read or write, dictation was out of the question. She became dreadfully depressed. We told her she could become a bard in the old sense like Homer, but alas, she took that to be a slur on her sexual proclivities.

WISDOM: How did she . . .

REX: She locked herself in her cell this morning and felt herself for hours and hours, starting at her toes. When she found what she was quite sure was her throat, she slit it.

WISDOM: Oh!

REX: With her 1679 prayer book—a collector's item, holy relic combined. She honed its right front cover in shop.

WISDOM: What a horrible death.

REX: Oh, I don't know. There was a certain grandeur to her end. She died ecstatic, singing Mozart, or what she thought was Mozart. Being deaf, she'd lost her ear, so to speak.

[NUNCLE *stops her interpretive dance gracefully.* REX *and the* HEAVY NUNS *who have set down the litter applaud*]

REX: Brava, Nuncle, again. Isn't Nuncle a divine dancer? She worked with Martha Graham until she twisted her spine in a relaxation exercise and found God. But come, Father Wisdom, Nuncle, and my ladies—I hear the noise of a play starting. [*They all freeze in place and listen. No sound is heard.*] Do you hear? They are hustling and bustling, last-minute props to build and paint, the set to go up—and yes, a line rehearsal. [*They stop and listen. All is silent.*] Come, come! Into the litter, little Augie, come, Nuncle! [*They all climb into the litter. The* HEAVY NUNS *start off.*] Come, ladies, faster. Sit closer, Father Wisdom, my skin disease is contagious.

[WISDOM *screams.*]

BLACKOUT

Scene 7

The recreation room, mostly as seen before. This time the raised platforms are being used as a stage. A draw curtain is hung in front of them with a false proscenium. The proscenium is in rococo style, the curtain has a very distorted Fragonard painting on it. There is a small organ in front of this stage. There is one "box" near the stage with a seat in it. On a slightly higher group of small platforms is a stool for GOD. MAD NUNS *mill about with great excitement. Whispers are heard of words like "Hell's Angel" and "Priest." The* NURSES *patrol, including a few with crossbows.*

NURSE: [*Virgin Mary, running forth*] Sisters! Sisters! The play's about to begin. Collect yourselves. Remember Catholic modesty, obedience, reserve, gentleness, and flagellation!

ANOTHER NURSE: [*Infant of Prague*] [*Bangs her steel rosary on the floor when the* NURSES *show signs of not responding.*] Look, bitches! You don't stop the shit, it's no play for you, and Stations of the Cross instead!

ONE MAD NUN: I always wanted to grope the Infant of Prague!

[*A trumpet blast as this* NUN *is beaten.* GOD *enters and sits on the stool.*]

GOD: Now, sweet sisters, in the name of my son and wife mother, collect yourselves. [NUNS *quiet down, grumbling.*] Good, dear sisters. Now, at the top of the page, what do we say? What do we pray at the start of the play?

NUNS: [*Mumbling*] To the greater glory of God.

NURSE: [*Infant of Prague*] Again!

NUN: [*Louder*] To the greater glory of God!

[*A Fanfare.* REX, NUNCLE, *and* AUGUSTINE *enter carried by the* FOUR HEAVY NUNS. AUGUSTINE *is greeted with screams. There is violence in this response. Hands, clutching, reach out; tongues are run over lips.* WISDOM *starts back in terror.*]

WISDOM: I can't . . .

REX: But, dear Father, you must.

WISDOM: No!

REX: And why?

WISDOM: Why!? What do you mean, why? Look at them! Listen to them! Monsters all—foul dogs every one! No, I won't. [*Makes to leave.*]

REX: [*Holds him back.*] But, Father, you aren't going to disappoint these poor sisters who have worked hour after hour enflamed by the promise of your presence at this, our play, are you? [*He is about to reply; she stops him.*] Oh! Don't say yes to that question, tragedy it is that it be asked. It is heartless of you and unthinking too! They will cry "Why?" to heaven if you go!

[*At a signal from* REX *the* MAD NUNS *cry out "Why, why?" Some of the* NURSES *join in. This reaches a fearful noise of lamenting. They all reach up to* GOD, *crying out "Why?"* GOD *looks down, wipes away a tear, and calls back down to them through her megaphone.*]

GOD: Why? Why?

REX: Oh, hark, ye reckless one, to those pathetic cries. The cries of the behumbled, the wounded, the vulnerable, the forgotten, the beaten-down-by-this-sawmill-universe! Oh, list to those heart- and soul-wrenching

cries. These cries of longing for warmth, these cries of
starving children . . .

WISDOM: Exactly. Starving.

REX: You're not afraid?

WISDOM: Yes, I am afraid. I am afraid at golf tournaments,
bingo, and boy scout banquets.

REX: [*Changing her accent to that of a regular guy*] Aw,
come on, you ain't gonna letta bunch of crazy nuns
scare ya off, are ya?

WISDOM: What the hell are you? Look, I'm sick, I'm old. . . .

REX: Thirty-two, in perfect health. Have you forgotten
your physical?

WISDOM: I have a premonition.

REX: [*Having dropped the accent*] Obsessional neurosis
merely. Come, come, you can watch me perform, it's
rude if you leave.

WISDOM: You're an expert at rudeness. Good-bye.

REX: All right, sisters, eat the priest!

[WISDOM *screams.*]

REX: It's either watch the play or be eaten alive. I appreciate, believe me, an educated man's aversion to the
theater. I've felt it myself on occasion. But, frankly, I
think being eaten alive is far more disagreeable and far
less aesthetically pleasing than any action on a stage.

WISDOM: I'll watch tonight. Tomorrow, I leave.

REX: Sisters, sisters, our guest agrees to watch. [*At a signal from her they cheer.*] Now come, Nuncle, we must
prepare. An actress prepares, Father Wisdom. Conduct
the priest to his box. [*Giggles.*] His first. Beg pardon,
Father. [*Leaves with* NUNCLE *and goes behind the curtain.* WISDOM *is led to the box and seated, very nervous.*]

GOD: [*Through the megaphone*] Let the play commence.

NURSE: [*Dressed as Virgin Mary*] Let the play commence!

[*A* MAD NUN *rushes to the organ and bangs, producing
a burst of loud incoherent sound. The curtains are
jerked open. The "Host" comes forward. This is a* MAD
NUN *in tails and top hat over her nun's garb.*]

HOST: Good evening! Good evening! Everyone live
clean! How are we this evening? How are we this evening? How are we this evening? How are we this evening? How are we this evening? How are we this eve-

ning? [*She is hit by a softball thrown from the wings. It hits her in the head. She goes into a soft-shoe immediately with no transition, singing.*] "Once in love with Amy, always in love with . . . [*Stops and speaks earnestly.*] We have a really good show for you this evening. From our stage here live, for the first time, [*An organ barrage*] the Feast of Family, by [*Another barrage*] the late and better Sister St. Ignatius Loyola! And now, our very own sisters act!

[*A sisters act comes on stage to wild cheers. These are* THREE YOUNG MAD NUNS *dressed like a grotesque version of the Andrews Sisters.*]

SISTERS ACT: [*More or less singing together, more or less in harmony, more or less accompanied by* MAD NUN *at the organ, singing*]

Hey, good-lookin'
Whatcha got cookin'
Cookin' up somethin' good for me!

[*And so on.*]

HOST: [*Comes forward, applauding them.*] Aren't they wonderful, folks? Great, guys! I tell you viewers at home and audience in the studio, I know a talent when I see one and I step on it before it spreads. [*Throws the oldest in the group down and steps on her. Much advice on how far to go from the audience. The* HOST *stops suddenly.*] But seriously, folks, these girls are wonderful guys full of courage and bicarbonate of soda. [*All the* SISTERS ACT *burp. Then they sing. The two left standing dance erratically. The one on the floor smiles, looks dazed, and tries to keep up with the song.*]

SISTERS ACT:

There ain't nothin' like a meal,
Ham or pork or veal.
Last night I ate a heel
And was he sad he stepped on me!

[*They step on the* THIRD SISTER *already on the ground.*]

HOST: Let's have a clap epidemic for these girls, folks, they're just too wonderful for words. [*As the applause builds*] Oh, girls, you're so wonderful, I could just eat you! [*Much seconding from the audience. One of the remaining two comes forward.*] Tell me, my lovely duckling, haven't we met in a summer oven?

SISTER: No, but you're full of gas! [*Kicks the* HOST, *who falls down.*]

HOST: [*Oblivious of her changed condition*] Come on girls, change the set!

[*The* HOST *and* THIRD SISTER *are helped up. Then all change the set onstage, dragging on set pieces to make up a living room. The set pieces are schizophrenic cut-outs of furniture and many holy statues, most with erections or vaginas exposed. During this, a* NURSE *sells hot dogs to the* NUNS.]

NURSE: [*Dressed as a Virgin*] Step up, sisters, and get your baby on buns!

[*As* NUNS *run up to buy, she asks each if they want mustard or ketchup.* WISDOM *talks to* GOD *during this.*]

WISDOM: Really, this entertainment is terrible. I had play after play of mine rejected and refused—by agents, by producers, by actors, by directors, by androgynous seminarians, by the sock sniffer under the sofa in the rectory—refused by all. And yet look, just look at the tripe that gets on. Horrible, why, even the worst and most fledgling of mine was better, far better than the best of this. It's an insult even to a retarded, or a bankrupt intellect.

GOD: Shut up. [*Has a hot dog handed up to her. A pause.*]

NURSE: [*Virgin Mary, selling hot dogs*] Baby on bun! Mustard or ketchup?

WISDOM: Really, you have no conception . . . why, my plays were so much better. In one, there is a man, wandering after death. He sees what he takes to be his mother in the dark world below. Hail, he says to her, hail, seer, holy one, thou who foretellest destinies . . .
[GOD *spills mustard on* WISDOM.]

WISDOM: Damn you, God!

GOD: Blasphemer! [*Dumps a bucket of water on* WISDOM, *who screams in surprise.*]

[*The set is more or less ready. It is a peculiar version of a "modern" suburban living room. Typical furniture as been painted on strangely distorted cardboard cut-outs. The religious statues brought on—and there are many—are all ,deformed in some way. A few have wildly enlarged genitalia. Now the light on the stage within the stage goes to pink. The youngest and most attractive of the* SISTERS ACT *dances on with a Sacred Heart statue with the heart exposed. She bumps and grinds, then slowly eats the Sacred Heart. There is much applause at this. The* HOST *dances on with a penis-shaped crucifix. Then the* HOST *and* SISTERS ACT *bow to the audience and run off. The curtains are closed.*]

WISDOM: I'm catching pneumonia!

GOD: Thou shalt not take the name of the Lord thy God in vain. Another baby bun, Virgin. [*The Virgin Mary* NURSE *hands her one.*] Ketchup this time. [*Pours enormous amounts of ketchup on* WISDOM.]

WISDOM: Hey . . . hey!

GOD: Don't mind it, Father Wisdom. It's our ritual cleansing and anointing.

[*The curtains are jerked open. Onstage is a tableau.* MOTHER, *an older nun dressed as a mother superior;* SISTER, *a younger nun who is* NUNCLE, *heavily made up;* BROTHER, *a still younger nun dressed as a friar; and* REX, *who crouches near the doorway playing the dog.*

REX *growls to her audience and waves a paw. Much applause.*]

MOTHER: [*She and everyone else in the play within the play speaks in an oratorical manner. They use large, unrealistic gestures to express themselves. All play front resolutely.*] Here we be, *en famille*, waiting for Father to bring home the food.

SISTER: I'm hungry!

BROTHER: I'm hungry!

MOTHER: I'm hungry. [REX *howls.*] Quiet, Rex. Where is Father with the food?

[SISTER, *in sudden frenzy, runs and snatches the penis-shaped crucifix and tries to ram it into her vagina through her habit.*]

WISDOM: Oh, I can't look!

MOTHER: Sister, I say, sister, I say, sir, cease. Arrest thyself, impure maid. A bad example you are to Brother and you're giving me ideas! Sister! And I say, your technique looks inefficacious. An engineer you are not! [SISTER *fails to get very far with the cross. In disgust, she throws it down.*]

SISTER: I'm giving up religion. It disappointed me!

BROTHER: I'm hungry, yes, hungry, how hungry!

SISTER: I'm hungry, yes, hungry, how hungry!

MOTHER: And I'm hungry, yes, hungry, well, hungry. [REX *howls*.] Quiet, Rex. Where is Father with the food? Hunger is hard to bear. Harder even than children, and just think of the pain that entrails. And the deformation. Yet sometimes have I wished to be a bitch like Rex. With seven tits all bloated with milk and seven sisters and brothers there to suck me. Ah! Ecstasy then. Seven tiny brown nipples, swollen and blue veins protruding, and all sources of anguish-joy, like Father only more flexible than he and squirting, after all, not mere man's slime, but nourishment.

[BROTHER *falls to the ground and appears to be masturbating through his habit.*]

MOTHER: Brother, no! You know how hard be that on a *mère*'s heart. And when your rod grows long it draws lightning and we all know what that does to the male protuberance. Sparks fly from it and it is electrified.

BROTHER: Then I'd be a source of heat and light!

MOTHER: Ah, until it burned out. Then like a spent candle you'd be, all wick and no wax. Let us pray. [REX *howls*.] Thank you, Rex.

SISTER: [*Slouches center stage, reaches under her habit, and pulls out a dead rabbit.*] Ma, guess what—in nine months I'll be doin' that with a baby. [*Puts the rabbit back up under her habit.*]

MOTHER: Alas! What hear I? *Ai, ai,* what does this mean? And worst of all—what a cliché. Cliché of clichés, *aii.* Say no more—domestic tragedy in store for family of four [REX *growls*.] and dog. *Ah me, ohimè,* as they say in the Italian opera.

REX: [*Singing*] *Ohimè!*

MOTHER: Thank you, Rex. Can it be you are to willy-nilly experience that greatest joy of all—motherhood?! [*Organ blast*.] Mayhap, mayhap, my daughter, you wish to feel a stirring down there in murky regions 'neath that heaving bosom. You wish to have your belly swelly with a new kind of food. You wish to become heavy, as they say, with child. To grow a mustache in the seventh month, to walk with a granitic waddle-waddle. Oh, glorious motherhood. To open up and drop! How often wished I myself a bitch like Rex, oviparous, able to

spawn twelve, fourteen at a time—drop, drop, drop,
drop, drop, drop, drop, drop, drop, drop, drop, drop. Or
in the latter case, drop, drop. Ecstasy then, ecstasy, my
daughter. Ah! [*The* ORGANIST *plays loudly but inco-
herently.*] With cosmic music fills my mind, the organ
swells, the strings tighten. My daughter—soon to be a
mother!

[MOTHER, SISTER, REX, *and* ORGANIST *all howl. An
ovation ensues from the audience along with cries of
"Encore, encore!" The howl is encored.*]

GOD: [*To* WISDOM] What think you, my son?

WISDOM: I don't like absurd plays.

GOD: Absurd? This is life!

WISDOM: No, it's art, bad art. You see, I think good art,
art which is, you might say, truly art, is an affirmation
of life—ultimately. [*Removes notes from pocket and
reads from them.*] I mean, I think art should ultimately
affirm and be an—how might I say it—affirmation.
Death, in its way, is an affirmation of eating. Eating is
a tragic process. It has all the necessary rhythms and
segments of tragedy. For example, a problem or di-
lemma is posed: should I eat lamb with mint jelly or
veal scallopini? A choice—mark that word—a choice is
made. The veal is chosen. Conflict ensues: the veal
clashes with that day's lunch and three martinis. The
problem and choice are rehashed. Should I have chosen lamb and mint jelly after all?—curse the fate that
weighted my hand toward the veal. Ah! Wicked veal
scallopini—I mash you, I chew you, I masticate you, I
slobber on you! In short, havoc is wreaked. The lull
before the storm and terrible suspense. Was it too heavily seasoned for an aging digestive tract? Catharsis—
defecation. The choice is ground out, excruciating, yet
uplifting. Painful, yet a relief. In the highest tragedy,
of course, it all backs up and causes an explosion—spar-
agmos in the truest sense. You see? [*Looks up from
notes.*] That was verbatim a lecture I delivered to my
class, "Towards a More Christian Drama."

GOD: Resume the play!

WISDOM: That is why I reprehend Genêt and Becket.
Their plays are too lean. *Great Expectations* but no
Twist at the end.

GOD: Resume the play!

[*An organ blast as the play resumes.*]

BROTHER: [*To* MOTHER] Will someday be I a mother, Mom?

MOTHER: No, my son, but genital males have their compensations.

BROTHER: As when I vent me little turdlings as diminutive as sister but more graceful?

MOTHER: Oh, be ye not trite, my boy. A mother can bear anything but to have encountered her children somewhere before in bad fiction.

WISDOM: My mother used to say that. She was a failed artist and had written much bad fiction in her youth. Often about failed priests and their dead brothers. Hence, in a sense, she had created us before she had created us. That doesn't make her any the more sympathetic, of course. There are many failed artists but that doesn't imply that they are nice people.

MOTHER: Line?

REX: [*Prompting*] No, my child, you a creator must be. . . .

MOTHER: No, my child, you a creator must be.

WISDOM: Failed artists are often destructive. If they can't create, they destroy. Thus my mother willed Chris dead to destroy me. It sounds simple, doesn't it? But oh, the reverberations, my God, the reverberations!

MOTHER: [*Continuing*] A creator—music, poems, novels. . . .

WISDOM: Chris! In course of dialectical aesthetic I'd forgotten him. He was so fair and beautiful. A fantasy figure fleshed forever, leaping like a golden trout.

MOTHER: A true creator! Oh, the glories of art . . .

WISDOM: It is trout who leap, isn't it?

MOTHER: Through the swollen electrified rod, the shock of inspiration tingles up and down the male's spine. To the untrained eye, 'tis merely orgasmic, but to one who knows, 'tis artistic process. And what spurts out the rusty peephole is not man's slime, not even milk, but art. My son a creator, my daughter a mother! What more could a mother want?

[REX *howls, then whimpers.*]

MOTHER: Yes, Rex, I know, food. Were you both more appetizing, my children, Rex and I should make a meal of you. 'Tis a mother's right, after all, and a mother's chief talent. I'd do it, be assured, with grace and charm. First I'd slit your throats, to bleed ye, then edit out those dissonant organs, add an egg or two, some chili pepper, and mayhap a dash or two of squash—indeed, indeed, it is almost tempting. . . .

[*Suddenly* REX *howls and barks, on all fours runs to the door, scratches it, hurls herself against it in jubilation.* MOTHER, SISTER, *and* BROTHER *all act joyful in their highly artificial way.*]

MOTHER: What is it, Rex?

SISTER: Is Father nigh?

BROTHER: Oh proximate genitor!

MOTHER: Yes, yes, I see him on the river!

SISTER: *Er kommt!*

BROTHER: *Er naht!*

[REX *barks and howls.*]

MOTHER: Oh, rejoice, my kindlings, thy father comes!

SISTER: Our begetter begathers!

BROTHER: With meat for his starvelings!

MOTHER: Dearest spousekin mine, be welcomed!

["FATHER" *enters. He is an older* NUN *dressed as a Bishop. He pulls a cart on which stands a cross. To the cross is bound a* HELL'S ANGEL. *He writhes but is gagged.*]

MOTHER: Wondrous near-widower be welcomed.

SISTER: Unfeigning father!

BROTHER: Be feted.

[REX *howls jubilantly.*]

FATHER: Oh, see the food I've brought ye!

MOTHER: Ah yes, today is Thanksgiving Day and you've brought us a wonderful tom!

[*The cart is pulled downstage. The audience's joy is tumultuous. When the* HELL'S ANGEL *has been brought in,* WISDOM *has stood shocked.*]

FATHER: He cost a pretty penny but should go far. [*Much seconding from the audience.*]

WISDOM: That's my brother! Chris! Chris! [*Jumps onto the stage from his box. Much confusion.*]

GOD: Come back here!

WISDOM: Chris, it's you!

HELL'S ANGEL: [*Through his gag*] Mumph, mumph, sscgfhghf!

[*There is great confusion and uproar. The cast stops the play bewildered.* MAD NUNS *rush toward the stage, wanting to attack both men, but are held back with difficulty by* NURSES. GOD *stands ready for action, looking worried.*]

WISDOM: It is you, you, my Chris! Why did you pretend to be dead? Why did you leave me alone?

HELL'S ANGEL: [*Gagged. Makes hysterical noises.*]

GOD: [*Through the megaphone*] Father Wisdom, in the name of God, come back here! Pull yourself together, this is not a happening! Nurses, get him off the stage. . . .

REX: No, wait, God, he wants to join the play. We must let him. Sisters, sisters, be quiet, your attention! [*The* NUNS *begin to quiet down at her command.*] The play, the play is still ongoing!

WISDOM: [*Eyes tearing*] So I remember you—blond, beautiful, my Chris! I looked to you for myself, hoping to see mirrored in your blue eyes—what? What I never was, never could be, my dreams, my past, my death— who knows? Chris! I have here a haiku about myself inspired by you. [*Reaches into a pocket and removes a sheet of paper. He reads from it.*] Tree-lined street / leaves windblown / me, knifed by autumn winds / loneliness / In short, my life.

REX: That's nineteen syllables, Father Wisdom! A lousy haiku. It also sounds like Rilke. That means you're not only a bad poet but a cliché'd one.

WISDOM: Oh no, I won't listen to that!

[*At a signal from* REX, *the actors start improvising around the* HELL'S ANGEL *and the* PRIEST. WISDOM *seems dazed and disturbed suddenly. He is deeply moved evidently and has lost all sense of time and place.*]

SISTER: Why did you bring home two turkeys, Dad?

FATHER: The older one was a gelding, he was being given away. No one wanted him. I thought at the least we could devil him, then put him in the soup.

WISDOM: I am not a cliché.

BROTHER: I want the young one's thigh.

SISTER: *I* want his thigh.

WISDOM: Chris! [*The* HELL'S ANGEL *continues to writhe and make noises through his gag.*] I am no longer what I was. Little that I was. It's all trickling out!

MOTHER: There will be more than enough thighs to go around.

WISDOM: Dead on a pongi stick in the war, I was told, you, my Chris, and here I see you. [*Reaches up and undoes the gag.*]

HELL'S ANGEL: [*Screaming*] They're gonna eat me, they're gonna eat me, goddamn it, man, eat me! Help!

WISDOM: Help me, Chris, help me. [*Falls sobbing at the foot of the cross.*]

REX: Let's skin the turkey! [*Runs on all fours and sniffs at* AUGUSTINE *and the* HELL'S ANGEL *like a dog.*]

WISDOM: Get away!

MOTHER: Get the spices, sister!

SISTER: I have them right here. [*Takes two small bottles out of her pocket.*] Frankincense and myrrh! [*She sprinkles* WISDOM, *who seems suddenly to recover himself. He stands with sudden dignity and speaks to the assemblage.*]

WISDOM: Sisters in Christ, I speak as your priest. This play runs counter to Catholic teaching and good Christian thought. As an honorary member of the legion of decency I give it an X. That is a forbidden rating. Ban it to all Catholics and order it closed.

GOD: Overruled!

REX: Thank you, God!

MOTHER: [*Continuing with the play*] We must clean these turkeys, they are foul!

SISTER: I want the young one!
[*All start crowding in on* WISDOM *and the* HELL'S ANGEL.]

BROTHER: The young one is mine!

WISDOM: He's mine, you can't have him!

REX: [*Barks, then speaks.*] But dear Father Wisdom, he's on our stage, in our madhouse, and possession is nine-tenths of the law.

GOD: Ask any devil!

WISDOM: No! By blood he's mine!

REX: Father Wisdom, I'm going to count to three. If you're not off our stage by then, all of us are going to attack you and all hell is going to break loose! One . . .

WISDOM: [*In a fury*] No, bitches! He is mine! You won't have him! All my life I've been ruined by women, these beteethed slits have ripped at me, and now, now for my revenge! [*Suddenly draws a knife.*] I'll penetrate any one of you who comes near me and not in the way you hungering kites wish, but lethally! I know who sent you all, I know whose creation you are—that final bitch mother who bore both Chris and me! But she hadn't reckoned on the new Wisdom, for I've murdered bitches, I've murdered your kind, I've bathed in their blood! Over and over! Didn't think that pansy Augustine had it in him, did you? But I've stabbed and strangled, squeezed pretty necks and ugly ones, and ripped out the prettiest bowels in the West, and I'll continue to do so! Those foul mouths of your won't suck me back in! I'll slaughter all of you!

REX: [*With reason*] Two . . . You are mine, Father Wisdom, the Hell's Angel is theirs for the feast of Thanksgiving. You won't win against all of us. It isn't a matter of who is more manly, of which is man and which woman, but of hunger. Our hunger is greater than yours, our needs are also. And three!

[*A riot breaks out. The* HELL'S ANGEL *screams through it all.* MAD NUNS *press toward the stage but* GOD *gestures* NURSES *to let only a few join those onstage. The actors crowd around* WISDOM, *who fights ferociously.*]

WISDOM: No, he's mine! [*Grabs* SISTER, *stabs her, and kicks her when she falls. She screams.*]

SISTER: [*Dying*] Help me, Rex!

REX: Nuncle, Nuncle!

[REX, FATHER, *and* BROTHER *drag* SISTER *offstage.* MOTHER *tries to flee with them, but* WISDOM *catches up with her, tackles her, and stabs her. She screams.*]

WISDOM: Bleed! [WISDOM *now turns on a* NURSE *and kicks her.*]

REX: [*Returning*] Keep the priest alive, for he is mine, but numb him with a dart.

GOD: A dart for the priest—a raise for her who hits him!

[WISDOM *keeps fighting.* REX *watches concerned.* WISDOM *stabs another* MAD NUN *and is wreaking havoc, taking on two and three as often seen in the movies. Although the* MAD NUNS *continue to scream at him ferociously, only a few are brave enough to run to fight him.*

A VIRGIN *raises her crossbow, fires, and misses.*]

GOD: Some virgin you are!

NURSE: [*Virgin*] It's hard to hit a moving target!

GOD: Give me that crossbow. [*Rips it away from her, takes aim, and fires. She hits* WISDOM *in the arm, who, with a scream, looks up, then falls, still conscious.*]

REX: Beloved sistern, the Hell's Angel is yours!

[*With screams of joy the cross is tossed into the group of* NUNS, *who hurry offstage with it. Their screams and those of the* HELL'S ANGEL *fade a bit.*

WISDOM *has been left alone on stage with* REX *and her party of* HEFTY NUNS. *He reaches out his hand after the cross is offstage.*]

WISDOM: [*Whispering*] Chris.

REX: No use, Father. They are now feasting on that young man.

WISDOM: Ah . . . [*Collapses. The dart has paralyzed him, but he still is conscious.*]

REX: Be happy, my little prelate. A much, much better fate awaits you. [*During the following, the lights dim out to a more mysterious hue.* REX *reaches up under her habit and pulls out an orange.*] Want half an orange? You sure? Just trying to make friends. When I was a child in the orphanage they used to say carry fruit, make friends. On my weekly walk once I offered an apple to a group of playing children, my age, about ten. Two of them went into convulsions. So much for the salubrious effects of kindness and so much, alas, for my weekly walks. I didn't get out of that orphanage again until I killed two nurses and the night watchman and escaped. Oh, they caught me, eventually, even though I am a mistress of disguise. But they pardoned me since I'd killed those people ingeniously—they were admirers of ingenuity. But all that was in the orphanage before my vocation. Actually, I never had a vocation. I just got wise and pretended. Orphanage to convent—I traded one home for the crippled for another. I've always managed to be of use though, and that's got me through. Oh, I haven't always been this authoritative. Before they'd just use me, whether I wanted or no. For instance: in the orphanage I wrote poems. In the course of time, I was found out and they used me to show that poems are written by ugly, deformed people. And it follows, amongst them outside, that being ugly one is also evil. Then, in a ceremony, they flushed my poems away. I'd written them on toilet paper, the institutional kind, hard and thick. It was the only sort of paper I could find, since it was a government-funded orphanage. It wasn't used toilet paper, although that would have been fitting, since everything else in the orphanage was used—teachers, food, staff, clothing. . . . I don't remember much about my poems save that they demonstrated a delicate sensibility. [*Laughs.*] A delicate sensibility in a body like mine! I was a walking irony.

Then I entered a teaching order as a skullery maid. I was also used as a teacher's aid. Every time one of the kids did something the nuns didn't like, I was hauled in front of the class. Then the nun would say, mustn't do that, children, or God'll turn you into this! After a while it didn't work so well. They'd haul me up thirty, forty times a week. Soon the kids were saying: God doesn't have much range, does he, he punishes every crime the same way! So the sisters got somebody else—the janitor. He had a birthmark the whole right side of his face, purple it was, and pulpy. He also had psoriasis everywhere and a humpback too, only more pointy than mine, with larger pimples in it. He had a blue-colored glass eye which was too small and which used to slip out a little ways when he'd bend over in intense conversation. He called himself Lancelot.

So they had a replacement for me. Can you move a bit, Father Wisdom? I'm curious as to how much the dart is wearing off. Can you move your feet? [WISDOM *can.*] Your legs? [WISDOM *does but with obvious difficulty.*] It is wearing off. Soon, Father Wisdom, soon.

Well, there I was. They were no longer interested in me. Never put too many eggs in your basket of uniqueness, Father. Uniqueness is a sadly transient thing. They wanted to cast me out, claiming erroneously that I was a bad skullery maid, and an indifferent votary of our Lord Jesus Christ. But I intrigued and murdered and manipulated the system. I was very good at it, from watching others for so long. And I had very many weapons. You'd be very surprised—all I had to do was show my hump to some people for them to give me anything I wanted.

Eventually, at my request, I was sent here. By no other

than his Holiness, the Pope. After my ritual strip for
him he even gave me his ring—see? [*Shows him her
ring.*] Move your legs for me, if you please. [*He does
more easily.*] Good. Raise your hands. [*He can only
with great difficulty.*] Soon then, soon.

The place was re-created to my orders. And I make my
own rules, as you have had many an opportunity to
discover. I even leave for brief times and do modeling:
clothes for the ugly, or clothes for the deformed. I
played Banquo the wolf in a Disney animal feature.
And when here, I delight in fostering the arts. I love
to be in our plays. I've played dogs, night, the angel of
death, and once I played Salome. I even did the dance.
[*Does a bit of the dance seductively for him.*] Mine is
the soul of the actress! Raise your arms. [*He does.*] Ah,
time is nigh.

I've made a satisfactory sort of life. It's a bit short on
love but that doesn't bother me as much as it used to.
Sometimes the reactions I get as I hobble down the
street are worth more than the serenading of a young
lover—sometimes not. Which is why you are here,
Father Wisdom. Can you move your arms and legs at
the same time? [WISDOM *does with ease.*] I know, you
are still a bit dazed. That will pass. Meanwhile, I desire
you.

[*The lights are mysterious and caressing.* REX'S HEFTY
NUNS *hum and dance evocatively. A lyre is strummed
with romantic music.*]

REX: Incense, my sistern, incense and sing! [*Incense is
wafted toward* REX *and* WISDOM. *The* NUNS *sing words
of love.*] How beautiful is this night, Augustine, and
how it caresses us. You've been washed and anointed.
You are ready. Kiss me. [*Kisses him passionately on
the lips.*]

WISDOM: [*Dazed but very uncomfortable*] Ah ... get
... away ... from ... me ...!

REX: My ladies and I will dance for you. [*They dance.*]
I dance the seduction dance, the night dance, the sucking dance, the dance of the secret caress, the dance of
the loving tearing, the dance of the tender night....

WISDOM: [*Trying to wake up fully*] No!

REX: Come, my pure beloved, come! Know the secrets of
my body. Touch my breast. [*Picks* WISDOM'S *hand up*

and forces it to caress her breast. WISDOM *screams.*]
My lover laughs as he plays with my breasts! His teeth
gleam and long for my twin fruits. Come, beloved.
[*Forces* WISDOM's *head between her breasts. He is nauseous.*] Oh, the spasms of anticipation my lover feels. . . .
[*Begins to undress, always moving.*]

WISDOM: Oh, my God . . . Jesus, Jesus, my savior, help
me! [*Crawls as best he can to the curtain and tries to
haul himself up. However, he succeeds in pulling the
curtain down around him.*] Hail Mary, full of grace, the
Lord is with thee, blessed art thou amongst women . . .

REX: Blessed am I indeed, blessed as my lover mutters
the tenderest words . . . [*The dancing nuns pick up the
fallen curtain and hold it up, still moving their bodies
sinuously.* REX *goes behind it and rapes* WISDOM. *He
screams and screams.*]

REX: [*Behind the curtain, as the humming of her attendants grows louder and louder*] Ah yes, ah yes, you are
what I need, you are well sent, yes and yes and yes!

NUNS: [*Singing and chanting loudly, these words emerge
from all at different times.*] Thank you, Virgin Mary,
for the priest!

REX: [*Behind the curtain, crying out*] Yes!

NUNS: [*Moaning and crying out loudly*] Thank you, Virgin!

REX: [*Crying out*] Yes!

NUNS: Thank you!

[REX *emerges from behind the curtain. She is now a
beautiful, mature woman, carrying her hump and
wooden leg.*]

REX: Sistern, sistern, sistern in love. It has happened yet
again. The miracle attendant on our sacred rites has
again occurred. Give thanks, my sisters!

NUNS: Thank you, Virgin, for the priest!

REX: Give thanks, my sisters, I am whole anew. The Virgin has made me whole anew.

NUNS: Thank you, Virgin, for the priest.

REX: See my hump! [*Holds it out.*] See my crippled leg!
[*Holds out the very stagy-looking wooden leg.*] My
eczema! [*Opens her hands and lets fall what appears
to be eczema.*] My old, blind eye. [*Drops an egglike
cone, which splatters.*] For this month I am again a
whole woman!

NUN: [*Various crying out and singing and dancing. They let the curtain fall on the prostrate* WISDOM.] The Virgin be praised, be praised!

REX: Thank you, Virgin, for the priest. [*This becomes a triumphant cry. There is suddenly a scream and cry off.*] The feast of Thanksgiving is still on! The feast giving thanks for my miracle. Let us join them and gain strength from the angel who fell amongst us! We'll save the priest for later!

NUNS: Amen! Glory, Hosanna, Hosanna, Gloria!
[*All run off. There is a moment of silence. Then offstage enormous cries of joy and feasting are heard. Slowly, under the curtain,* WISDOM *stirs and comes to himself. He raises himself partly up.*]

WISDOM: Oh ... where? [*He remembers.*] Oh, my God ... my God. [*He has huge wrenching spasms of horror and terror.*] The ugliness, human ugliness, the ugliness ... sucked dry, mouth, Mother—the ugliness, my God, the ugliness ...
[*An enormous shriek offstage. Then silence.*]

BLACKOUT

Scene 8

Green and blue scarves descend from the flies masking the upper part of the stage. These scarves undulate and are lit to suggest a sea. The lighting is dim and mysterious. A boat appears. Two figures ferry it, REX, *now a beautiful woman cradles the barely conscious* WISDOM. *The boat wends its way across the stage slowly. Suddenly a tall shrouded figure rises and whistles the song:* "Memories." WISDOM *stirs*

WISDOM: [*Dreamily*] What is that old sad tune that revives me with its plaintive sound? What is the meaning then, thou old pathetic ditty, of all thy sighing sound? On evening's breeze thou sadly rang when as a child my father's death news chilled me; through morning mist thou stole when news—news so sad was brought

me of my brother's fate. And now to hear thee yet again,
asking always, asking what is the fate before me to
which my monster–mother bore me? What is the fate?

REX: [*Quietly, kindly*] Oh father Wisdom—you learned
Tristan from the Angel recording—though I think
you've forgotten some of the words ... Be comforted,
little prelate, soon you'll know ... soon ...

[*The mysterious figure continues whistling, swaying
in the mist. The boat disappears.*]

BLACKOUT

Scene 9

*The scarves part to reveal a mountain of candy kisses,
at the top of it, as in a beautific vision, stands a radiant,
apparently living,* CHRIS. *The boat bearing* WISDOM *arrives,* REX *has disappeared.* WISDOM *sits up in wonder.
The two ferry people help him out of the boat, lovingly.
The scene is brightly lit and very beautiful.* WISDOM
gapes about him, then sees CHRIS. *His entire being is
illumined with joy*

WISDOM: [*To* CHRIS] Chris, brother, beloved—I see you
now, as I always saw you, angelic, radiant, the light
streaming from you—and atop the mountain, a mountain of candy kisses! [*Eats a candy kiss*] Oh how beautiful this is—do you mean, there is surcease, and peace
after all? I am dead I suppose and this must be—is it?
Dare I breathe the word? Heaven? [CHRIS *nods and
beckons to* WISDOM *who joyfully climbs the mountain
toward him.*] Oh Chris, my Chris, am I now to possess
you—? Excuse me for a minute. [*Stops and eats a
candy kiss.*] Fresh! [*Continues his climb.*] Chris! Chris!
Chris! [*Reaches the top of the mountain.*] Then this
has been my *gradus ad parnassum*, my tortured climb
slowly out of hell to the summit, the summit of joy! Oh
Chris my Beatrice, and that ... that creature my Virgil
must have been—Chris you are mine! Mine! [CHRIS
opens his arms to WISDOM. *His white shining robe falls*

away revealing CHRIS *totally naked and beautiful.*
WISDOM *gasps*] Chris! [WISDOM *slowly, relishing every
second, approaches* CHRIS *to kiss him when suddenly*
REX *comes between them.* CHRIS *disappears.* WISDOM
falls back with a cry.]

REX: [*Stern but resplendent, her breasts revealed under
a transparent robe*] Fool! To believe that pablum they
taught you, and you taught them—Heaven! [*She laughs.
Her laugh is echoed by the* MAD NUNS *offstage*] There
is no peace, no surcease, no end to the agony! No end!
[*The* NUNS *echo "no end."*] There is only grief and desire, longing eternal, hate and need and more agony
and more agony and more pain and more grief and more
and more and more and more and more and more and
more and more. [*The offstage* NUNS *take up her chant.*]
And more and more and more and more and more and
more . . . [*She and the* NUNS *continue this chant.* REX
grasps WISDOM *by the throat and slowly strangles him
as the chanting builds. For a moment she covers him
as her robes billow. When she uncovers him his body
is lying limp in her arms. She starts swinging the
corpse—in time to the chanting—over her head more
and more wildly as the chant builds to a scream. Suddenly she releases the corpse into the theater.*]

SUDDEN BLACKOUT